Sandersville

Ned Kellar

Sandersville
Copyright © 2023 by Ned Kellar

ISBN: 978-1639457625 (sc)
ISBN: 978-1639457632 (e)

All rights reserved. No part of this publication may be reproduced, distributed, or transmitted in any form or by any means, including photocopying, recording, or other electronic or mechanical methods, without the prior written permission of the publisher or author, except in the case of brief quotations embodied in critical reviews and certain other noncommercial uses permitted by copyright law.

The views expressed in this book are solely those of the author and do not necessarily reflect the views of the publisher, and the publisher hereby disclaims any responsibility for them.

Writers' Branding
(877) 608-6550
www.writersbranding.com
media@writersbranding.com

This book is dedicated to:
Dorothy

The love of my life. Thank you for standing with me during the year in Sandersville and for standing with me for over fifty years.

Kent
Our son, conceived in Sandersville, born and reared in Florida. No father could ask for a better son.

Kim
Whose tenacity and energy kept her father at the task of finishing this book. I am indebted to her for editing the manuscript at least three times.

My other children: Karen and Steve and to my two grandchildren, Phoebe and Madison whose openness and acceptance of all people gives me hope for a better world.

And to the good people of Sandersville who received a "liberal pastor" and loved him in spite of it.

Introduction

I was in my sophomore year of high school when the Supreme Court declared the "separate but equal" school system was unconstitutional. While it made news in my home state of Mississippi, I could not recall any upheaval in my life. I was busy playing sports, chasing girls and doing what sixteen year old boys do. The principal of my junior high school had urged us to alert our parents of the coming "disaster," but it did not seem that important to me at the time. Compared to today, media exposure was limited. Besides, if it did not appear on the sport's page, I was not likely to see it. What I did learn through reading the sport's pages was that state colleges were not allowed to compete against blacks in athletic events. There was some talk among the students that "niggers" may try and come to our high school. This was followed by boasts that "if any nigger comes to this school, he would be a dead nigger." There were elaborate plans to close the public schools before allowing a black to enroll. The local community had gone to elaborate lengths to forestall integration by erecting a new black school that was newer and better than the white schools. The reasoning was that no black family could complain about unequal schools with the new George Washington Carver High School in West Picayune.

All of the hullabaloo created by the Supreme Court seemed far removed from my life. I do not recall having any reaction to the perceived threat of school closure. I do recall sitting in class on a hot spring day hoping an attempt would be made to integrate our school so we could get out and play some baseball or go swimming at the creek. However, I was oblivious to most of the reactions taking place around me. Besides, I had black friends that lived just down the street from my home and I did not see them as a threat in any form or fashion. However, I did have conflicts with some white friends and relatives because of my association with the black neighbors. That was more confusing to me than anything else.

As time passed, the "problem" became more personal. A cousin observed me shaking hands with a black friend and immediately began to attack me for doing so. We actually got into a fight over the issue. On another occasion I responded to a black lady by saying, "Yes ma'am." I was reprimanded and told "a white person never says ma'am to a nigger." We too, ended up in a fist fight over the issue.

It was experiences like these and many others that caused me to focus more and more on the whole issue of race. I began to notice articles in the media that reported conflicts between the races. As I recall, it was not a conflict as much as it was an attack on black people. In this book I have outlined some of those events and how they impacted my life. Up until I went away to graduate school, I continued on the real important issues of life – like football, basketball and baseball.

I began writing this book in 1964. It has been a work in progress for more than 45 years. I chose to write the account of that year, from June of 1962 to June of 1963, because I wanted my children to know about the lives of their parents during a difficult time. They have heard talk of it and read about some of what happened and often asked questions. Hopefully, this book will answer the questions they may have asked. It may well inform them about their father and mother.

As you will read, the book was prompted by an experience I had while the pastor of a small Methodist Church or churches, in and around Sandersville, Mississippi. I have tried to recount the experiences I had during my one year of ministry in that community. Because of a fading memory, I may not have listed accurate dates of experiences, but I do recall the events. I have purposely changed the names of some of the characters I encountered. The events I describe are accurate. It is a memoir of a person in a specific community. There were a total of 28 Methodist Ministers who signed a statement titled, "Born of conviction." That statement triggered an upheaval that would forever change our lives. I was one of the twenty-eight. While we all had common experiences, I would remind the reader that we also had unique experiences and reactions. This is a recording of mine.

Table of Contents

Chapter One: Welcome to Mr. Harvey's Neighborhood......1

Chapter Two: The Town, and Charge, of Sandersville.......15

Chapter Three: Welcome to Our "Little Preacher" 29

Chapter Four: "We're Common Southern Folk" 40

Chapter Five: Meeting the Religious Establishment..........49

Chapter Six: Sandersville Society..55

Chapter Seven: The Honeymoon is Over............................65

Chapter Eight: Move Over Billy Graham............................80

Chapter Nine: The Ole Miss Incident.............................102

Chapter Ten: Fall: Football, Leaves and Nesting............114

Chapter Eleven: How Did I Become a Minister? 128

Chapter Twelve: If I Get Where I'm Going, Where Will I Be? 137

Chapter Thirteen: Hidden Haven: The Beginning (or the End) 148

Chapter Fourteen: The Bomb Drops 158

Chapter Fifteen: Threats and Letters, Letters and Threats ...168

Chapter Sixteen: Expected and Unexpected Conflicts..........181

Chapter Seventeen:	Expected and Unexpected Support 191
Chapter Eighteen:	Saturday Morning Meeting with Larry Hosey 208
Chapter Nineteen:	To the Ivory Tower then Back to Reality ... 220
Chapter Twenty:	The Decision to Leave 237
Chapter Twenty-one:	The Final Straw 245
Chapter Twenty-two:	Final Chapter 262
Bibliography 277	

Chapter One

Welcome to Mr. Harvey's Neighborhood

It is strange how one thing stands out in my memory. The first thing I noticed about the parsonage at Sandersville was a huge oak tree in the backyard of the house that was dead. Its gray skeleton stood out like an ugly scarecrow against a background of oak and pine trees dressed in the green of late spring. All the leaves had fallen as had some of its branches. The old oak, once a grand tree, now stood as a sad, ugly, rotting skeleton that stood tall in stark contrast against the clear blue sky of that summer morning. It was useless except as a source of firewood. I continued to stare at that old tree as I got out of the car, remembering I had a U-Haul trailer to unload.

"That tree has been here longer than I have."

The voice startled me. I was so dreadful unpacking that I allowed the old tree to capture my thoughts for a moment and had not heard anyone approach. I turned to see a smiling gentleman approaching. He was older, a bit short and overweight. The first thing I noticed about him was his hair. It was completely gray and cut in a flattop style. I had worn my hair in a flattop for years but it looked different on him. Maybe it was because his was gray, and he was old.

Before I could introduce myself, he announced, "I'm Harvey Hinton, your neighbor and the lay leader of the Sandersville church. I've come to officially welcome you to our church and to our community."

I introduced Dot and myself, and we shook hands.

"I noticed you've been looking at that old dead tree. It's a shame it died. It has been here a long time – a lot longer than I've been here," Harvey announced. Without waiting for an answer he continued, "Now you can see by the wrinkles in my face and the color of my hair that I've been around for many years. But that tree is falling apart and we'll have to cut it down one day so it won't fall on the parsonage." With that he gave an impish grin.

In the next few minutes Dot and I learned more than we wanted to know right now about Harvey, his wife Jewel, and his grocery store. As Lay Leader of the Sandersville church, Harvey was its spokesperson. He told us about the parsonage and presented a set of keys.

"Guess y'all will need these, but it's not locked right now." he said and started to walk away. "By the way, I didn't have to walk too far to visit you. I live just across the street. I can keep an eye on our preachers." Harvey again gave his impish smile. "Why don't you and your wife come and have supper with us after you finish unpacking? My wife Jewel is a great cook."

We accepted his invitation and he left us the task of unpacking and settling into our new home.

The Sandersville Methodist Church parsonage was a small frame house covered with asbestos siding. It stood on a corner lot and was comparable to the other homes, except Harvey's house. His was considerably larger and well landscaped with azaleas and shrubs. The parsonage had a few shrubs that were in sore need of trimming. The lawn had patches of grass and larger patches of bare clay. Several large trees substituted for the lack of landscaping. The one exception was the dead oak tree. The house itself had a screened back porch and a modified patio for the front porch. It was listed as a three-bedroom, one-bath house. The three bedrooms were very small. In addition, there was a dining room, kitchen, and living room. The kitchen was the smallest room in the house. It opened to the screened back porch, which was at least six feet above ground level. The driveway circled the rear of the house and unloading meant climbing the seven or eight steps to the porch.

Like all Methodist parsonages, it was completely furnished. It was not Ethan Allen, but it was much better than what we had in seminary. While at Emory, we had lived in a one-room apartment with a Murphy bed. In three years of marriage we had accumulated one chair and a television set. We were more than happy with the fact that Methodist Churches always had a furnished parsonage. Moving in consisted of transferring clothing, silverware, books, our one chair, and a television set from the U-Haul into the house. In a short time we unloaded the trailer and were putting our belongings in their proper place. Most of the day had passed by the time we finished and took a few minutes to rest.

As Dot moved things around to suit her tastes, I relaxed. All I could think of was being in Sandersville. It still seemed strange that I was the pastor of Sandersville Methodist Church. It suddenly dawned on me that I was the pastor of three churches that made up the Sandersville Charge. This was our first pastorate after seminary and we still were in a state of shock. It all seemed more like a dream than reality. No, on second thought, it all seemed like a nightmare. Sandersville was the last place in the world I wanted to be a pastor and yet here I was. I wondered if Harvey read the body language that shouted loud and clear that I did not really want to be there. I am confident that I did not display much enthusiasm.

I had lost track of time but now I remembered it had been two weeks since we packed our meager belongings into a U-Haul trailer and left Emory University. After two and one-half years in the big city of Atlanta, Dot and I had come home to Mississippi to begin a career in ministry. This would be a good indicator of how quickly I would move up in the conference. A good start usually meant that a minister was in good stead with the appointment makers. I wanted an appointment to the Seashore District which consisted of towns and cities along the Mississippi Gulf Coast. If there was a liberal area in Mississippi, it was along the Gulf. I had decided I would fit in quite nicely in that area. Besides, it was near my home and I knew every little community in the area.

The appointment system in The Methodist Church is unique among the Protestant denominations. The Mississippi Annual Conference, made up of towns and cities in South Mississippi, consists of six districts with each district containing several churches. Each district has a supervising pastor who carries the title of District Superintendent. Overseeing the superintendents is the Bishop of the Conference. The Bishop is elected by his peers and serves until retirement. The process for the Methodist Church is to appoint a Bishop to a conference and the Bishop appoints the superintendents. It is important to note that Bishops, District Superintendents, and ordained pastors all possess the same credentials. We were all Elders in the Methodist Church. While the credentials of a district superintendent were no different from that of an ordained preacher, the power of his office made him special. These were the leaders of the conference. They, along with the Bishop, appointed the preachers to a church. Debate over appointments was out of the question. To do so was to jeopardize one's career.

I was impressed with most of these men. Some were honorable men who looked out for their churches and the pastors who served them. However, I had learned enough about the Mississippi Conference to know that it was divided between the good guys and the bad guys, depending on your point of view. The division was satirized in a book titled *The Stained Glass Jungle*, written by Gregory Wilson. I was very familiar with the book. One group was led by J. W. Leggett, the power broker of the Conference. The younger seminary graduates, along with a few of the long-time members, were on the other side. Naïve pastors, if there are such beings, believe all superintendents were honorable men who prayerfully consider each appointment. That was simply not true, and it was a well known fact. The Mississippi Conference had six District Superintendents. Each of them held the future of about thirty men in their hands. The Superintendents played politics with their appointments. I knew that and wanted to catch the eye of Tom Prewitt, the D. S. of the Seashore District. I combined a trip home with my attendance at the gathering of the annual conference to find out what decisions these honorable men had made concerning my first appointment.

The Mississippi Conference meets in June of each year. Usually the conference was at Galloway Methodist Church in Jackson, clearly the largest Methodist Church in the Mississippi Conference. However, for reasons I cannot remember, that year the conference was held in Biloxi, one of the larger cities on the Gulf Coast. Perhaps this was an omen for me. What better place for me than in the very heart of the Seashore District, my home district? Besides, Biloxi had the reputation for being a wide-open town with many great places to eat and play. I had frolicked on the beaches many times in my life and could recall a lot of good times. I was excited to be out of school and anxious to begin my career journey.

En route from Emory, Dot and I stopped by her parents' home and parked our U-Haul trailer. It was a relief to be out of school. We stayed just long enough to catch our breath, eat some of Mrs. Dickinson's cooking, then departed for Biloxi. It was an exciting time as we anticipated our first appointment. The Annual Conference was also a time of renewing old friendships and meeting other ministers. The conference was a time to visit, politic and exchange war stories. We had made reservations at the Friendship Motel, which was situated between Gulfport and Biloxi. Amazingly, it was the same hotel where we had spent our honeymoon just three years earlier. More amazingly, we were placed in the same room as we had on our honeymoon. Perhaps this was another good omen. My first visit to the motel had been very special.

The conference began Monday and was scheduled to last until noon Friday. Most of the sessions focused on the program of the conference. However, most clergymen were trying to discover where they were being appointed. Every man in the conference, theoretically, faced the possibility of being transferred to a different church. At least, that is what the first-year clergy thought. We would receive the appointments Friday at noon. It was a ritual and no one left until they heard their name read. However, they released the appointments Thursday evening so the Friday readings were merely confirmations of the appointment. Once read, it was cast in stone. Those men receiving new appointments, and those men moving from one church to another, had until the following Thursday to move. It was reported that more moving trailers were rented in Mississippi on Wednesday of the week following the annual conference than any other week of the year.

By the time Thursday evening came, I was a nervous wreck. I was standing on the front steps of First Methodist when Dr. Brunner Hunt of the Hattiesburg District approached me. We knew Dr. Hunt as a solemn man without a hint of a sense of humor. His trademark was an old leather briefcase that he carried everywhere he went. There were those who said that he slept with the thing.

With a briefcase in hand, and with the emotionless manner that was characteristic of him, he stopped and announced, "Brother Kellar, we are sending you to Sandersville. You will like it up there, and they will like you. They have big plans for that church."

All I heard was Sandersville.

"They told me that if I sent them a seminary graduate they would increase the salary and go full-time. In a year you will have one church appointment. However, right now it is a three-point circuit with a church in Vossburg and one at Goodwater. Their lay leader has told me that they will be willing to pay $4,000 when they go full time. Right now it is a minimum salary church."

Dr. Hunt continued to talk about Sandersville. The name echoed in my mind. I could not have been more shocked than if my doctor had told me that I had terminal cancer. I think I would have almost preferred the cancer diagnosis.

As I previously stated, my feelings are hard to disguise. The shock I felt must have come through. I hoped this was some kind of cruel joke. Didn't everyone know how much I did not want to go to Sandersville? I had told everyone I knew in the conference that I would quit the ministry if ever appointed to that church. I knew about Sandersville for two reasons. One, the man I had followed at a student appointment church in Hattiesburg was the Sandersville pastor. I never liked the man and did not want to follow him again. The second reason was, on our trips back and forth to Atlanta, Dot and I had to drive through the town. It was one of the least attractive places

I had ever seen. Every time we drove through I would announce with conviction, "I will not serve this place."

Brunner Hunt was not joking. He never joked. They had appointed me to Sandersville. My worst nightmare had come true. Momentarily, I reverted to my old theology from the Baptist persuasion and thought this must be punishment for some sin I had committed in the past. That's it! This is God's punishment. But what could I have possibly done to deserve such a fate?

There was another good reason for not wanting to serve Sandersville. Beside the previous pastor being a jerk and the town being ugly, the politics of the area were completely incompatible with mine. These were the most conservative people in the whole state. Jones County, Mississippi was a long way from the Gulf Coast area and the Seashore District, both geographically and socially. The locals boasted of Jones County as The Free State of Jones. This translated to mean it was the heart of all the prejudice and hatred so predominant in the Deep South. Didn't the bishop know that I had been active in a group while at Emory that plotted and planned to do something positive about the race issue in Mississippi? Those evenings when I sat around with other students and talked about making a change in the state would be wasted if I was sent to Sandersville. I knew these people would never appreciate my ministry because I was one of those liberals on the race issue. The more I thought about this appointment, the more I realized there was not one reason for my being appointed to Sandersville that made any sense.

I wandered about the lawn of First Methodist in a daze. The sound of Hunt's voice kept ringing in my ears. It was like a slap in the face. I was deeply hurt and disappointed. My whole world had collapsed, and my career had ended before it started. I was in a world to myself when my closest friend, Wilton Carter, came rushing up and asked where I was going. I stalled and asked him the same question.

"I'm going to Lake Methodist Church. It's up near Newton and Forest. It is a four point Charge. Now tell me, where are you going?"

It took every ounce of strength I had to say "Sandersville. It's a three point charge."

"You're kidding. Come on now; tell me where you're going."

"Sandersville," I said.

He could tell by the look on my face and the sound of my voice that I was not joking. Wilton had been one of those to whom I had boasted about quitting before I would serve Sandersville.

"Isn't that the church that you said you would never accept?"

I could have responded, "Yes, it was, and now I'm eating crow." Instead, I said nothing.

"Does Dot know?" he asked.

My God, what do I say to her? This was supposed to be the happiest moment in our life but it was, at least for me, the most miserable moment. This was not how it was supposed to be. I agonized about telling her. The drive back to the motel only took about fifteen minutes. I wished desperately for more time to think through just how to break the news to her. Embarrassment made me want to think up some excuse. After all, I had only myself to blame for making the rash statement about quitting the ministry if the decision involved Sandersville. As I drove into the parking space in front of our room, I remembered that we were staying in the same motel, and the same room, as on our honeymoon. What could be more ideal than to celebrate the beginning of our ministry in the same room we had celebrated the beginning of our marriage?

Sitting in the car in front of that room, my mind drifted back to that cold December night just three years past. Dot and I had joked all the way from Hattiesburg to the Friendship Motel. Dot took glee in telling people that I had stopped about one-half of the way between Biloxi and Hattiesburg to buy a flashlight. The reason was clear to me. We were traveling on a dark highway and, should we have a problem with the car, I was prepared. To this day I think Dot was afraid that I had some kinky sexual thing in mind.

I found myself smiling to myself recalling our first night together. Dot had been committed to remaining a virgin until we were married, though I had tried everything I could think of to keep her from achieving her goal. Throughout our courtship, I had chased, pursued, manipulated, pulled every manly trick, to get in bed without success. She won out, although there were some close calls. I may have made a run at first base but I never made it. Tonight, I would hit a home run. That drive was the longest trip I'd ever taken. All I could think of was getting to our room and into bed.

It was well after 10 p.m. when we arrived. Naturally, Dot was hungry. We went to a restaurant for a drink and a sandwich. Dot drank one glass of wine, put her head down on the table, and went to sleep. I laughed out loud at the memory. Getting her awake enough to get inside the room took some effort, but once there, she remembered she had not eaten a bite. At 11 o'clock that evening, on our wedding night, I trudged to the restaurant for two roast beef sandwiches. I literally ran back to the room to make sure she was awake. There was no way I was going to wait any longer. She ate her sandwich and noticed that I was not eating mine. Frankly, food was not primary in my life just then.

"Can I have your sandwich?" she asked.

Without waiting for an answer, she took it and ate it. Is this a stall, I wondered? Then she excused herself, went in to take a bath and get dressed for bed. I waited for her to exit the bathroom. It was both exciting and scary. We had been dating for over a year and there were so many things I did not know about her. At that age, I thought I knew everything about everything. The door opened, and she stepped out of the bathroom dressed in a beautiful white gown. My heart was pounding. I could see the outline of her body as she stood there. It was a beautiful evening, and all the waiting made it even more beautiful.

And now, three years later, we occupied the same room.

The reality of the events of the day returned. I realized that I had been sitting in the car for several moments. The excitement and good feelings left as I remembered the task ahead of me. How do I tell her? What do I say? I briefly rehearsed a few lines to see how they would sound. "Honey," I would say, "do you remember those silly statements I made about what I would do if they sent me to Sandersville? Well, I was only kidding." Yet humor was not in my soul then. I was embarrassed and angry and deeply disappointed. I wondered if it would be as upsetting to her as it was to me.

"Where are we going?" she asked when I went inside. She must have noticed that I was disappointed and asked what was wrong.

When I told her we were going to Sandersville, Dot was disappointed. Her disappointment was more for me than for herself.

"At least it's not too far from home, and we can eat with Mama and Daddy occasionally."

Here I had been thinking that my appointment had absolutely no redeeming factors, but as Dot reminded me, it was close to home.

I was not going to give up without some effort to stay out of Sandersville. That evening, as several couples gathered in our motel room in Biloxi to discuss the appointments, I slipped out to search for a telephone. I was going to call a man I had worked for in North Georgia and see if I could get an appointment up there. I found a phone booth and began a lengthy conversation with the one person who could save me from my dire situation. But the call to Georgia did not give me what I had hoped for. It looked like Sandersville or leave the ministry.

Dot noticed that I had been missing for several minutes and sent a friend to look for me. She confessed with a laugh that she thought I was so despondent that I might have thrown myself in the swimming pool.

"Take this box into the bedroom." Dot's request brought me back to the reality of Sandersville. It was late in the afternoon, and we were tired and hungry. We surveyed the furnishings and utensils and found all the switches to turn things on and off. There was still time to take a quick drive to the Sandersville Church to look it over. I drove the quarter mile in silence.

The church was a rectangular building with a meeting room on the west side of the sanctuary. The whole building was covered with asbestos siding, as were the homes nearby. The church itself was located one block off U.S. 11, the main north-south artery in that section of Mississippi. The inside was as attractive as the outside. The pews were dark brown and straight backed. Behind each pew were attached hymn racks containing well-worn Cokesbury Hymnals. Unlike the larger Methodist Hymnal, the Cokesbury was an abbreviated form of hymnal.

The chancel area consisted of two chairs, a pulpit, a piano, and a small choir section. An altar rail and a table where flowers were placed for the services fronted the area. The ceiling was acoustical tile which had turned yellow due to aging. There were dark stains showing where rain had soaked into the tile then dried. As I stood and looked at "my church", I had ambivalent feelings. I felt like a parent who had seen their newborn baby for the first time and realized that the baby was not very attractive.

Sandersville Methodist Church was not the most beautiful, but I finally accepted that it was mine for at least a year. When I considered my alternatives I really had no choice.

There was an adjoining room, which served as the fellowship hall. It was a plain room with a concrete floor. There were the usual folding chairs and a few folding tables. Also included in the furnishings was a ping-pong table, which delighted me. I thought of myself as a pretty fair ping-pong player and immediately planned to find the best player in town and challenge him or her to a match. It would be my way of letting the people know there was a new sheriff in town. I actually laughed out loud at my thoughts of "ping-pong superiority". As I looked around the room, I noticed that there was a large crack in the floor that ran completely around the room close to the wall. It was not a small crack but one that was almost one-half inch wide. It appeared that the floor was sinking. I made a mental note to ask Harvey about it at dinner later that evening.

When I returned to the parsonage, I shared my impressions of Sandersville with Dot. While I had been resigning myself to my assignment, Dot had completed another miracle in homemaking. The parsonage had been transformed from a drab house into a warm, inviting place to live. I was not too surprised, having experienced her dab hand at converting our one-room apartment at Emory University into what seemed a multi-roomed home.

That evening we joined the Hintons for supper. One blessing about being a pastor of a rural Methodist church was the availability of meals with parishioners. Actually, it was both a blessing and a bane, because not all were good cooks. Jewel Hinton was an exceptional cook if the meal we had that evening was an indicator. She prepared a meal that was traditional for a preacher. It consisted of fried chicken, butter beans, okra and creamed corn, along with hot rolls. The rolls were homemade and the aroma alone could add five pounds to anyone. The Hintons were very nice people and seemed to have much more depth than I first suspected. Harvey and Jewel not only ran the local grocery store, they also managed a small farm consisting of several head of cattle and a large number of chickens. They were among the wealthiest families in the area and the most respected. Both had been Methodists most of their lives and were the backbone of the Sandersville church because of their support, financial and personal.

After supper, Harvey and I retired to the living room while Dot and Jewel cleaned up the kitchen. Harvey seemed anxious to talk about the church and the community.

"Jewel and I help the preachers at Sandersville every way we can. We'll give you a discount on your groceries at our store. We always give our preacher a steak or two each week." It was obvious by the look on Harvey's face that he took pride in doing his special part for his preacher.

After telling me about his benevolence to preachers, he began to talk about the dynamics of the church. "I told the D.S. that we were ready to go full-time and get rid of those other two churches," he began. "That's why we wanted an educated preacher. We've never had a man who went to seminary. Most of our preachers had very little education."

Going full-time meant that the churches would have to stand on their own. I knew that most of the small churches in Mississippi were joined with at least one other church on what was known as a Charge. Harvey's idea pleased me because there was a certain status attached to a single church ministry.

"What do the other members think about your plan?" I asked.

Harvey began to fidget with the armrest of his chair. After a brief pause he said, "I haven't talked with anyone about my plan yet. I thought I would wait until we grew a little and then talk to people about it."

My excitement abated. I wondered if Dr. Brunner Hunt had been told of the details, or lack of details, in Harvey's plan. I suspected he thought as I had thought – the plans had already been worked out with the congregation.

The conversation quickly moved to the church and the congregation. I told him that I had visited the church earlier that afternoon and shared my impressions.

"By the way," I said, "the floor in the fellowship hall is cracking. Have you noticed that?"

Harvey smiled. "Noticed it, hell! I don't even go in the room because I think it will fall in." He began to laugh. "Preacher, that room was built by the men of the church. They had a supervisor with the same first name as you have, Ned. His real name is Edward but we call him Ned. Anyhow, he was the supervisor for the job and designed the plans for the foundation. He's hardheaded and you can't tell him anything. He left the wire out of the concrete. I knew it would crack and separate from the footer."

"Is it a serious flaw?" I asked.

Harvey did not hide his feelings about Ned and the building. "It probably won't fall in, but it looks like hell. You can't talk about it because he can be a mean man. No one mentions the crack. I doubt if anyone would say a thing, even if they fell into the darn thing and broke a leg."

"Maybe," I suggested, "we can patch the crack so that it won't look so bad."

Harvey's smile slowly went away. "Preacher, I suggest you let the crack stay, and not mention it. Please don't ask Ned about it."

I felt uneasy. Was this a warning to me to avoid this man named Ned, or was Harvey just advising me to not stir the waters? The answer was not clear. The tension was broken when Jewel and Dot returned and announced that they had washed and dried all the dishes and put them away.

The remainder of the evening involved more gossip than anything else. Harvey, with Jewel's help, gave us a run down on the congregation. He was quick to point out that he had both a brother and a sister in the congregation, and the Hinton family had several other relatives in the church as well.

"My brother, Earl, is the song leader and has been for several years."

"Harvey," added Jewel, "don't forget that we also have a very nice pianist in Sarah Lewis."

They covered several other church personalities that evening. They gave some of them good marks, but they did not treat everyone with kindness. Harvey did most of the reporting while Jewel sat quietly and listened, offering a nod of agreement occasionally. Harvey mentioned his sister Emma. She was the post mistress but never came to church.

Harvey was an outspoken man and evidently enjoyed a place of power in the community. I was now "his preacher", and he reminded me that I could always turn to him for help. They obviously expected me to turn to him for help just as they expected I would shop at Hinton's grocery.

It was late and Dot and I were tired. I reminded Harvey and Jewel that I had to visit the other churches before Sunday. We excused ourselves and thanked them for dinner. Later that evening, Dot and I discussed the events of the day. Maybe Sandersville would not be as we had assumed. The Hintons were nice enough people, and the house was not so bad. Maybe Sandersville wouldn't be as bad as I thought it would. I had selected Paul's statement, "All things work together for good…" as my favorite scripture. Somehow, I had to accept that Sandersville was a part of "all things."

Chapter Two

The Town, and Charge, of Sandersville

We arose early the next morning more out of discomfort than anything else. The first night in a strange bed is restless at best for both Dot and me. Getting up early was not a bad idea, especially in a small community where most of the community can see your home.

I recalled a practice that a friend of mine used in Georgia. He was serving a small church in a farming community and would get up at five in the morning and go into his study and turn on the light. He would then go back to bed and sleep until seven or eight. "Man," he said, "we impressed those farmers with their preacher who got up at five every morning to work on his sermon and do his Bible study. They kept telling me how pleased they were to see my light on each morning as they drove past the house." At least the Hintons would be impressed seeing both of us up and busy at daybreak.

The first order of business was to scout out Sandersville then find my other two churches. After breakfast, I set out in my car to see the town. Our house was a block from the main section of town, and I made a note that next time I would walk to the town center. If getting up early impresses people, I was confident that walking to work would do even more to boost my image. As I approached the downtown area from the south, I noticed many sights which had contributed to my negative image of Sandersville. On my left, (west) were the railway tracks for the Southern Railroad. Several trains, mostly freights, used the railway system each day. The tracks gleamed with the reflection of the June sun. On my right, to the east, was a row of homes some no more than 30 feet from the highway. Highway 11 was a major north-south thoroughfare and heavily traveled. I could only imagine how loud the train and automobile noises must have been. Farther north was the town proper. The first business was a barbershop, the next was a drugstore. Both buildings were old. The paint has peeled off revealing old, gray wood. The owners had nailed a large metal sign advertising Coca Cola, Phillip Morris cigarettes, and other items to the side of the buildings. The drugstore also contained the office of the town's only doctor, an eighty-five year-old man. Next to the drugstore was Harvey's grocery. A common porch connected the two buildings and, like those that grace the screens of western movies, the sidewalk between the two buildings was wood. Each building had screen doors that had seen better days. The door at Harvey's store had been reinforced with a large Royal Crown Cola sign. The drugstore screen door was mostly wooden frame void of screen.

The next building, much newer than the other buildings, was a truck stop/restaurant combination. There were gas pumps for cars and a diesel pump for the large tractor-trailer trucks that frequented Highway 11. A little further north, and across the side street, was another business that sold dry goods. The next building was the post office, the newer and one of two brick buildings in town. Harvey had mentioned it was run by his maiden sister, Emma. The only other occupied building on the main street was a garage surrounded by several junk cars. The last building on the main street was an empty, two-story structure. I later learned the building contained a hive of bees. Some townsmen talked about the abundance of honey in the old building.

The railroad dominated the west side of the town. The only building on that side of the street was the depot, a brick building that was the busiest place in town. Every day freight trains would stop and pick up loads of paper wood for the mill in Laurel. At least two passenger trains passed through the town daily, but neither stopped.

Like most small southern towns there was an abundance of churches. I estimated the seating capacity of every church in town could hold the entire population of Sandersville three times over. There were three major churches in the town: Baptist, Presbyterian and Methodist. The largest was the Baptist, which made sense because Sandersville is in the heart of the Bible Belt. The Methodist Church, my church, was next in size, with the Presbyterians a distant third. None of the churches were on a main street. Each was one block east of U.S. Highway 11. Interestingly, all three churches were within a block or two of each other. Houses were scattered around the town, most painted white with large front porches and a clothes-line in the backyard.

There was no industry in town except a pumping station for a gas-line that ran from Texas to Florida. The line supplied natural gas for several states and was maintained by a small crew of men. One of them was Harold Boone, a member of the Sandersville Methodist Church. The station, or pump house, contained two large pumps designed to keep the flow of gas moving to other pump stations. The pumps were so powerful that the ground shook when they were turned on, which averaged twice an hour. Harold's job was to monitor the pumps to make sure they continued to function. Morbid curiosity made me ask Harold if there was a chance that the line would rupture and, if so, what would happen.

"Well, Preacher, you really do not want to know. Let me say that there would be quite an explosion. Those homes near the station would disappear. We try not to think of such a thing happening." If Harold, who worked at the station, did not want to think about an explosion, neither would I.

Sandersville had its own elementary school, junior high and high school, all at the same location. The schools united the whole community. Like most small southern Mississippi towns, the local high school was the one rallying point for the community. This was especially true during football season. I was to learn that the entire community closed Friday evening so that people could attend Sandersville games.

I learned, also, that the community closed even if there was not a game, but the stores closed an hour earlier on game nights.

The away games involved a trip of no more than thirty-five miles. Also, as with many small towns in the Deep South, everyone in the area was an expert on football. Not only were they experts, but they shared their expertise with anyone who would listen. The most difficult job in the area was that of football coach. Win, and he was a hero; lose and people wondered why he was kept on as coach. The coach at Sandersville, Butch, was a local boy and his father was a Baptist minister. I met Butch and really liked him. The coaching staff consisted of him and the line coach. He was less mature than Butch but exuded energy all the time. Talking to him was as exhausting as running laps. But because I loved football, I was to spend many hours with Butch and his staff.

The Sandersville Charge

Sandersville was a three-point charge. This meant there were three churches that jointly shared a single minister. Jointly does not mean equally. Sandersville, being the largest church, would have most of the minister's time. The other two churches, Vossburg and Goodwater, would have to split the remainder of the minister's time. There was not much time to get to know three churches. We had moved in on a Thursday and Sunday was just a couple of days away. It was imperative that I establish contact with the other churches before Sunday. For one thing, I needed to know their location and the quickest route to get there. Harvey gave me written directions on how to get to each church. With his note in hand I set out to find the other two churches of my three-point charge.

Dot elected to stay at the parsonage and continue redecorating to fit her tastes. This was a formidable task. Besides, she would see the other two churches soon enough.

The Other Churches: Vossburg and Goodwater

I set out early Saturday morning to find Vossburg and Goodwater. According to Harvey's directions, Vossburg would be my first stop. It was about twenty miles northwest of Sandersville. The drive took me north on U.S. 11 for about fifteen miles to a small community named Stafford Springs, once a booming resort. It was no longer the "place to be" and was so rundown it was almost a ghost town. There was a time, Harvey told me, when famous people from all over the world visited the spring, but those days were past. I turned west from Stafford Springs and continued for five miles. The road from Stafford Springs to Vossburg was narrow and winding, passing through what once must have been farmland. It was now covered with oaks and small pine trees. Scattered across the landscape were the remains of old barns. Most were only shells of what they had once been.

I arrived at Vossburg within thirty minutes of the time I had left Sandersville. I made a mental note of the travel time so that I would know how fast I had to drive on Sunday. The schedule for the worship services had been set by the previous pastor and called for alternating services between Vossburg and Goodwater at nine a.m. with the services at Sandersville beginning at eleven a.m. every Sunday. This meant that I had to finish preaching at Vossburg or Goodwater with enough time to drive to Sandersville.

I had no idea what to expect at Vossburg. What I saw as I approached the little town was depressing. The first sign of civilization was an old, unpainted building with a sign that indicated it was the general store. The sign was so worn that much of the lettering had faded enough to make it hard to read. The next building was Billy's Beauty Parlor. Scattered about were some homes in various stages of ill repair. That was Vossburg. A few houses, a general store and a beauty parlor. There were a couple of vacant buildings about to collapse from non-use. Several old homes dotted the area. The Methodist Church was the only church in the area that was unusual. This was southern Baptist country, and there was a Baptist church for every twenty people. I did not know whether having the only church in a community was a good omen or a bad omen. What did the other churches know that the Methodists did not?

The church was the largest building in the area. It was a large white frame building that looked much like a huge cardboard box. It, like the other buildings in the area, was in bad shape. Its active membership numbered about twenty persons, many of whom were elderly. Most of the people had lived in the area their entire lives. I had researched the finances of each church and the annual salary as paid by Vossburg was $300, an amount that would not come easily. Harvey had briefed me on the status of the community. His remark that it was a poor community was a gross understatement. What little bit of industry that once kept the area alive was gone. All, that is, but the general store and the beauty shop. Of the two, the beauty shop was the busiest. As I later learned, most ladies got their hair done once a week, usually on Saturday.

My intention was to simply locate the churches then return home to complete my sermon preparation. As I stopped in front of the Church, I noticed a couple of people looking out from their screen porches. They were obviously curious about the stranger walking around their church. I waved to those I could see but there was not a return wave. It was a little eerie and unnerving. Like many churches in the Deep South, the door to the building was unlocked. I entered and took a look around. The Sanctuary would seat over one hundred people. The chancel was elevated from the floor level and there was a choir loft along with a piano. The pews were brownish oak and quite nice. The ceiling was stained proving a leaky roof. It was apparent the building had not been maintained very well for several years. There were a few Sunday school rooms adjacent to the sanctuary but I did not examine them.

I walked outside and looked around the property. Finally, a man drove up in his pick-up and parked next to my car.

"Hello. I'm Ned Kellar."

His simple reply was "Howdy." Nothing else.

We stood a few feet apart and looked at one another. Finally, I told him I was the new preacher, and he immediately shook my hand.

Sandersville

"I heard ole Brother Wilson had left the church. So you're our new preacher." Without waiting for my response he shouted to the two people who had been watching me, "It's the new preacher. Now what did you say your name was?"

"I'm Ned Kellar."

Another shout to the onlookers. "Says his name is Brother Kellar."

One of the ladies shouted back to this man who had forgotten to introduce himself, "Well, Woody, invite him in for coffee."

"The missus wants you to come and have some coffee."

I turned down the invitation suggesting that I had to get over to Goodwater before it got too late.

Woody turned to the onlookers and shouted, "Says he's got to get over to Goodwater before it gets dark. He doesn't want to get caught in those woods after dark."

A voice came from the other porch, "Can't say that I blame him. I wouldn't want to be caught way over there after dark. Taint a safe place if you ask me. Iffen you had a wreck you'd lay there until the next morning 'fore anyone found you."

It amazed me that these people carried on a conversation about me while I stood there. Not a single one of them introduced themselves nor, with the exception of Woody, spoke directly to me. I reminded Woody, and anyone else listening to our conversation, that I had to get Goodwater and then back to Sandersville.

Woody said, "I'll be seeing you every first and third Sunday. If you need anything up here, just let me know. By the way, I'm your song leader."

As I drove off toward Goodwater all I could think of was how strange that whole meeting had been. My curiosity was running amok. What will worship be like in that church?

It was much later than I thought, and I drove as fast as the road allowed. My mind was on getting to Goodwater then back to Sandersville before dark. Frankly, I was a little nervous. I kept thinking about the remark the woman on the porch had made about the danger of being on these roads after dark. I increased my speed and, just as I did, a chicken darted into the road. It was too late to even attempt stopping. I hit the chicken. In my rearview mirror all I could see were white feathers flying through the air. It looked like it was snowing. What do I do? I could stop and see if I could find the owner of the chicken, but then I would be even later getting to Goodwater. I kept driving and prayed that God would forgive my hit and run.

I also prayed no one had seen me.

Goodwater was about fifteen miles from Vossburg and no more than fifteen miles from Sandersville. It was a narrow asphalt road with no center stripe. There were very few houses along the way. The road ran along the top of a ridge with a lovely view. I could see far across the valley to the south. At times the road would go through an area where the embankments on both sides rose about ten feet above the pavement. The soil consisted of red clay and everything around the road carried a reddish tint to it. What caught my attention were the caves which appeared to have been dug into the red clay banks. Some even had doors. I made another mental note to check that out at a later time.

The Goodwater church was in the middle of the woods, literally. The nearest house, a farm, was at least a quarter mile away. The church was picturesque. It was a small, white building with a high-pitched roof and arched windows. It reminded me of the church found on Christmas cards. It belonged in some village in New England. What also struck me was how small it seemed. The door was unlocked, and I went in to see what the interior looked like. It was even more beautiful than the exterior. The floors were a high glossed pine, as were the pews. There was a small organ and a choir loft that could seat no more than six people. The pulpit and chancel area were in scale with the rest of the church. The pulpit, however, was very close to the rear wall. The pastor's chair was immediately behind the pulpit with only knee room separating the chair from the pulpit. Thankfully I was not the roaming type. I would have very little room in which to roam. One small gas heater abutted one wall. There was no restroom. There was no plumbing at all for that matter. And, unlike Vossburg, there were no curious people nearby. I did not see a single person during my visit. I left the church thinking that God has given me a lovely diamond in the midst of these woods.

Reporting on the Charge

Excited as a kid, I told Dot about my diamond in the woods. I also gathered my courage and confessed to killing the chicken. She was pleased about the first, wary about the second. But it wasn't long before I had her laughing over the "chicken flurries" I left behind.

This being our second day in the parsonage, we needed to go to Harvey's for groceries. We drove up to the store and parked out front. This was my second time seeing the store, and I still could not get over how ugly it was. Once inside the store the scene was a little different. The counters were filled with every item anyone could ever want, and then some. Besides food, hardware and some clothing were for sale. It was the type store where the shopper gave the clerk a list of items needed, the items would be collected and brought to the shopper. The exception was the meat market, which was a separate operation. The shopper was expected to go to the meat counter and tell the butcher what they wanted. The meat would be cut and wrapped and brought out to the counter.

Harvey greeted us and announced to everyone in the store that I was the new preacher. He also let everyone within earshot know that he always gave his minister a ten percent discount. I had always believed in paying a man a fair salary and not using discounts to supplement a salary. Discounts always embarrassed me for I never knew what to say in response. Nevertheless, I gave Harvey a list of what we wanted and he helped us find where things were. After putting together our first bag of groceries at Harvey's, we started to leave the store.

It was then that Harvey shouted to his butcher. "Frank, cut the preacher and his wife a steak, and put it on my account." With a twinkle he reminded us of what he had promised at supper the evening before. Dot and I came to discover that the same ritual would take place each time we visited Harvey's store.

The first Sunday of my new ministry was drawing near, and it was time to prepare my sermon. It also meant that I had to print the church bulletin. The equipment available was archaic at best. Dot had an old typewriter, a portable Smith Corona. She typed the stencil for the mimeograph machine. The stencil had to be carefully cut in half and each half typed independently. The typewriter ribbon had to be removed so that the letters would be cut into the stencil. Once that had been done, the stencil was glued back together. This too had to be done carefully lest the bulletin be out of balance with one side higher than the other. The system never produced the product we hoped for. One side would be higher than the other, or one side would be tilted while the other was straight.

The mimeograph machine was probably the first ever produced. After fitting the stencil onto the drum, the goop called mimeograph ink was applied to the inside of the cylinder with a paintbrush. This process was always a disaster. Once the process was complete, a single sheet of paper was fed into the tray beneath the cylinder. A crank was turned to feed the paper through the machine. If good luck prevailed, the finished product would be a readable, relatively clean bulletin. It rarely was. Because the ink was slow in drying, each bulletin had to be laid out to dry. Two problems occurred immediately. The desk space I had would not hold the fifty bulletins I had to print. The second problem was the ink could only print five or six bulletins before being used up. This meant reapplying ink at least ten times during the printing process. I learned to wear old clothes because it was impossible to keep from getting covered with the black goop. It was also very hard to remove the ink, especially from around and underneath fingernails.

After finally finishing my preparations for my first Sunday, I retired for the night. It was a sleepless night because I kept reviewing all of the things I was supposed to get done. I wanted everything to be perfect for my first service. I was going to show these people that I was a lot better than my predecessor. After all, I was the first educated preacher to serve these people. I would wow them with my preaching and my preparation.

As I lay in bed that night, I thought about my ministry. Tomorrow I would preach at my first appointment after finishing seminary. For the rest of my life I would be moving from church to church, meeting new congregations and living in a different home. It was my call to be a Methodist preacher. This is what I had prepared for the past eight or nine years.

My memory came alive as I lay there thinking about being a preacher. For four of those years, I had been the preacher at three different churches. One of those years was spent as a student assistant at a Methodist church in Chamblee, Georgia. I discounted that year in my memory bank because I had preached only twice. The senior pastor did not want the student pastor to get too much exposure, probably because it could cause problems in the church. It was another way of saying that if the student pastor was the better preacher, the congregation would want him to preach more often. But tomorrow would not be the first time I had the responsibility of preaching at a church.

It is funny how thoughts can cover so much ground in so little time. I must have been fifteen or sixteen years old when I dedicated my life to full-time Christian service. I assumed that God had called me to do that. As I reflected on my decision, it occurred to me that God does not always issue a clear call. One influencing factor for me involved my childhood, a life of poverty. I wanted to be like my minister, Brother Maddox. He had a nice car, always dressed well, and lived in a lovely home. In a way I made my decision to get into Christian service so that I could have what he had. I believe that God uses whatever means possible to get the call through to whomever he wanted to preach. Later, my decision to move to another denomination had more to do with the girl I was dating than anything else. I am confident the Lord knew of my interest in lovely young ladies. Had I not met Joan Ennis, the daughter of Brother David Ennis, the local Methodist minister, would I have become a Methodist? The answer to that question was a resounding no. My relationship with Joan was mostly typical of the times. The only difference was she was a preacher's daughter. I don't know what I expected from a preacher's daughter but Joan surprised me. She was wild.

As I lay there trying to sleep, my mind raced. I closed my eyes tight and tried to visualize a peaceful scene in the hope that my mind would close down. No such luck. It seemed Joan Ennis was still influencing my thoughts. I felt guilty being in bed with my wife thinking about a high school relationship. Firmly, I pushed the memories of Joan out of my mind and, in a few moments, I was again focused on the experiences that brought me to the ministry, and ultimately to Sandersville. Instead of counting sheep, I counted the churches I had served and the people I had met.

"I want you to serve at Byrd Chapel and Wesley Chapel. Both churches are near Crossroads, which is close to Pearl River Junior College." That was the extent of the District Superintendent's request, or better put, his directive. I was just beginning my sophomore year at Pearl River College, a junior college in nearby Poplarville, Mississippi. I knew as little about preaching and administering a church as any atheist. I had completed my studies to be a licensed preacher, but I was surprised that I would be pastoring a church so soon. At that age I was so cocky that I thought it would be a snap. Nothing could intimidate me. I was now a preacher and had my own church.

I thought back to my time at Byrd Chapel and Wesley Chapel. Both were within ten miles of Bogalusa, Louisiana, home to a large paper mill that often sent its smelly smoke across the Honey Island Swamp to settle in and around the churches. Byrd Chapel was on a hill overlooking the swamp, while Wesley Chapel was situated on the edge of the swamp. Byrd Chapel was a lovely building more than 150 years old. Wesley Chapel was a white frame building in a state of ill repair.

My God, I thought as I lay there in bed, Wesley Chapel is just like Vossburg. I tried to recall the people I had met at the two churches. There was Shelby Smith and his two sons from Vossburg. Never had I met a more gracious and devoted Christian family. I could not recall a single name from Wesley Chapel. I did recall that their pianist had only one arm. I almost laughed out loud when I recalled how fast she could move that one arm, especially with some of the more upbeat hymns. I stayed at that appointment for only one year and I marvel that the two churches survived. I was only a sophomore in college and not ready mentally or emotionally to minister to a congregation. But God being God kept them going

The next year I moved to Mississippi Southern College which necessitated a move to a church close to that campus. In my junior year, I moved to Hattiesburg and began serving two churches, Bonhomie and Arnold Line, as a student pastor. Both were small churches. Bonhomie was a very poor congregation made up of ex-mill workers for the Tatum Company. The church had been built by the owner of the mill, and was a replica of a little church the Tatum family attended as children. It was a beautiful A-frame building nestled in the midst of tall pine trees. Most of the congregation lived in the company's old mill town even though the mill had closed several years earlier. The mill town housing was adjacent to the church property and rented for $10 per month. The homes were small with only one or two rooms, but many housed two or three families. Quilts were suspended from the ceiling creating makeshift walls. Teen pregnancy was rampant, along with a high dropout rate and unemployment. I saw in real life what my sociology textbooks said about poverty stricken rural southern states. It was by far the poorest area in Hattiesburg and, for a white community; it was the poorest in southern Mississippi.

The other church was Arnold Line, Dot's home church. It was a family church, in the literal sense. Well over half of the congregation was related to her family. That allowed for some of the more interesting experiences in my pastorate while in Hattiesburg.

Dot's mother, one of the most enjoyable people I have ever known, helped make those two years exceptional while she worked hard to promote her daughter to her preacher. Mrs. Dickinson would invite me to Sunday dinner and announce, as I enjoyed the food, that Dorothy had prepared each of the dishes. If I showed particular interest in a dish, Mrs. Dickinson would announce that it was one of Dot's best dishes. By the end of my first meal with the Dickinson family, I was convinced that not only was Dot beautiful, she was also a culinary expert. I later learned that Mrs. Dickinson did not tell the whole truth. Not even part of the truth. She was the real cook, not Dot. I found out shortly after our marriage when Dot attempted to make a pie crust and the thing disappeared in the oven without a trace. Because of her looks, personality, and advertised culinary skills,

I asked Dot for a date. She accepted. This led to a relationship that evolved into an engagement.

I found that dating a member of my church presented some problems. One was the perception that ministers do not have a sex drive, nor are they interested in any kind of physical exchange. Dot shared with her friends how guilty she felt about kissing her minister. God knows how she must have felt once she discovered how sexually aggressive her preacher could be. I had to literally chase her around the car one evening just to get a hug.

I stayed at that appointment for two years, and it was from the earnings of that church that I was able to pay for my education. As I write this journal, I realize that my entire education was provided by income from the Methodist Church. I was a pastor, and at the same time I was a student. Even after being at Emory, and serving a church in a neighboring community, I was still first and foremost a student.

As I lay in bed that night recalling my ministry, I realized this was the first time I would be a real pastor of a real church. My feelings were mixed. On one hand, I was excited about it. On the other hand, I was scared. I thought of the people I had met and of my first sermon waiting to be delivered. Tomorrow I would speak at Vossburg and Sandersville. The anger I had felt when first appointed to Sandersville had ebbed. I found myself liking the people I had met. The evening was not very restful, and I was reluctant to get out of bed when the alarm sounded.

Chapter Three

Welcome to Our "Little Preacher"

After breakfast I got all of the materials for my first Sunday, dressed in my dark suit and, with Dot at my side, set out for Vossburg. The trip did not take as long as it had on my trial run. Perhaps I was anxious to get to the church and drove faster than I had on the first trip. Most likely, it was because it was Sunday and the traffic was light. Dot was no more impressed with the landscape than I had been. Never having been a person who minced words, Dot affirmed just how ugly the area was. When she saw the church, all she would say was, "My God!" In any case we arrived almost an hour before the scheduled service. Unwittingly, I was slowly but surely conditioning the people of the Sandersville Charge that I was an early riser and early arriver. Neither had been characteristic of my behavior prior to getting to my new appointment. Arriving early allowed me to fully scope out the church. While I had seen the inside of the church, I was still shocked to see it from the pulpit. The inside was about as lovely as the outside. Now I could see the stained ceiling better than I had on my first visit. It had to be more than a simple leak to cause so much staining. The acoustical ceiling tiles sagged where most of the water damage showed. Once upon a time the church must have been a first class operation for a town the size of Vossburg. There was a choir loft that would hold at least twenty people. The seating capacity far exceeded the needs of the current congregation. Everything had been done in a dark brown. Time had aged the furnishings, and the last coat of paint must have been added thirty years before.

The service began a few minutes late because Woody, the pianist, did not arrive on time. When he finally struck a chord, he led the congregation in a rousing hymn. After a prayer and an introduction of Dot, it was time for the sermon. I introduced myself and began my first sermon. I was preaching to about twenty people. Woody assured me that this was a large crowd because people wanted to see their new preacher. After the service, as I stood at the door, Woody introduced me to each attendant.

"This is our new little preacher," he would say as each person filed out. "Our new little preacher" became the standard introduction not only at Vossburg but at Sandersville and Goodwater as well. Woody and the others were half right. I was new, but I was not little.

The handshaking took longer than I had anticipated. A quick glance at my watch told me I had just enough time to greet the last couple of people and begin my drive to Sandersville. Among the last people to leave was a very attractive lady who was much better dressed than the others. Another thing that stood out about her was her lack of expression. Her name was Anne Woods and she was among the higher income families in the area.

Woody introduced me and quickly added, "Preacher, this is the lady that owned the chicken you ran over the other day."

My face burned. I fumbled through an apology and made a poor attempt to say I was sorry about her chicken. The feather snowstorm in my rearview mirror had been amusing, almost enough to balance my embarrassment at being caught in the hit-and-fly.

Ann Woods stared at me and said nothing. Evidently the chicken incident was a problem for her. After a couple of seconds, which seemed more like several minutes, she said, "It is all right about the chicken. We will talk about it when you visit next week." There was no doubt that Miss Ann, as she was called, liked to be in control.

My first inclination was to regain control so I looked her square in the eye and said, "Yes, ma'am."

As Dot and I got into the car Woody shouted, "Be careful, and watch out for chickens."

The drive back to Sandersville was an adventure. My Studebaker Lark hugged the curves of the country road as I sped toward my next preaching assignment. Dot and I talked about some of the people we had met, and both of us concluded that they were an unusual group but very nice. I also knew the time would come when I would do some visitation in the community. Recruiting new members was out of the question because most of the people in town were already members of the church.

I made it to Sandersville with just a couple of minutes to spare. As I drove up, I noticed that several people were standing outside the door of the church. They were waiting for their new preacher and, for most, it would be our first meeting. I quickly shook a few hands at the door of the church and rushed in to begin the service. Time did not allow for lengthy introductions. The congregation was in place as I made my way to the pulpit. Someone had volunteered to be the usher and had distributed the bulletins. As I straightened out the notes on the pulpit, a tall elderly man approached and asked for the numbers of the hymns. I gave him the numbers, which were printed on the bulletin, and he wrote them on a small piece of paper.

"I'm the song leader unless you want to do it yourself," he announced. "By the way, I'm Willard, Harvey Hinton's brother. I've been leading the singing here for more years than I can count."

Willard did not look anything like Harvey. He was much taller and not nearly as extroverted. He appeared older than Harvey but retained a full head of hair. He was also toothless. Having someone leading the singing is a great idea when I am the only other alternative. I love music, can read a little, but my singing conflicts with, rather than complements, the music.

After welcoming the crowd and telling them how happy I was to be their minister, I asked them to stand and sing the first hymn. Willard rose, walked to the center of the church and began to lead the singing. His voice was quite good and he was loud enough to drown out my voice. While the lack of dentures caused him to slur some of the words, he still did a very good job. As was the custom in Deep South churches, the first act after singing a hymn was to have a prayer. Usually someone was called on from the congregation to lead the prayer. Since Willard was standing so close, I asked if he would lead in prayer. To my shock and amazement, he shook his head no. I did not know just what to do, and it took a few seconds to collect my thoughts. I led the prayer and the rest of the service moved along without any more surprises.

The church was almost filled. I was to learn that most of those present were members of the church and attended regularly. Some were there out of curiosity. There were very few visitors. It was my first time to see my church members and for them to see their new preacher. Following the service, I moved to the door of the church to shake hands with those in attendance. I was careful to listen to the introductions of each person so that I could remember their names. I had been taught that that was critical in the ministry because on Monday morning I would be asked by the first person I met that had attended the service, "Do you remember who I am?"

The first person out the door was a rather small lady named Rose. She was about five feet tall and had the look of a very capable and confident lady. I had a feeling that I was going to like her.

She grasped my hand and told me her name. "So, you're our new little preacher. Glad to have you here. By the way, it seems no one told you about Willard. He refuses to pray in public. If you ask me, I don't think he prays in private either." Her sassy talk and frank opinions further convinced me that she was going to be one of my favorite people.

The next person to take my hand was Dale. Dale was also short in stature, but he had red hair and a muscular build. Standing next to him was his wife Jean, a tall, attractive brunette. They struck me as being an odd couple because of the difference in their height.

"Welcome to Sandersville," Dale said. "This is my wife Jean, and we have two young'uns, both boys. You'll meet them at MYF this evening. We'll be seeing you around town this week."

As they walked away, I turned to face the next couple. Their names were Billie and Larry Hosey. Billie was a demure, shy blonde lady and Larry was about six feet six inches tall and might have weighed 150 pounds. He was balding, withdrawn, and apparently relied on his wife to carry the conversation. Billie was a lovely lady who spoke in a soft voice.

"We're glad to have you as our minister," she said in a voice just above a whisper. "Larry and I want to have you and Dot over for Sunday dinner soon. We hope you like Sandersville."

Larry shook my hand, impressing me with his strong grip. "Hope you're a football fan because that's about all we talk about in the fall." He then extended an invitation to join him for morning coffee at the local restaurant. "We sit around and talk about Ole Miss and what kind of team they have. Meet me there tomorrow at about seven and I'll buy the coffee."

I assured him I loved to talk football and also was a fan of Ole Miss. I decided to get to know Larry better.

Some of those who were present just shared their names and went on their way. Toward the end of the line were Harvey and Jewel.

"Looks like the Bishop sent us a good one this time. Jewel and I enjoyed your sermon. You'll be good for Sandersville. Let me introduce you to the chairman of the Official Board. His name is Ned, at least that's what we call him. His real name is Edward but don't call him that. This, here, is Ned and Ann Dillard." Ann was an attractive brunette in her forties and Ned was a tall, large man whose face revealed a tough life.

While Ann smiled readily, Ned kept a stern look on his face. "Hope you can cut it here," he said. "We are not very slack with preachers if they can't do the job" he warned.

"Aw, don't listen to him," Ann responded. "His bark is a lot worse than his bite. By the way, we want you and your wife to come and visit us sometime. We live out in the country. I'll call and give you directions."

Harvey and Jewel walked away. Harvey's parting shot was, "Guess you know not to call on Willard for prayer again." He gave me an impish grin as he took Jewel's hand and walked to their car.

Ned and Ann stood with me at the door for a few moments and talked a little about the church. He told me how the church had added a room and then said with some pride, "I was the foreman, and I put together the work crew that built the room."

It dawned on me he was the man responsible for the poor foundation, the foreman everyone feared. After meeting him, and hearing him talk, I could better understand why he was feared. It was apparent that Ned felt he was in charge, and he did not want anyone to think otherwise. Finally, he and Ann left.

Most of the crowd had departed. Only one couple remained.

"We're your neighbors, the Kellys. My name is Jack and this is Mary and my son, Jack, Jr." The man had a warm smile surrounded by two scars. His wife was a round faced lady who could be described as warm and caring. There was also a fragile nature about her. Their son, Jack, Jr., was a very polite young man. He was handsome, about fifteen years-old, and well mannered. He stood back until introduced, then extended his hand and told me that he was pleased to meet me. I was impressed with his manners and concluded that the Kellys were a fairly sophisticated family.

"We live next door to you. Sorry we weren't there when you moved in. We would have helped with the moving. Why don't you and your wife drop by this afternoon for coffee or iced tea?" Mary asked.

Dot and I assured them that we would take them up on the invitation. Of all the people I met that day, Rose, Larry and Billy, and the Kelly family impressed me. If we were to have friends at Sandersville, it would probably be these families.

Inviting the preacher to Sunday dinner is a ritual in most Southern communities. The tradition was alive and well in all three of my Charge communities. We were invited to dinner by the Hintons but, instead of going to their home, we were taken to Phillip's Cafe. I think Harvey wanted to show off his new preacher.

The restaurant was filled with churchgoers by the time we arrived. Harvey assured me we would find a table because the Baptist church did not let out until 12:30. The owners of the restaurant were Phillip and Dot, both from New England. They were, as many noted, the token Yankees in Sandersville. They had been in the area long enough to be adopted as Southerners by the locals. The food was excellent and plentiful. By the time we had finished, the Baptists were coming in for lunch. Harvey ribbed two of the latecomers by reminding them if they were Methodist they could eat at a decent hour. While Sandersville was a small community, it was clear that lines did exist between the churches. Lunch always included some socialization. It was a rite.

Sunday meals in general were special. The locals took great pride in preparing meals. Sunday dinner was a tradition in the Deep South and Sandersville was as deep in the South as any place could be. There was also a friendly competition among the ladies as to who was the best cook in the area. If there was a challenge with this tradition, it was the zeal with which the different ladies in the church tried to outdo one another in preparing meals for the preacher. Even among those families where income was limited, the meal included two meats and three or more vegetables. Weight gain was imminent.

A small issue for me involved the types of foods usually served. I let the congregations know, tactfully, that there were some foods I did not enjoy. At the top of that list was squash. I despise it. Call it yellow squash, purple squash, zucchini, or anything else, I hate it. A squash by any other name...

A second food I detest is meat loaf. Running a strong third is tuna fish. I do not like the smell, the taste, or the aftertaste of tuna, regardless of how it is prepared. It was a constant challenge to convince those who tried to change my tastes that I do not change easily. Had I been paranoid, I would have sworn that there was a conspiracy to place squash, tuna casserole, and meat loaf, on every Sunday table. The problem was how other people handled my food prejudice. Once I mentioned the foods I do not like, the more determined members became to prove they could prepare any food on my hate list and turn it into a favorite. The very next time I had dinner with one of those families, I could count on squash and meat loaf being served.

"You'll love my wife's meatloaf," the man of the house would announce. Most of the time it sounded more like a directive. As a result of this type of pressure, I developed a method of moving the offensive food around my plate without eating a bite.

"My wife's tuna casserole is the best in town," was another phrase I heard too often.

"Have you ever had summer squash prepared like this?"

I never relented, much to the chagrin of my hosts. No one can prepare squash, tuna fish, or meat loaf in a way that appeals to me. Trust me – many have tried and all have failed. So I mastered the art of moving food. One does what one has to do.

Actually, I enjoyed most every Sunday meal served. There were a great many meals in a great many different homes. My memories make my mouth water. I believe those southern Methodist cooks, male or female, are the best in the world. However, the after-church dinner meetings provided an excellent opportunity for getting to know the people of my parish. It did not take long to realize that these were good people who struggled like everyone else. What they had that I loved was a good, old-fashioned view of religion. I never sat down for a meal without grace being offered, and I never left the table hungry.

Following that first Sunday, after returning to the parsonage, Dot and I talked about the churches and about the people we had met that day. It was not as bad as I thought it would be, and the people were not as I had expected. My fear had been that the congregation would be an uneducated, narrow-minded group. All the times I had sworn I would never serve Sandersville, I had conjured up an image of people who could neither read nor write. While there was that element at Vossburg, even those people were friendly and receptive of their new "little preacher." I knew that term as one of endearment from my previous ministry in Mississippi while a student at the University of Southern Mississippi. It was a way of recognizing my youth. I felt a bit guilty because these people seemed to genuinely like me, and I had arrived with a negative attitude toward Sandersville.

Jack and Mary Kelly were delightful people. They shared much about the area and the personalities in the community.

"You'll meet some real characters in Sandersville," Jack said. "Some of them you'll like, and some you won't. By and large, it's a good place to live. Laurel is just a few miles away, and you can find some good stores down there. Of course, you can buy your groceries at Harvey's."

As is the custom in the Deep South, the men and women separated for "men talk" and "women talk." Jack and I had walked to the front porch to talk about the weather and other inane subjects.

Then Jack turned serious and said, "The racial thing in this area is not so good right now. You'll hear some of these people talk about this being 'the Free State of Jones County.' I don't know what your thoughts are, but I can tell you the feeling of many of these people is pure hatred."

I found it hard to remain quiet as he talked about the attitudes of the locals. To this day I have difficulty controlling my tendency to say what is on my mind. When much younger, I attributed my knee-jerk responses to be a result of my idealistic youth. Whatever the reason, I said to Jack, "Well, I don't think the attitude of the average person in Mississippi toward the black person to be very Christian."

He looked at me without saying a word but his body language suggested that I had said something out of order. I thought about what I had said and remembered what one of my professors at Emory had told me. "Don't try, nor expect, to change people overnight. Remember, these people have been living with their attitudes and beliefs for a long time. Try to change them, and they will attack you." Obviously, I had not heeded his advice.

After a moment, Jack said, "I sure hope we are able to settle this matter without killings."

"Killings?" I blurted out. My heart began to beat faster.

Jack's demeanor changed and I could tell that he was choosing his words carefully. "Preacher, folks around here do not feel kindly toward the colored people. In fact, some down right hate coloreds. Not everyone around here would take kindly to someone showing any sympathy toward them."

"Tell me about yourself and about your family," I asked, subtle or not. He let out a heavy sigh, perhaps a sigh of relief that we were not going to discuss the black/white issue any more than we had.

I learned a lot about Jack Kelly that afternoon. He was not a native of Mississippi but had lived in the area for the past several years. He came to work at Masonite, a large wood product company in Laurel. He told me that several of the church members worked at the plant, as well as several of the townspeople. I also learned Jack was a veteran of World War II and had been wounded more than once. The scars on his face came from wounds during the heavy fighting shortly after the invasion of Normandy. He was a real hero, not that he boasted of such, but he did discuss his experiences. His job in the war was to plant explosives in the hedgerow to create openings for the troops to advance. He placed explosives in the heavy growth while under fire from the Germans. He described how he planted the explosives, lit the fuse, ran for seven seconds then fell to the ground. As soon as the explosion occurred, he was up and moving to the next target. He was wounded two or three times but never left the front lines. I was enthralled with his description of his action and could have listened for hours. But time moved swiftly and I had to get home and prepare for evening service.

Jack and Mary Kelly were good parents, good citizens and good church members. Jack was a hero but a common man. He appeared to be a deeply sensitive man who cared for others. I noted a deep love in his heart when he talked about his son. Jack, Jr. was the apple of his eye. He beamed with pride every time his son's name was mentioned.

"Brother Kellar, I worry about the future because of Jack, Jr. The racial thing we were talking about is a threat to our community and to the whole South. I fear for our children."

For a moment I thought I had heard that sensitivity and caring include not just Jack, Jr. but all people. Maybe, I thought, just maybe, Jack is not a racist. Dot and Mary came out, and Dot reminded me I had MYF and evening worship at the Sandersville church.

I met with the young people of the church for the Methodist Youth Fellowship later that evening. It was easy to put each child with the parents I had met earlier that day. The Dillards had a daughter and a son. The daughter, Maryann, was as cute as could be and very popular with the other young people. She was a junior in high school and a cheerleader. Ned and Ann Dillard's son, Ned,

Jr. wanted to control everything even though he was younger than most. Amazingly, he frequently got his way. Few challenged him. Like father, like son.

Dale's two sons were as different as Dale and Jean. The oldest son, Billy, was tall like his mother and very athletic. He was a star on the high school football team and very polite. The younger son, Keith, looked just like his father. His hair was a deep red and his face was covered with freckles. If ever looks suggested mischievousness, Keith had it. Not only did the children look like their parents, their mannerisms were very much like their parents too.

The evening service was less formal than the morning service, if that was possible. The order of worship included several hymns, of which only two verses were sung, and a few prayers. I was careful not to call on Willard for prayer. The crowd was not as large as it had been in the morning. After the service was over and people left, I was reminded that several people would not come out in the evening because they did not like to drive at night. It was somewhat ironic that people would not come out after dark to worship when the service ended at around 7:30 p.m. which was broad daylight in the summer, but those same people would attend a Friday night football game and even drive to the away games. But that was football. This was a church.

All in all, the day had been good. The worship services went well and I enjoyed meeting the members of the church. Tomorrow, I would get up early and have coffee with Larry and meet the townspeople.

Chapter Four

"We're Common Southern Folk"

The people of Sandersville were like those in any other little southern town. Everyone I met had all the traditional manners, which are a part of Southern communities. It was always yes sir, and yes, ma'am, and hats were removed while inside a building. Everyone said grace before meals, even if they were on a hunting trip sharing a can of pork-and-beans. His or her religion was very important and no one ever admitted to being unchurched. I never heard of any atheists in the community. Frankly, I do not believe they would have survived. Southern Christians can be a real mean bunch if someone questions the existence of their God. To my knowledge there was not a single Jewish family in the entire area. The same attitude directed toward the nonbeliever would have been directed toward the Jews, if any had lived in the area.

Apart from religion, there were three classes in the area. Unlike most areas where there are an upper-, middle-, and lower-class, Sandersville divided its class system into white, Negro and Indian. The Indians were those who had been tossed out of the Choctaw Reservation which had been in the Sandersville area. It had since been moved to Philadelphia, Mississippi, and word had it that some were not allowed to move with the tribe. Sandersville had the dubious distinction of having a class of people lower than the blacks.

Within the white community there were the three traditional socioeconomic groups. The wealthy class was very few in number. These were the landowners and the large farmers who just happened to have oil wells on their property. The middle-class consisted of those people who worked at the Masonite Plant in Laurel. The lower class was made up of the local laborers whose income was minimal. The blacks, or Negroes, were largely out of sight of the community. There was a section south of Sandersville, which made up the "quarters," a term still used even though it belonged to the Old South and slavery. What stands out in my mind is that everyone called the blacks by their first name. I also remember that most blacks would stand back and wait until someone asked them for a response.

The other "class" of people, the rejects from the Choctaw tribe, fell just below the blacks. These were the poorest of the poor and rummaged through garbage cans for food. They were the most pathetic people I have ever seen. Amazingly, in a southern town where most anyone would receive help if it was needed, these people were treated as if they did not exist. They were easy to spot because of their style and color of dress. They wore dark clothing even in the heat of summer. The other residents never recognized them or their needs.

The wealthiest person I knew was Harvey Hinton. In addition to his grocery store, Harvey owned considerable acreage and several head of cattle. The church had a few families who made good money. The budget of the church gave an indication of that wealth. At the Methodist Church the annual budget was $5,703. Of that amount, the minister made $1,400. We were the second wealthiest church in the town. Using these figures as an indicator, it is easy to see that wealth is relative.

Sandersville's "Personality"

The personality of the community could best be described as friendly, with a touch of suspicion. Like most Southern towns, it had its peculiarities. There were the usual prejudices, particularly toward blacks. I attributed this to what was happening in the South at that time. The civil rights issue clouded everything with suspicion and anger. The local news media presented a slanted view of the news, often ignoring facts. When it did report the real facts, it was careful to editorialize in opposition to anyone who advocated fair treatment toward blacks. The television station did the same as the local newspapers. Mississippi was right and the rest of the Union was wrong regarding the injustice of segregation. With everyone feeling targeted by the outside media, the townspeople had only one another to trust. It presented a kind of glue that held the community to a single focus. It increased the paranoia that had been fed to locals by hate groups, some of which were located within the community itself. The Ku Klux Klan was reported to have a presence in the area. The community, like most small towns, felt threatened by the possibility of blacks gaining voting rights and entrance to their schools.

Prejudice was not limited to blacks. Like most Southern communities there were historical prejudices. A common decorative tag could be seen on any number of pickup trucks and family cars, as well. It was one that portrayed a short Confederate soldier standing next to a Confederate flag proclaiming, "Hell No We Ain't Forgetting". Some thought the Civil War had not ended. Yankees, defined as anyone north of the Mason-Dixon Line, were suspect. Stories appeared in the local papers about someone with New York license plates, or Illinois plates, who was harassed by a group of young people in a pickup truck with a Confederate Flag attached to the antenna.

This was not a new experience for me. I grew up hearing that anyone from the North should be treated with distrust. My grandmother, who was alive during the Civil War, despised all Yankees. She referred to them as "Blue Bellies" and enemies of the South. Others in my family would make the same remarks. One of my cousins swore he had seen a Yankee and his belly was as blue as blue could be. I am embarrassed to admit that I was in junior high school before I learned that Yankees did not have blue bellies. While I never heard anyone in Sandersville refer to Northerners as having blue bellies, they still did not like them.

Sandersville had the same attitude about Northerners as those where I grew up. It began to make sense when I learned more about Jones County. The county, in which Sandersville was located, called itself "The Free State of Jones." The rest of the South may have rejoined the Union, but Jones County still considered itself free of any link to the United States. I know some of the residents realized this was simply a motto adopted in humor, but some actually believed it to be true. The only Yankees that graced the town of Sandersville were those who stopped for gas as they passed through the city. If a resident of Sandersville happened to meet a Yankee, and liked him or her, they simply adopted them as Southerners and denied their Yankee heritage.

As I mentioned earlier, a group most often associated with prejudice, the Jewish, were not represented by a single family in Sandersville nor the surrounding community, as far as I knew. I am certain someone would have mentioned it to me. Making certain I was aware of Jews living in the area would be typical of most Southerners. In my youth, I had been taught that Jews were evil people. My learning experience came through an uncle who delivered freight to different businesses in my hometown. On occasion, he would let me ride with him and help unload the boxes from his truck. I vividly recall delivering items to the Boston Store, the only clothing store in town that sold clothes other than overalls. The owner was a man named Jacob Carp. He was a huge man who wore the largest shoes I have ever seen. I remember them always being polished and shiny, and he wore a dark double breasted suit. My uncle reminded me that Mr. Carp was Jewish and explained that Jews were condemned to hell because they were the ones who killed Jesus. I believed that was true because my uncle was a Christian man and knew such things. However, I liked Mr. Carp and that upset my uncle. It was the first time I had been told that I should not like some people because of their religion. Strangely enough, most of the good Christian folk shopped at the Boston Store, as would I in my high school years. I mention this because I do not recall being told that I should hate "niggers." I guess it was assumed that all whites in Mississippi hated blacks. However, I did not have to worry about anyone's attitude toward Jews in Sandersville. There weren't any.

Phillip's Café and Truck Stop

Every community has a place where the local characters hang out. Phillip's Cafe and Truck Stop was that place. While it served as the meeting place for Sunday dinner, on weekdays it was a hangout for locals. It also was the only restaurant in town so deciding where to hang out was easy. I need to add that it was a truck stop restaurant which kept the tables full all day. You could buy gas, have a tire changed, and eat breakfast, lunch and dinner at the same place. It was also the male gossip center of the community. Everyone knew what everyone else was doing.

The building was concrete with white stucco. The front was largely glass and, painted in bold, bright lettering were the words, Phillip's Café and Truck Stop. It could be seen for quite a distance if you were approaching from the north. Harvey's Grocery blocked the view from the south. The first thing I noticed as I walked into the cafe was the long counter with metal stools covered with a red vinyl. There were four or five tables scattered throughout the dining area. A row of booths fronted the large window. Behind the counter was an opening to the kitchen area. Next to the opening was a glass-enclosed cabinet filled with pies. The cash register was located near the door. There was the usual array of chips and candy bars and a large jar of pickled pigs feet. It was like most of the restaurants in small cities across the South.

Ironically, the owners were a couple from New England who spoke with a heavy Boston accent. As I have mentioned, they had been in town long enough to become accepted as "converted Yankees." Phillip had developed the skill of real Southern cooking, thereby shedding his Yankee status. It was strange to hear the two of them use Southern terms with a Boston accent. If it bothered anyone, they did not make an issue of it. Both were always on the move, him wiping tables and hustling orders, and her bringing the food to the tables. It struck me as a good place to hang out and read the paper, have a little coffee, and listen to the gossip. It was not a place for intimate conversation because everyone in the room was part of the conversation. People would come and go, return, drink a cup of coffee and be off again, only to return an hour later. Obviously, it was a place where everyone knew your name and your business and whether you and your wife were getting along. It was also a sports information café. Everybody talked about football and how the state teams would fare in the coming season. If there were loyalties to a particular team, it got lost in the constant bantering and kidding. I knew I would like Phillip's Café. I could see most of my congregation on a given day, so it saved me the effort of visiting their homes.

I began what I hoped would be a ritual. I would get up, eat breakfast with Dot, and head for Phillip's Café for coffee to read the Clarion Ledger and visit with the community. It did not take long for me to establish the ritual, and I was a regular within the first week of my stay in Sandersville. On the first day I met Phillip and his wife, Dot. I was greeted warmly and referred to as Preacher. There were at least two other preachers in town and each was referred to as "Brother" so and so. I never did figure out why I was referred to as a Preacher but it didn't matter. I was always warmly greeted and soon struck up acquaintances with several people. I grew to really like Larry Hosey, the local Southern Railroad depot manager. He was also an avid fan of Ole Miss, and football in general. I usually arrived around 9 a.m. and he would drop by about ten minutes later. We sat and talked sports and listened to the local gossip until about 10 a.m. then went our different ways. That ritual repeated itself at least four days each week. The only difference would be the newspaper I would select for reading. I had three choices: the Clarion Ledger, the Mississippi Daily, or the Times-Picayune from New Orleans.

I had once been a contracted sports reporter for the Times-Picayune. I would phone in the high school basketball scores, and they would pay me a couple of bucks. It looked good on a resume but, in all honesty, they never spelled my name correctly. I was Ned Kexlar to the Times-Picayune. Since the paper didn't give me a byline, it hardly mattered. The most important thing to me was that my bank cashed the checks. I also wrote a sports column for my high school paper and dreamed of being a famous sportswriter. In study hall, I spent the whole hour reading sports pages from newspapers across the South. My favorites were the Nashville Banner, Miami

Herald, The Atlanta Constitution, the Clarion Ledger, and Times-Picayune. Now I was limited to the Ledger or the Picayune. The Times-Picayune focused on Louisiana schools like LSU or Tulane. The Ledger focused on the Mississippi schools. Frankly, as long as there was a sports page I was reading it.

In Sandersville, whether it was the Times-Picayune or the Clarion Ledger, the mornings were mostly the same.

I read a columnist who reported that Ole Miss would be great as usual, and Mississippi State would win one or two games. That was good news about Old Miss and sad news about Mississippi State. Just as I finished the article, Larry Hosey came into the café. I remembered him from the previous Sunday. He had attended church and, on the way out, mentioned that he hoped I was a football fan.

"Have coffee with me at Phillip's next week" he had suggested. So we did. Exchanging greetings, he sat down at my booth and we immediately began discussing the upcoming football season. Larry was very pleasant and far more verbal than I dreamed he would be. His job was to operate the depot for the Southern Railway. The depot was across the street from the café, so close he could practically answer his phone before it stopped ringing. The passenger trains had ceased to stop at Sandersville but the depot was still active, serving as a freight stop and mail pickup and drop station. Larry's job was not physically demanding but he had to be present at the place from 8 to 5, five days a week. That is except for the morning coffee break.

Philip's Cafe and Truck Stop did not claim gourmet status. It was a greasy spoon and did not have any pretense of being something different. The method of cooking was limited to frying or baking. In spite of the heavy aroma of grease, the food was great and service was good. The two major meals served were breakfast and lunch. Phillip and Dot kept the cafe open every day from sunup to sunset. Breakfast usually consisted of two eggs, grits and bacon and biscuits. The proper way to eat such a breakfast, according to the clientele of Phillip's, was to place the eggs on top of the grits. The egg yolks would then be mashed into the grits resulting in a yellow-white mass. After adding salt and pepper, the concoction was ready for eating. While I had grown up in the South, I had never seen grits and eggs mixed. As a child, I was taught to add sugar and butter to grits. I mentioned my past history of grit eating to Phillip.

"Only Yankees eat grits with sugar on them," he said.

It seemed rather strange that Phillip, of all people, the only Yankee in the place, would tell me that people in the South knew how to eat their grits.

My initial impression of Larry was on target. He was one of the nicer people in Sandersville. He was an avid Ole Miss football fan and could tell you anything you wanted to know about the Rebels. He did not attend Ole Miss, but most of the local people were Ole Miss fans and not a single one graduated from the university. Still, they were more fervent than most alumni, and thought head coach John Vaught could walk on water. In the late 50's, Vaught's teams dominated the Southern teams, and everyone in the nation knew about Ole Miss. It was the one thing most Mississippians could boast about. The people in Sandersville were no exception. Even though Mississippi Southern College was only forty miles away, it was Ole Miss when it came to picking a team to support. This bears mentioning because football was the main topic of conversation. And a safe one. When political issues were discussed there was always stress and anger. To diffuse the tension all someone had to do was switch the topic to Ole Miss football.

This first Monday in Sandersville passed quickly. By the end of the day, I had met many of the locals and seen several church members. I found that I could do most of my Sandersville parish visitations by going to Phillip's Cafe and Truck Stop and Harvey's Grocery Store. My visitation for the Vossburg and Goodwater churches would be limited to Sunday afternoons unless there was an emergency. If there was to be an exception, it would be Goodwater. The community was lovely, and driving through the area was a positive experience.

A part of the responsibility of a minister is to visit those who are sick and confined to either their homes or hospitals. In Sandersville, the task was relatively easy. The hospital was in Laurel and it was a fifteen minute drive. However, for Vossburg and Goodwater, it was a different matter. The nearest hospital to those communities was in

Quitman, a small town about thirty-five miles from Sandersville. It took at least an hour to make the drive to Quitman, and the roads were poor at best. It was obvious that I would put many miles on my car just to keep up with routine duties. The roads were rough and would destroy the best automobile in a short period of time. Visiting hospitals is not an option but rather a responsibility for the minister. Neither one of the churches paid travel expenses, and the trips to the two outlying churches were an added financial burden.

Chapter Five

Meeting the Religious Establishment

While at Emory University, my most enjoyable times were those spent with other ministers discussing theological or sociological issues and their religious significance. Of course there were the Monday golf outings, but little theological or sociological issues were discussed on the golf course. I enjoyed good discussions and had hoped it could continue with the ministers of the local churches. There were only two other pastors in the community. There may have been more, but they served small, non-denominational congregations outside the community. The two mainstream churches were the Sandersville Presbyterian Church and the First Baptist Church. Like most Southern towns, the Baptist church was the largest with more than 150 members. The Methodist was next in size followed by the Presbyterians. It took one meeting to realize that the days of sitting around discussing theological issues were long gone. The two ministers were as different as night and day. Neither was open to discussing anything with the other. I learned that preachers in small towns tend to be territorial with their members.

Brother Hester was the pastor of the First Baptist Church of Sandersville. His church was a red brick building with four white columns in front. According to Brother Hester, the four columns stood for the four Gospels: Matthew, Mark, Luke, and John. Surely, I thought, he would have assumed I knew the four gospels. But there is nothing like informing the uninformed. Reverend Hester was the oldest of the three mainstream pastors. I never saw him without a gray suit, a starched white shirt, and a conservative, solid color tie. The suit never changed. His ties were always some shade of red. He let me know that his church was the largest and that some of his members once had attended Sandersville Methodist. He also told me that he was a staunch believer in baptism. When I told him I was too, he quickly added his definition of what real baptism was.

"It is submersion, Brother."

In a small town there is considerable pride in being the biggest and the best, and First Baptist was no exception. Like most Southern Baptist churches, it was a closed shop theologically. The opportunity for a give and take discussion with Mr. Hester never presented itself. His "the way and the truth" left little room for debate.

In the year I was at Sandersville, I never got to know Mr. Hester better than that. We were poles apart theologically and socially. He reminded me of another Baptist minister I had met while at Byrd Chapel. His mother was in my church and was a fine Christian lady who loved her church and worked hard as a layperson. When she died, her son, the Baptist minister, lamented that his heart was broken because his mother was going to hell. The reason was that she had not been baptized but only sprinkled.

"Anyone who really knows the Bible," said her son, "knows that you have to be immersed in order to truly receive salvation."

His mother had been a Methodist all her life and had been baptized as an infant. Since she was not immersed, she was not saved. I had always thought of that attitude as being the most unchristian philosophy I have ever heard.

The Presbyterian minister was a tall, unattractive person who was a quiet, shy man. His name was Albert Spencer and was known as Brother Al. The casual name did not go with the demeanor. He was not very open, nor even friendly. His mannerisms suggested that he had very little self-confidence. He was nice and appropriate but somewhat formal. His face was pale and he looked to be suffering from some illness. Brother Al was not the type of person I would likely spend time with. He gave me the impression of being rather pious, a man without much training or, if he was well trained, he kept it a secret. Like Brother Hester, he too, wore a suit. Only his was dark. Later I was to discover that it was a suit given to him by members of the church. Not one of the ministers wore robes, so the dark suit was fit for preaching on Sundays, for funerals and weddings as well as other special services. I also learned that Brother Al had been the minister of the Sandersville Presbyterian Church for more than 20 years. It was unclear whether he wanted to stay at the church or whether the church could not afford anyone else. Brother Al was not a dynamic person. As one local put it, "His sermons could put coffee to sleep."

I have never met another minister who did not think he could out preach other ministers. After meeting Brother Hester and Brother Al, I felt confident that I would be the best preacher in town. I also had the better education of the three of us. I had the fantasy of drawing from the other churches and making Sandersville Methodist Church the largest of the three. But I was to learn something about small towns and churches: people do not move from one church to the other, particularly in the town of Sandersville. The community would be more accepting of a person who ran away with a dancer from the circus than they would if he changed denominations. This was especially true for the Baptists because they had been taught that the Methodists and the Presbyterians were not true Christians. It was the baptism issue that separated us from them. While a person may want to change churches, going to hell was a huge price to pay. That reduced the likelihood that many new members would join the Methodist church because everyone in the community professed to already be a member of a church.

There were two other churches in the area. Both were Holiness churches and appealed to the less affluent in the community. Both had preachers who were not full time. Consequently, neither ever participated in community activities. The reason they did not was because they did not believe in any public celebration. It was easy to spot the members of those churches, especially the women because of the lack of makeup. While I never attended any of their worship services, nor their revivals, I was told that they were unusual. Larry used to joke that their worship services would turn into "holy rolling" sessions.

"Why," Larry would laugh, "they have more moves than Elvis Presley."

On a good day, Sandersville had a population of 700 people. Those five churches served the white community. There were a couple of black churches on the outskirts of Sandersville but no one knew who their leaders were. Since no one acknowledged the Choctaw Indians, their religious inclinations were a mystery. Ironically, all three mainstream churches had mission programs directed toward African Americans and other far removed populations, but none had any type program for the Choctaws. The Baptists outnumbered all the other churches combined. The town was religious in the sense that most Southern towns are religious. The Christian Church holds a considerable power over the lifestyle of small Southern towns. Mississippi was a "dry" state and did not allow the possession or sale of alcoholic beverages. A popular saying of the time was the state would stay dry as long as the Baptists could stagger to the polls and vote against the sale of liquor. In all honesty, many Methodists could be added to that group of staggering voters. There were other influences wielded by the churches that were more subtle. It was early on in my pastorate that I learned about one of the no-no's as it pertained to clergy. We did not have a clothes dryer so Dot hung our laundry on an outside clothesline to dry. On one occasion, the laundry included a pair of Dot's shorts. A church member stopped by for a visit and noted the shorts on the clothesline.

"My Lord," she said with tongue in cheek, "I can't believe what I see. The preacher's wife wears shorts. What will the church women's circle think about that?" Tongue in cheek or not, wearing shorts was something that good Christian women did not do, especially the preacher's wife.

The religious community also condemned any kind of dancing where one sex held another closely. The explanation for the negative attitude was that if any man held a woman closely, he would be tempted to commit a sexual sin, in thought if not reality. This was a long held position, particularly with the Southern Baptists. I remembered that as a junior in high school in my hometown of Picayune, Mississippi, the local Baptist minister held a party for the Christian young people the same night as the high school prom. Those who attended the minister's party would not be subjected to the wild debauchery which supposedly took place at dances. There was tremendous pressure placed on members of local churches to go to the Christian party and not the prom. As a young person attending the Baptist church in Picayune, the Baptist Student Union (BSU) would have a hayride party on occasions. No dancing was allowed but young men and women were allowed to sit, and in some cases, lie close to someone of the opposite sex, in the back of a large truck without chaperones. If the church leadership had known what took place in the back of those trucks, dancing would have been the least of their concerns.

The Christian churches were the moral voice of small Southern communities. Sandersville was no exception. The community's morals were the minister's responsibility to keep straight. It was assumed that my church would be a part of that voice. I found I did not have to declare my position on any issue. It was assumed that because I was a white Southern Christian, I would be in full agreement with the other ministers and "righteous" laymen. The church was expected to preach against blatant sins such as gambling, drinking and anything else inconsistent with the lifestyles of the rural southerner. Conversely, the expectation was that every minister would speak out against such issues as integration of public schools. In this arena, not only was the church the moral voice of the community, it was also the enforcing agent. Those who violated the rules were ostracized and branded as sinners. In certain areas of the state, some local ministers were leaders in the KKK and other groups created to keep the "niggers" in their place. On the whole, the church chose to speak against issues. They were against dancing, mixing of the races, and sin, as they defined it. Few ever spoke about the positive aspects of Christianity. That kind of preaching was branded Bible preaching which was the calling of every minister. In reality, it is preaching the Bible as interpreted by the local's mores.

Never having been a "Bible thumping, scripture quoting, hellfire and damnation preacher," I must have caused concern with many of my members as I focused most of my sermons on social issues and on the importance of relating to one another. However, I was young, a good speaker, and everyone seemed to like me. I had learned from one of my professors at Emory to go to a new community and appear to be as happy as a lark. He also told his students that the wise thing was to praise your predecessor. I was able to accomplish one out of two. I was as happy as a lark. I did not like my predecessor. I could not act as if I did. It may be a flaw, but I have a difficult time being nice to people I do not like.

It was the interaction with the churches in the community that led me to feel homesick for Emory University and the "ivory tower" offered by academia. I had thought getting out of school was the one thing I wanted most. It did not take long to begin missing the camaraderie of close friends. I missed, too, the discussions in the cafeteria or in the hallways of our apartment house. There I could be as liberal as I wished without fear. I did not have that opportunity in Sandersville, and I missed it. Sandersville had a narrow-minded view of life and there was little or no opportunity to enter into discussion with other ministers. To do so, I needed to travel forty miles to visit with my good friend, Wilton Carter. My $3,000 salary did not allow for too much traveling. But, I was preaching to good crowds, and things were going well. I thought about the future and how my ministry would progress. Perhaps, I thought, as things settled down, I would get over my homesickness.

Chapter Six

Sandersville Society

To call Sandersville a culturally starved community was an understatement of significant magnitude. The town closed at dark on weeknights. The only evening activity was found in the churches' prayer and committee meetings. The only social gathering was the local Lions Club, the lone civic club in the area. It met once a week and was the only gathering where there was a cross section of community persons. I was extended an invitation to join the group by Harvey Hinton. I agreed to do so only after Harvey agreed to pay my dues. Frankly, I cherished the opportunity.

Sandersville's Lone Civic Club

The Sandersville Lions Club turned out to be a good social outlet for its members. I found it enjoyable and an ideal way to meet people who were not members of my church. The only other minister in the club was Brother Hester. Every meeting started with the Pledge of Allegiance, followed by a prayer. Prior to my becoming a member of the club, prayer had been Brother Hester's responsibility. Now that another minister was a member, the responsibility for praying rotated between the two of us. I perceived just a hint of jealousy on Brother Hester's part. Soon after the rotation started, Brother Hester increased the length of his prayers by at least two minutes. I am sure that if I had increased my prayer time, he would have increased his even more. In consideration of the meeting length, I conceded that Hester could pray longer than me. Besides, I have always been one who believed in short prayers. The competition did not escape Harvey. As we rode home he would joke about how short my prayers were and how long Hester's were.

"Can't you keep up with Hester?" he would ask. Just as quickly, he would explain that he was only joking, and I did not have to pray longer on Sundays.

The club meetings were an ideal place to keep up on all that was happening in the community. This was especially true of various rumors about the community personalities. One member, a huge person originally from another community, was the unofficial leader of the club. He had been a member of a Lions Club in his home community and knew more about Lions International than anyone else. He would keep the actions of the club in line with what Lions was all about. His name was Alfred and was known as Al. Al was not a shy person and had a reputation of being kind of pushy. Not everyone liked him. However, no one ever confronted him. His rulings on the proper behavior of a Lion were never questioned. He spoke with authority about Lions' matters.

There was something else about Al that made him different from the other members: he did not always agree with the actions and statements of Ross Barnett, then governor of Mississippi. While this may seem like politics-as-usual to some, Ross Barnett was the savior of the segregationist stance in the South. To question his position on any issue was to run the risk of harsh rebuttal. Al apparently couldn't care less what anyone thought or said. I liked Al and enjoyed talking with him. If I had any reservations, it was that Al was not a religious person. He put down the churches and seemed to take glee in knocking the church in conversation with Brother Hester. This caused considerable consternation with Hester, which was highly entertaining to some of us.

The annual "Ladies Night" at the Lion's Club was the only social event that occurred in my tenure at Sandersville. It was a semi-formal dinner which meant the men had to wear ties and jackets. It was held at a restaurant north of Sandersville. Phillip's Café was not elite enough for such a gathering. It was a grand event by Sandersville standards, and everybody dressed in their Sunday best. There was a speaker, dinner, dessert and then adjournment. The event started at 6:30 p.m., and by 8:30 the party was over. The strongest beverage served was iced tea. The only entertainment, other than the speaker, were the comments made about the cooking.

The thought of having a dance in conjunction with the meeting was entertained only by Al, who asked irreverently, "What we need to have is a good old-fashioned dance at our ladies' night shindig. What do you think about that, Brother Hester?"

It must have made Hester's blood boil but he never said a word. While I do not know for sure, I am confident Hester's sermon the next Sunday had some reference to the evils of social dancing.

The cultural deprivation at Sandersville was more difficult for me than Dot. I have always enjoyed going out and being with crowds. One of the many things I loved about Atlanta was the many places to go dining. To be sure, growing up in Picayune did not afford many social opportunities either. Being in college at Southern Mississippi afforded some opportunities for social activities, but it was moving to Atlanta that really introduced us to "high society." One of the first things we did was go to a fancy restaurant for dinner. We selected the Kings Arms, a well-known eating establishment in downtown Atlanta. The restaurant had a doorman, and we were impressed with having someone opening the door for us. We both noticed his extended hand. I thought he wanted to shake hands and welcome us to his establishment. But, of course, he expected a tip. He must have had a few laughs over the visit of these high rollers from south Mississippi. We visited other special places and enjoyed our new lifestyle.

After mastering the better restaurants in Atlanta, we decided it was time to visit a nightclub. The Carters joined us one evening, and we drove to the Domino Club on Peachtree Street. Wilton and I wore ties and jackets, and Dolores and Dot dressed in their finest outfits. The Domino Club was not a gathering place for theology students. It was known for its decadence. The hostesses were beautiful young ladies who began by offering drinks. We tried to be cool and act as if a night at Domino's was a regular routine. Our cover was blown though when Dolores announced she was not staying because the hostess was obviously not wearing a girdle. After a couple of years in Atlanta we adapted to the practice of women not wearing girdles, and of being offered drinks when we dined out. By the time we graduated, we were pros at participating in the nightlife of the big city. But living in Sandersville meant the only nightlife was an annual Lions Club Ladies night.

There was one other "club" in Sandersville that included locals. It was the "White Citizens Council of Mississippi". Newspapers spoke of it often, but I had never met anyone who professed to be a member. Many of the state's prominent bankers, lawyers, doctors, and politicians were members of the council. Local newspapers wrote openly about the strategy of this aggressively racist council. In a nutshell, the White Citizens Councils sole purpose was to preserve Mississippi's "sovereign right" to maintain a segregated society. This group held a strong influence over the state but it seemed far removed from sleepy little Sandersville.

Later in the year, I was asked to serve on a committee to select the most valuable member of the Sandersville High School football team. It was an annual award made by the Lion's club and was the only award given to the team. This was done in November and I, unwittingly, created a stir. The quarterback's father was a member of the club. His opinion, and others, was, no one deserves the award more than the quarterback. I, however, had noticed a young halfback who hustled at every game and was all over the field. Unfortunately for him, his parents were not active in the community. I felt he was the most valuable player and voted for him. My opinion must have carried some influence because he won the award. The quarterback's father was irate. I had made my first enemy in the Lion's Club.

An Ill Wind Gathers

The first several days at Sandersville were mostly pleasant. The townspeople were good folk who would do most anything to help a neighbor. I believe they were as Christian as they had been taught to be. Many tithed their income and served their church with a loyalty and commitment that was admirable. The "coffee" sessions at Phillip's Cafe were a delight and much of the time was spent laughing and trading "war stories" with one another without too much regard for fact. Most were simple people with simple ways. This is not to say that they were ignorant and unaware of the real world. It is to say that they had so much to do that they did not have time for the big world.

There was one exception. Besides, as I have learned over the years, it is easier for someone else to think for you, than to think for oneself.

Temper of the Times

The racial environment in Mississippi had always been tense but as long as the black person stayed in his place there were minimal problems. Mississippi was involved in the slavery business for as long as slavery existed. Contrary to what many think, there were not too many slave owners in the state. Only the large farmers and landowners could afford slaves. The average citizen did not own slaves nor were they involved in the slave trade. However, many were dependent on the large farmers and landowners for their livelihood. The simple reason for the continued existence of slavery was economics. Of course the slaves were the only people who would do the work in the fields and not charge a fee. Slave owners argued that they could not produce cotton and food crops were it not for slaves. Even after the Civil War blacks were considered lower than second class citizens. It was easy for the communities to treat blacks with little regard.

This attitude continued into the 1940's and 50's. The school systems used one room schools for blacks and proclaimed they were treating them fairly.

In the early 1950's, there was no case against "equal but separate" school systems in the South. In my hometown, the high school for whites was a one-floor, modern school building. They decided to build a new two-story, wood frame school building for the black high school.

"No one can say that the black school is not equal to the white high school," was the new cry.

It was all for naught. The U. S. Supreme Court struck down the "separate but equal" argument in the famous Brown versus Board of Education in 1954. Some would say this is when the "problems with blacks" began.

By the late 1950's, the bent was toward declaring the entire old South system unconstitutional.

As a member of the Sandersville church told me, "They didn't have to do that. We treated our niggers real good." She went so far as to declare that slaves were well treated. After all, they had a place to live and food to eat and they were taken care of by their owners.

After the Brown versus the Board of Education decision, discussion of racial attitudes — in the South — was limited to those who opposed the ruling. Anyone agreeing with the decision did so at their own risk. The thought of segregated schools being outlawed was not only unacceptable, but unthinkable for most people. The line had been drawn and the South would never yield to this "communist inspired" ruling. The South did not believe that blacks would ever set foot in a white school. If the government tried to force the issue the state would simply close all public schools.

I went to Sandersville in 1962, eight years after the Supreme Court ruling, and the attitude was still the same. I mention this because, in my opinion, most of the residents of my new parish never thought for a moment that the schools would integrate. For most it was beyond comprehension thus making it a non-discussion issue. For others the mere thought of the Southern way of life ending was a call to arms. Organizations were created to ensure this ruling never took effect. For those people, it was war, and all is fair in war.

This is not to say that everyone in the community was a part of some club or clan determined to fight the government to the point where they would withdraw the court ruling and things would remain as God intended them to remain. However, whether a member of such a group or not, the general population either agreed with those groups or remained silent, giving tacit approval for any and all actions that would prevent "niggers" going to a white school.

The issue was constantly fanned by an aggressive media controlled by people who sided with the segregationist position, or as some would put it, "to preserve the Southern way of life." It was also the rallying cry for every politician in the state in the South who were self-appointed protectionists of the way of life enjoyed by our forefathers and everyone who was a true American Southerner. Hardly a day passed without some political ad, an editorial and/or letter to the editor, damning anyone who remotely suggested that segregation was wrong. The blame was placed on outside agitator's hell-bent on destroying "our way of life." Acts of violence were increasing at an alarming rate.

The prevailing attitude made any discussion of the merits of a single school system impossible. I recalled a time when a friend of mine attended a service while I was a pastor of Byrd Chapel. He challenged a statement I had made in a sermon. All I had said was that Jesus taught us to love all people. He took it to mean I supported desegregation. This man went on to be elected as a State Representative from my home area as a staunch advocate for racial segregation. To me, he was an egomaniac who liked to rant and rave. I gave him very little thought except to consider that any pastor's remark could, and would, be taken in whatever manner the listener saw fit.

I had hoped that, while I had been away from Mississippi, that attitude had changed. Not only had they not changed, they were much worse. Sandersville was no exception. While there, I felt comfortable discussing any topic except racial views, especially if they were interpreted to be sympathetic toward blacks. It just was not done. For me, who had had many discussions about the problems of segregation while at Emory, it was like being unable to talk or hear or think. I felt suppressed by rules that were in place and must not be violated. The only race-related remarks I ever heard were wholly negative toward blacks.

The fact of the matter was that I never heard the term black, only nigger. No one ever gave that term any thought. It was the word used to describe black people.

I often had to bite my tongue since it was assumed that I felt as they did. Someone would tell a joke deriding blacks and they would begin by saying, "Preacher, you being a native of Mississippi will appreciate this joke..." Everyone would laugh without a hint of concern about the plight of the black person and his/her consequences. It was a way of life.

One experience stands out in my mind. The wife of a prominent member of our church was visiting the parsonage. The KKK came up and I made mention of my dislike for the organization.

"Preacher, the Klan has done a lot to keep the niggers in their place. You ought to be thankful they are around," she immediately responded.

I knew that before I came to Sandersville, but I did not realize just how bad it was. I let it go. If there was a Klan in Sandersville, her husband would have been a part of it.

The state of Mississippi was obsessed with the whole segregation issue. It was busy making sure that integration would never happen. Legislation was passed setting up a special commission designed to "protect the ways and lifestyle of Mississippians." The state legislature passed law after law, which ran counter to the Supreme Court's decision on segregation. They even created the Sovereignty Commission which was in support of the white Citizen's Council, a group like the Klan but given a new status. This commission was designed to block integration and root out those who would support the same. (It was later revealed that this commission funneled thousands of dollars of tax money into the council.)

With each passing day the state hardened its stance against integration. Not only did Mississippi refuse to integrate its schools, they even altered the state constitution to permit Mississippi officials to close schools to avoid desecration. The state legislature went even further and outlawed common-law marriage. This meant that many black children were suddenly considered illegitimate in the eyes of the state and, under another Mississippi law, ineligible to attend public schools.

It was strange to see people who would lead prayer in church sit in a booth in a local cafe and talk about killing a person without conscience if that person threatened Mississippi's sovereign right of segregation.

Few spoke out against the injustice. One man, Medgar Evers, a black man from Jackson, did speak out. He quickly became a thorn in the flesh of the segregationists in Mississippi. He was a member of the dreaded evil organization, the National Association for the Advancement of Colored People. Let Medgar Evers name be brought up and the collective blood pressure of most everyone present would rise considerably.

As the media began to report the events, especially the national media, the conversations in Phillip's Café gained a new focus. All of a sudden, football was secondary. Or so it appeared to me. It could be that I had walked into a long standing problem, and it just seemed like it was exploding. Many of the events discussed in Phillip's Cafe had occurred while I was still at Emory University. The Atlanta Constitution and Journal recorded the stories of the efforts on the part of the black community to gain their rights. While I read them, and was concerned, I was so involved in my own education that I did not give much thought to what was really happening. Besides, I would work to change things once I graduated and returned to Mississippi. I knew it was bad but I watched Atlanta integrate its school system with little violence. It seemed inconceivable that people were being killed in my home state. But now I was in Sandersville, in the "free state of Jones", and the events happening around the state were brought into my world and into my church. In the "ivory tower" of liberal Emory University, I vowed to do many things and had voiced many opinions. Obviously I had not followed through with my vow to leave the ministry if sent to Sandersville. Was I wrong about this, too?

Idealism from afar carries little personal threat. Idealism on the battlefront is a different matter. No, my attitude remained the same but being among those people did not allow for much verbalized idealism. Hatred, fear and anger had completely consumed those people. Reason and common sense had been replaced by a reactionary attitude that was closed to debate and discussion. For the most part, people continued with their daily activities without much ado. That is so long as no one mentioned the race issue in any positive manner. It was a ticking bomb, much more difficult than I had imagined.

Chapter Seven

The Honeymoon is Over

A good rule of thumb is that the first six months of a pastorate is a honeymoon. Like the traditional honeymoon, it is a time of getting acquainted when both the minister and the congregation are so overwhelmed with one another that there is no time for honest exchange. I learned that the smaller the church, the shorter the honeymoon. I realized my honeymoon was ending through one experience which occurred on or about June 21, 1962, just a bit over two weeks into my ministry at Sandersville. It was an experience that was beyond my control or the control of the congregation.

The first two weeks had passed quickly, and I had settled into a routine of getting up early, dressing, and walking to Phillip's Cafe for coffee and a visit with some of the locals. I had been readily accepted as a part of the group so mornings were a treat. On the way I stopped and picked up the Clarion Ledger. It was the only paper available on that day. The Times-Picayune was late arriving. Besides, the Ledger had the best sports section. I entered the cafe, greeted those present, and sat down to a cup of hot coffee and the paper. By the time I finished, the cafe would usually be half-full of locals ready to discuss the latest news, generally limited to politics and sports. Since few of the local people kept up with politics outside the boundaries of Mississippi, political discussions did not last long. Sports was another matter. Baseball was given a courtesy mention and then the talk turned to football. I thoroughly enjoyed the sports discussion. Of late, the political discussions had become too upsetting for me. Ross Barnett was governor of the state at the time, and he was one of the most bigoted men in the South. The political discussions always came to the same conclusion.

"Somebody ought to shoot that nigger Medgar Evers," and "Ain't no nigger going to a white Mississippi school."

I refilled my cup of coffee and began to look at the newspaper in earnest. On the front page was a story about an incident that had taken place in Forest, Mississippi about an hour's drive north of Sandersville. My interest was tweaked by two facts: one, it was near the church served by my good friend Wilton Carter. The second was the content of the story. The editor of a black newspaper, according to the story, had driven to Forest to investigate a report that a black man had been killed by the local police. The article reported that the editor was stopped by the local police and badly beaten. The article did not go into detail.

As I looked around the café, I was hoping against hope that no one had read the story. It would be one of those days where the crowd would rant and rave about the incident. I hated those kinds of days because I knew I would be asked for an opinion. I glanced around to see if anyone else had a paper. I saw a customer who was new to the café. Perhaps he was a truck driver passing through town. He was huge and wore dirty overalls and a baseball-style cap with the Caterpillar logo stamped on the front. The man was so large, and so mean looking, that I felt uneasy. He made his way to the counter and sat down. He turned the stool around so that he was facing the few other patrons in the cafe.

"You people hear what I heard on the radio?" Without waiting for any response, the big man reported, "Seems some nigger got his ass kicked up in Forest by the sheriff's men. They didn't kill 'im, but they came real close to killin' 'im. Them boys up in Forest know how to handle a nigger."

Some heads nodded but no one said anything.

"They should have killed the bastard, if you ask me."

No one responded. I stuck my face deeper in the newspaper. Phil walked over to him and whispered something. The big man looked directly at me and apologized for using profanity.

"Preacher, I'm sorry if I offended you with my language. As you can tell, I don't like niggers, and I don't like people who do."

I offered a weak smile and went back to reading my newspaper, hoping he would have his coffee and leave. The man was clearly agitated and wanted to talk with anyone who would listen. Soon, a couple of others began to share their views and the conversation was rolling. The more those people talked the more radical they became. Soon they were talking about killing a black man with the same emotion one would have speaking of killing a mad dog.

"A good riddance to all them niggers."

I kept trying to read but my anger blurred the words on the page.

Then the big man turned my way and said, "Say, preacher, we ain't heard from you. What do you think about that coon getting a little whipping?"

Before I could answer, another volunteered, "I'll tell you how any real Southerner feels. He ain't gonna sit by and let the niggers take over."

Soon everybody in the cafe was giving his opinion, each trying to outdo the other. I never did get a chance to respond to the big man with the Caterpillar cap.

Several long minutes had passed since the big stranger had entered the restaurant. All I could think of was the discussion taking place all around me. It seemed unrealistic that this group of men, some active in their Christian churches, were talking about how they would treat any black man who dared violate the Southern ways. They spoke so matter-of-factly about violence against a black person that my anger threatened to spill over and out of my mouth. How in God's world could anyone justify the beating of another person simply because he was black? It was difficult to understand that a man was nearly beaten to death by the very people who should have protected him.

I was terribly uncomfortable and my stomach felt queasy. It was not the first time I had felt that way.

My mind drifted back to another time and place. I was a senior in college at Southern Miss. A young black man had been lynched by a mob. I remembered the name of the black man, Charles Mack Parker. A young white couple had been driving north along a deserted stretch of Highway 11 between Poplarville and Lumberton. Somewhere along the way, the car developed trouble and the couple pulled off the road. After several minutes of trying to fix the car, the young husband decided to hitchhike into Lumberton to get help. He asked his wife to stay in the car. After he was gone, a vehicle pulled up alongside the disabled car. A black man got out and approached the stalled automobile. The woman saw him approach and locked the door. According to her, he broke the car window, opened the door, and dragged her out onto the ground. There he raped her and left her beside the road.

When her husband returned, she told him about the rape. The police were called. In a matter of hours the whole community was up in arms looking for the man who had raped that helpless woman. Using the description given by the woman, the police arrested a black man named Charles Mack Parker. Later the woman identified Parker as the assailant, though she admitted that she was "not really sure." It had been dark and she could not see clearly. A highway patrolman, according to reports, handed the husband of the white woman his revolver and told him to shoot Parker. The husband refused to do so because his wife was not certain that Parker was the rapist.

Parker was arraigned on charges of rape and put in the county jail in Poplarville. Word spread through the community that a "nigger" had raped a white woman and was in jail.

The same remarks now being made in Phillip's Cafe had been made in every restaurant and gathering place in Poplarville. In Forest there had been only a beating and a lot of talk. In Poplarville it had been very different.

One evening, shortly after Parker had been imprisoned, a mob broke into the jail. It was a well-orchestrated mob because they knew the exact location of the prisoner. The keys had been left on the desk in clear sight. The deputy in charge of the jail was away from his post. The members of the mob went into Parker's cell and castrated him as a lesson for "other niggers who may think about raping white women." They then took him out of the jail and drove twenty miles to the Pearl River, the state boundary between Mississippi and Louisiana. There, they shot him to death, weighted his body, and tossed it into the river.

The next day there was talk about the jail break-in. Some conjectured that Parker had actually been freed by some of the "northern niggers" and was alive and living in Chicago. The news media reported on the incident and quoted several of the people involved in the case. The judge who had held the arraignment made the remark that the "nigger showed no remorse and was even arrogant." The judge went on to say that he would have been in and out of prison.

"This way he will never rape another white woman."

The jailer gave an excuse for being away from his post. Others said in as many words, "justice prevailed." Some still speculated that there had been no killing because there was no body. Three days after the break-in, Charles Mack Parker's body was found floating in the Pearl River. Ironically, it was found on the Louisiana side of the river making his death a federal case.

The F.B.I. was brought in. The sleepy little town of Poplarville was now in the national spotlight. Soon many prominent people were being questioned about the lynching. The FBI brought in several agents who spread throughout the county and into neighboring counties looking for leads. The locals were not accustomed to the tactics of the feds. They discovered that these lawmen were very different from their own and were persistent in their questioning. There is a newspaper article with a picture, which stands out in my mind. It is a photo of a farmer sitting in his iron-framed bed with a shotgun in his lap. He was sure, the article said, that the FBI was going to break into his house in the middle of the night. It was one of the most pathetic pictures I have ever seen. That poor old farmer had been dragged into the middle of an event he thought was so simple. Now he had become the hunted, and the fear in his eyes was something I shall never forget.

Prominent people were being questioned about their involvement in the lynching. I knew the names of some of the people, and their children were friends and acquaintances. It all seemed so strange and unreal. People were quick to share their feelings, all of which were in favor of the mob that lynched that "damn nigger." For the first time in my life I saw the lengths some would go to keep the "Southern way of life." I did not, at that time, understand just how deeply entrenched cultural beliefs could become. A few weeks later, the newspapers would report that the county prosecutor refused to try the case even though the FBI had named almost everyone involved. The reason given was insufficient evidence.

I recall the reaction of family members when the news of the lynching first reached the papers. Dot and I were engaged at the time, and I spent more time with her family than I did at home. Dot had warned me that her dad was very prejudiced against blacks, or Negroes, as we referred to them. My first encounter with him over the lynching reinforced what Dot said. My father-in-law to be was a man who was as good as any person I have ever known, but he had a very deep prejudice toward blacks and was quick to point out that if a "nigger does that to a white woman, he ought to be shot." It was in his kitchen that I first witnessed the depth of his prejudice. When we sat there with the Hattiesburg American on the table with its bold headline about the lynching, I remarked that killing a man without a fair trial was wrong. Not only did he disagree, but the tone of his voice and the look he gave me reminded me that we had strong differences on the matter of race. Not wanting to jeopardize my place in Dot's family, I held my tongue.

I was brought back to the moment in Phillip's Cafe when someone raised his voice in condemnation of the media for "blowing out of proportion" the Forest incident. What I felt that morning was exactly the same feeling I had about Charles Mack Parker and the people who took his life. There was an ignorance that seemed so apparent to me, but no one there shared my view. The attitude of most can be summarized by a short, fat, balding insurance salesman who came to talk with Dot and me about life insurance. I remember not liking anything about him before he even spoke. I also remember him sweating a lot. He was unattractive and the type of person that was an expert on everything. Just minutes into our conversation, the Charles Mack Parker issue came up.

"You know," he started, "that nigger deserved to be shot. If it had been my woman or one of my family members, I'd've shot him dead. You know, the body they found probably ain't that Parker nigger. You know why dead men float?" Without waiting for an answer he continued. "It's because gasses form in their stomach and they pop to surface. All you have to do is rip their guts out and they won't float. Don't ask me how I know that. And, you know what them FBI men said about identifying him through fingerprints. Well, I know if a man stays in the water for three days he swells like a pig. His fingers would have split wide open. You can't get any fingerprint if the finger is split wide open." By now his face was red and covered with perspiration. "By the way," he said almost as an afterthought, "I hear you two are going to get married, and I want to talk to you about some insurance."

Again I was brought back to my booth in Phillip's Cafe when Larry shared with the group that some of the papers were touting Ole Miss as a possible Southeastern Conference contender. Just like that, the conversation left the issue of a black man being beaten by police simply because he was investigating a killing, and returned to the safe arena of football. Once the conversation drifted from beatings to football, the big man got up and walked out. That morning at Phillip's Cafe I had been reminded that feelings run deep and hatred was in the hearts of a lot of people. The death of a person did not matter when that person was black, especially if that black man was a "nosy, uppity nigger." I left the café with a bad feeling in the pit of my stomach. I hoped that the issue would end with that morning's discussion at Phillip's Café. It was wishful thinking.

Perhaps it was a result of the encounter at Phillip's Cafe that I began to notice the frequency of racial stories in the newspapers, or maybe it was because more articles were being printed about the racial strife in the state. I do know that I became more sensitive to the stories and more bothered about what was happening in Mississippi. I felt fear and at the same time guilt. Wasn't the pulpit a place where divisive issues were addressed? Didn't I have the responsibility to say something about all of the anger and hatred that seemed to permeate the lives and souls of this community?

The problem was not new to the state. Already the Student Nonviolent Coordinating Committee was working to register blacks to vote. There had been sit-ins in Jackson and in Amite County located in the rural southwest section of the state. I remembered reading about the incidents in the Atlanta newspapers while in school. There were stories about a black person being beaten and some being killed because they had attempted to register to vote. Some of the stories stood out in my mind. One black applicant was pistol-whipped by the white registrar. Another had been shot to death by a state legislator. Just two months before I began my ministry at Sandersville, a black soldier, Roman Ducksworth, was shot to death by a white policeman for refusing to sit in the back of a bus. This had happened in Taylorsville, Mississippi, just a few miles from Sandersville. But those incidents had been in some other community. They happened before my ministry. Now I began to feel the presence of blind hatred, and I was frightened. The look in the eyes of that big man in Phillip's Cafe haunted me.

I began, for the first time, to give serious thought about what I could do about this explosive issue. It was not the first time I have thought about ministering in a community where the racial issue was so dominant. While at Emory, a group of men from Mississippi met with Dr. Arva Floyd, one of the most genteel men I had ever known. The purpose was to discuss, with this great saint, ways we ministers could make a difference in our home state. We wanted to know how to make a difference. What is the appropriate way to provide an effective ministry to a people in racial conflict? We met in the home of Dr. Floyd and asked him what we should do. Not a single person in that room believed in the traditional attitudes held by most in Mississippi. Dr. Floyd began by advising each of us to be patient. He also reminded us to treat blacks with the same respect that we give to white people.

"Remember," he said, "these people have lived their whole lives believing that black people are inferior. They will not change easily."

I remember sitting in that room feeling somewhat disappointed. I am not sure what I had expected but "being nice to blacks" was not enough for me. I had always been nice to blacks. I wished he had told us how to change people and help resolve the anger and hatred. I was willing to be patient. I could wait as long as six months if necessary. I finally suggested that we needed to do something more concrete than just being nice.

"Remember," Dr. Floyd cautioned, "be patient."

After that meeting some of us talked about what had happened. The consensus was that Floyd's advice was good. I disagreed.

"When did you become such a liberal?" The questioner was Mel, a former Marine from the Gulf Coast of Mississippi who had entered the ministry in his thirties.

I could not answer his question. I didn't know when it was that I began to relate to blacks. I could not remember when it was that I did not like blacks. I did remember once getting in a fight with a cousin because I had answered a black lady by saying "Yes, ma'am."

"You don't say yes, ma'am to a nigger," he said.

"I'll say anything I want to say," I countered. One thing led to another and we ended up trying to punch each other out. Maybe it was before that. Living close to the "quarters" resulted in my playing with black children. I don't know when it began but I knew that I was bothered by the way my relatives and neighbors treated blacks.

"Your attitude is going to get you into trouble," warned Mel.

That would not be new for me. My sympathy for blacks had gotten me into trouble before.

One experience haunts me to this day. I was in a National Guard unit in my hometown. Most of my family had been in the military, and I took pride in my soldiering. Because of my "gung-ho" attitude, I was appointed to a leadership platoon. This resulted in my being part of a fifteen-man group that would take a long hike in full military dress with a rifle and backpack. We had marched about five miles then took a break. We all fell out and lay on the ground beside the road. As we lay there an elderly black man approached.

Red, one of the more bigoted of the group, shouted to that old man, "Hey nigger, better not pass this way." Others began to deride him. One even pointed his rifle at the old man, probably scaring him half out of his wits.

All the while he kept his head down saying, "Yassir, God bless all of you." He must have repeated that statement a dozen times as he walked past that group of young men. You could see the fear gripping him. It must have been overwhelming.

"Nigger, we are going to shoot you," someone shouted.

"Yassir, God bless you, God bless you."

My heart ached for him, and I could feel his pain. Soon he was well past the group and we continued our march. Brave men we were, with a rifle, combat gear and full uniform. We had just met the enemy, a 70- or 80-year-old black man, and we had instilled fear. I have never forgotten the feelings I had at that moment. I felt sorry for the old man and angry at my fellow brave soldiers.

Again we hit the road and marched about a mile further. We stopped again for a break. As we lay there in the grass, catching our breath, Red mentioned that I had not said anything to that "nigger." My response was something like, "I don't find much sport in intimidating an old black man." This set Red off, and he was ready to fight.

"Are you some kind of goddamn fuckin' nigger lover? If you are, I'll whip your ass right here!"

"I don't think you can whip my ass but if you want to try, let's get to it." My heart was pounding. In that moment I had enough anger in me to kill him. I wanted to do what the old man could not do and that was kick the ass of his tormentor. The lieutenant stopped the fight before it started. From that day on, Red and I never liked one another. In retrospect, I know that if Red and I had started fighting, I would not have had a single supporter among the other thirteen guys.

I do not remember how long I had been lost in those painful memories. After a while I got up and left the café. My heart was pounding. I was both angry and sad. My short honeymoon at Sandersville was over.

"Be patient," Dr. Floyd had said.

Others had reminded me that I had a responsibility to keep the church together. But, I thought, at what price to my conscience? The real issue in my life was how long I could keep my emotions together. I kept seeing that old man, frightened near to death, being taunted by a pack of young men just because he was black. I began to see a side of myself that I did not like. I could hate people like Red with a vengeance. I would not let go of the hatred I felt toward him and his cohorts. I could recall the anger with which I had attacked my cousin. I concluded that I needed to keep away from the issue. My plan was to stay involved with the daily activities of my ministry. Besides, all the real struggles were far away in Jackson or McComb.

It did not take long to settle back into my routine. Much of the time was spent writing sermons and trying to get the mimeograph machine to print. I tried to be a good pastor and visit as many of the members of the three churches as I could. This meant some extensive travel over winding country roads, most of which were paved.

The visits to Vossburg were the most difficult. It was not an attractive area, and the people were not as friendly as they were in the other communities. For example, on one occasion I dropped by to visit a lady who was active in the church. She had a lovely home and was the most sophisticated person in Vossburg. The practice was to just drop by and visit without advance notice. The lady of the house invited me into her living room and offered me coffee or iced tea. I selected the iced tea because it was July. It was hot outside and inside. As she prepared the tea her dog, a small breed of animal, came and stood near my feet. The little black and white dog looked friendly enough, and I reached out to pet it. As my hand approached the dog's head, the little bastard bit me. It was completely without warning. There was no growling nor barking, just a quick bite on my hand. I jerked my hand back and my impulse told me to kick the dog into oblivion. However, I controlled my impulse and studied the hand to see if the skin had been broken. The appearance of blood assured me that I had, indeed, been wounded. I was not surprised to see the blood because it hurt like hell. The lady of the house came into the room, saw the dog standing at my feet, saw the blood on my hand and asked, "Did she bite you?"

I was tempted to say, "No, I am so depressed being in your home that I cut my wrist." I laughed out loud at this! Again I controlled my impulsive nature and growing anger toward the dog and said that it was just a little bite.

"Well," this gracious lady said, "she doesn't like strangers, and she will bite. Do you take sugar in your tea?" I concluded that one visit a year to this home would suffice.

Visiting in the Goodwater community was much more enjoyable. The few people who lived in the community were simple farmers who treated guests like family. The one visit I remember most was to a man who was a leader in the church. He raised hogs. He boasted of having several hundred head of hogs on his farm. We spent about two hours together talking about hogs. Mostly I listened and he talked. Goodwater is in south central Mississippi and located on a high ridge. It was the closest thing to a mountain in that area, and you could see for miles on a clear day. The farmer told me it gets so cold that he has to take his pregnant hogs into his home so that they can deliver.

"Why, just last February I had an old sow that delivered twelve little pigs right there in my kitchen. Me and the wife helped her."

We were sitting in his dining room which was adjacent to the kitchen. As his wife brought a cup of coffee and a slice of pie, all I could think about was that 400 pound hog delivering her piglets on that kitchen floor. In my mind, the coffee smelled kind of funny, and the pie did not taste very good.

By the middle of July my routine was set. Each morning I went to Phillip's Cafe for coffee, reading the newspaper and sharing war stories with Larry and others. I would then go to the post office and check to see if we had any mail. That turned out to be one of the more enjoyable parts of my routine. The postmistress was Harvey's sister, Ruth. Ruth was a maiden lady in her 60's or 70's. She was a small-framed woman who loved to talk. There were rumors that she read all the postcards before placing them in the proper mailbox. One story had it that one of the young men was expecting a postcard that listed the time and place of a baseball game that he was scheduled to umpire. By the time he reached the post office the building was closed. He was frantic and finally called Miss Ruth. He told her of his dilemma and then asked, "Do you remember what time the game starts?" She was incensed and reminded him that the postal department forbade any employee from reading anyone's mail. He told her he was desperate and had to be at the game or he would be fired.

She then told him, "Well, I did not read your postcard but if I was you I would be at that ball park at 2 p.m. Sunday."

Following the post office visit, I would return home and do some chores around the house. The church furnished a lawn mower, and I mowed the yard about once a week. I remembered what Harvey had told me about the old dead tree so I was careful to mow around it as fast as possible. After my chores were done, I would set out to do my visiting or work on sermons. It seemed that sermon preparation was never ending. I had to prepare three messages a week, and I was new at the task. The Sunday morning sermon would be good for both Sandersville and one of the other churches. The evening sermon and prayer meeting were for Sandersville. This took much of my time and all of the talent I could muster. I took pride in my preaching and wanted each sermon to be awe-inspiring. I don't think I ever accomplished the awe-inspiring level, but I did pretty well most of the time.

About once a month Dot and I would travel to Newton, Mississippi, to visit with Wilton and Dolores Carter. Wilton's charge was about the same as Sandersville except that he had four churches. We met to discuss our progress and then play golf. Dot and Dolores would share stories about the parsonages and about the women's meetings. It was always a pleasant visit and we had fun. The distance was about fifty or sixty miles but the driving time was at least an hour and a half longer. The trip took the better part of the day. We did manage to visit Dot's parents at least every other week. I loved those visits because we would have a great meal. It was not that Dot could not cook. She had become the cook her mother said she was when I first met her. However, Dot would buy a pound of hamburger and make four meals out of the single pound. Visiting the farm was a refresher both physically and spiritually. Dot's mother had a sense of humor that was without peer. The only problem was that she would laugh so hard that she wet herself. I often thought how lucky Dot was to have a mother like that – at least the humor part. I shall never forget the time, prior to our being married, that Dot and I were a being a little amorous in Dot's bedroom. Dot vowed to be a virgin when we got married and she succeeded. However, it was one of those times when we nearly violated her vow. As we "made out" in the bedroom, Mrs. Dickinson came home. She must have realized what was going on because she walked around the house two times coughing loud enough for us to hear her. She must have been relieved when we went outside to greet her.

On occasion we would visit Dot's brother Buford, who was a pastor of a church in Decatur, Mississippi which was near Meridian. Buford and Jean, his wife, had two children, and we would spend time playing with the kids. It was obvious that Dot wanted children and so did I. We had worked to keep from having children while in school but now, seeing Tim and Kathy, we were ready for our own family. Tim once spent a week with us, and we loved playing the role of parent. Tim was toilet trained but always needed assistance after he used the bathroom. He would yell, "I'm through, I'm through," which meant one of us had to go in and help him get things back in order. Tim was very special to us, and I hoped for a son. Kathy was a beautiful little blond who controlled the whole house. Our visits with Buford and Jean and being around Tim and Kathy made us realize how much we wanted children.

The visits to Decatur were also a boost to our morale. Jean was one of my favorite people. She was, and is, a very talented lady. She is also one of the easiest going persons I know. If you ever want a definition of "easy going" just get a picture of Jean. I thought of myself as being easy going as well so I identified with her. Buford, on the other hand, was just like his father and his sister Dot. He was a very bright person but he never seemed to relax. While Jean and I would sit around and talk, Buford would pace the floor or fidget with something. He reminded me so much of Dot's dad. One of the first things Dot's dad said to me was how much he regretted that the

Lord did not put more hours in a day so that he could get more work done. Buford was the same way. As I recall, so was Dot and the rest of the family.

Chapter Eight

Move Over Billy Graham

Late in the summer, I received a call from a neighboring pastor and friend, Sam McRaney. Sam was the pastor of Philadelphia Methodist Church located in a small community about twenty miles away.

"Ned," he said with a Southern drawl that makes mine sound like a New England accent, "I want to invite you to preach at our annual revival."

It needs to be said that being asked to preach at a revival was a real compliment. In an effort to show modesty, I responded by assuring him that he could certainly find a much better preacher. My expectation was that he would say that I was the best, and he was lucky to have me.

Instead he said, "Ned, you're right but I waited too long to ask others and you're the only one left." He was dead serious. The schedule he set was for four morning services and six evening services. I was on cloud nine. Well, eight and a half.

Preaching that revival is one of the highlights of my Mississippi ministry. I loved being the visiting preacher. Not only that but I got paid $50 for the week's preaching. We had a song leader and all of the trimmings. After that week I was certain that the phone would ring off the hook with invitations to preach revivals. Unfortunately, that did not happen. So, when it came time for me to have a revival at Goodwater, I invited myself to preach.

As I have mentioned, the little Goodwater church seated thirty or forty people at most. That was twice the number of Methodists in the area. On the first night we had a standing room only crowd. The news of my Philadelphia crusade must have reached the small village of Goodwater. Unfortunately, I was told that when a revival was held, everyone in the community would attend regardless of who was preaching. There were two experiences which made that week unusual. On the very first night a family of seven came. I had never seen them before. The father was a heavyset man who wore a see-through nylon shirt. Only two buttons held the shirt closed and they were the two top buttons. The shirt flared open to reveal a very large, round and hairy stomach. His wife was also large. They had five children, the oldest being about seven and the youngest about three months. The entire family sat in the back row of the church.

In the middle of my first sermon, the mother began unbuttoning her blouse. I could not help but notice that she was not wearing a bra. Soon one of her breasts was fully exposed. I stopped preaching for just a moment. Luckily, I regained my composure and continued to preach. She lifted the breast and offered it to her youngest child. She continued to breastfeed her baby through most of the service. I was the only one taken aback by her action. The family attended every service and at the same time every night she repeated the ritual.

The other experience involved a soloist. Each night we would have special music just before the sermon. The first few nights the soloist would stand in front of the pulpit and sing. This was a wise move because the church was so small that the pulpit was less than three feet from the back wall. Between the pulpit and the back wall was the chair for the pastor. All I had to do was stand up and I was in place for the sermon. On this particular evening the soloist, a lovely young woman, made her way to the chancel area. Instead of stopping and standing in front of the pulpit, she proceeded to work her way between me and the pulpit. I had to swing my knees to one side and turn my head sideways so she could fit. Her rear was so close that if I had faced forward my nose would have touched her. I sat as still as I could, not even breathing, until she finished her song. Through the whole thing I tried to look as proper as I could with my knees sticking out to one side and my head turned away. I have never felt so much a part of a solo without singing.

After the service I confessed to Dot about my terrible, un-Christian thought that, with a simple turn of my head, I could have helped the soloist with the high notes.

The experience of conducting my own revival was one I shall never forget. What amazed me the most were the number of people who attended. I had driven through the entire community on several occasions and I never noticed many houses. After the revival I assumed the heavy woods obscured many homes. Otherwise, those in attendance must have driven many miles to hear me preach. The churches were the only social outlet for the Goodwater community and a revival allowed for five or six nights of socializing. People would gather a full hour before the start of the worship service to stand outside the church and visit with one another. Everyone visited with each other as if they were long lost relatives. It was a fun experience and I loved being a revival preacher, even if I am the only one available.

Storm Clouds Grow Darker

The summer was passing quickly. The routine of breakfast at Phillip's Café, dropping by Harvey's and picking up the mail continued daily with the exception of Sundays. We continued our bi-monthly visits to Lawrenceville to see the Carters. It was fun being with Wilton and Dolores. We could share our dreams of one day serving a single church appointment. We would end up with a church that paid $5,000 a year and had only two services. Sandersville was a difficult charge to manage but it was not as bad as Wilton's charge at Lake and Lawrenceville. He had four churches while I had three. Lake was near Forest, a small and extremely conservative county in the very center of the state. The nearest town was Newton, which had a population of about 2,000 people. It was farm country.

The visit routine was always the same. Wilton and I would drift off to play golf while the girls would look for sales. Golf was the only really relaxing thing we did. Having always been competitive, it was good to get into a game with someone with whom I could act as I wished. Wilton was a tough opponent and could hit a golf ball as far as most people on the pro tour. The course we played was in Forest and was rough by most standards but inexpensive. That was always a determining factor for two new ministers just out of seminary. We developed a practice while at Emory to seek out the cheap courses. Atlanta provided a variety and we played every one that did not cost over $5 for 18 holes. The course we played most often was the American Legion Course in Avondale Estates which charged a whopping eighty-two cents for 18 holes. It was actually a nine-hole course but we could play the same nine twice making the total cost less than a dollar. Forrest was much like the American Legion Course. It was poorly kept with fairways that received little attention. They were covered with a variety of grasses, which would cause a ball to bounce in strange ways. However, it was golf and there were 18 holes. At least the Forest Country Club had more grass than clay which set it apart from the Atlanta courses we had frequently played.

Golf was always followed by long conversations, discussions of our goals and stories about our churches. Wilton told about a man he visited who lived four miles from Lawrence. He had lived in the same home in which he was born seventy-five years earlier. He boasted that he had not been to Lawrenceville in four years, and had not been to Newton in more than fifty years. Once I told him about Vossburg, Wilton knew he had been topped again.

Many of our conversations were about our future appointments. When we compared office equipment, I clearly had the best. My mimeograph machine had a greater printing capacity than his. I could print almost fifty bulletins to his twenty-five before having to change stencils. I used that to offset the whipping he put on me on the golf course. With my competitive spirit any victory was better than no victory.

Wilton was my best friend though we were very different. He is one of the neatest men I have ever known. There was a joke in our apartment building at Emory that if Wilton had to get up in the evening to go to the bathroom he would brush his hair before he returned to bed. The guy's shoes were always polished and his clothes were clean and well-matched. Dolores would often remind us that every time she and Wilton had sex he would get up and shower. Hearing that did not make Dolores very happy, but that was Wilton. My mind would sometimes try and paint a picture of Wilton working over his mimeograph machine and keeping the ink from getting on his hands. It boggled my mind that he could do the messiest work and *still* not get dirty. We laughed a lot and enjoyed each other's company. Dot and Dolores were also very close. Knowing the two of them, having good times together and sharing our frustrations and our dreams, helped keep our sanity.

The summer grew longer and the temperature grew hotter. Unfortunately, the political climate kept in step with the summer heat. More and more news of racial conflicts made the local news. It seemed as if every one was on edge, waiting for the impending explosion. Between the racial issues, the threat of sit-ins, of riots, and of homes being bombed, disturbing news was a daily event. The White Citizens Council kept the pot stirred and declared that "all of the problems came from outside agitators. The people of Mississippi were not the problem; it was the Freedom Riders, niggers and other communist sympathizers." The local media only added to the problem. There were constant threats, some clear and some veiled, that promised any black or black sympathizer that came into Mississippi could possibly end up being carried out of Mississippi in a box.

"There will be a lot of dead niggers if anyone tries to integrate our schools or tries to eat at our restaurants." But the local community was not afraid because the Klan had vowed to not let anything happen in the "Free State of Jones."

Reading the Clarion Ledger's sports page was fun but the other articles stared out at me. These were the articles that reported people being hurt or killed all because of the racial strife that increased daily throughout the South. Try as I might, I could not just pass over them. I knew that others in the community would be reading the same articles, and I needed to at least know what was being reported.

I focused on incidents in Mississippi. After all, that was my home and where I would be serving the church for a long time.

The story about the black editor was an indicator of just how Sandersville reacted to media reports. It was in July that the following report appeared in the Ledger.

> *July 23, Albany, Georgia: The pregnant wife of a black civil rights worker was beaten while visiting her husband in jail. The beating resulted in a miscarriage.*

Keeping my mouth shut was becoming more difficult. I felt the need to be on constant guard lest I blurt out my wrath. I kept reminding myself of Dr. Floyd's advice of being patient. My exterior demeanor sent one message, but my interior was filled with rage. I questioned my practice of going to Phillip's Café on a daily basis. Was I just putting myself in a difficult place? However, I knew that I had to be there because I had to know what was happening in the community.

I had inquired about the big, mean looking guy in the dirty overalls who showed up at Phillip's Café after the Forrest incident. Everyone agreed that he was not a person you would want to hang out with or offend. He was known by "Bear". It was an appropriate name. He became a frequent visitor to Phillip's. My paranoia told me he was there to check out this new preacher. I had no proof that he had any idea about who I was, nor did I know of any reason why he would be watching me. Paranoia is a strange thing. It almost takes on a life of its own.

I learned that there were two things you could count on in Sandersville. One was that you had to be seen in the community, and the other was that all issues about the strife in Mississippi would be discussed at length at Phillip's. I wanted to know the attitudes of the community but, then again, I did not want to hear them repeated on a daily basis. It reached a point where I could predict what each person would say. If there was an exception it would be the vehemence of the remarks. "Bear" would remind the group that he would kill the blacks involved. Others would either shout an "amen" or at least concur that killing might be a good way to solve all issues.

The horrible story of the pregnant wife being beaten to the point of losing her child gnawed at my insides. I remember sitting there hoping no one would ask me what I thought. I prayed that I would not be called on to say what I would have done. The sympathies were always on the side of the white man's behavior.

"They should have killed the bitch," someone remarked.

"That is one nigger who ain't gonna cause any problem," intoned another, referring to the miscarriage.

Even though I had heard the remarks many times, I still found them repulsive. I could hear Dr. Floyd's reminder to be patient but I was ready to cry out, "How long Lord, how long I must hear this stuff?" My fear was that my silence would indicate that I agreed with the violent behavior of the people who acted out against the blacks. Strangely enough, the men, when using profanity, would turn to me and apologize. My God, I thought, you're talking about killing someone and are fearful your profanity will offend me! Never was a thought given about the victims.

Bear continued in a chilling voice. "There's gonna be a lot of killings before them nigras learn that in Mississippi you don't stir up the whites."

"I'll tell you what it is," another said. "It's them damn outside agitators. They come from Chicago and places like that." Several others would join the chorus and talk about how Mississippi had always handled their problems with the nigras.

"We don't need any outsiders coming in here and telling us that nigras can vote or go to our schools."

One day I had to get out of there before I went mad. I found a reason to leave early. I cowardly left that café feeling that I had failed everything I believed about justice and caring for the person involved. I knew that the question would come sooner or later. It was the one I hated the most. "Preacher, what do you think about all this stuff?"

I left before anyone asked the dreaded question. I am sure most thought I would have sided with them because I was a Mississippian. Dear God, if they only knew what I felt that day. It was the same feeling I had when that fat insurance salesman described how you keep a "nigger from floating." The discussion brought turmoil to my gut. I was literally shaking with anger. My soul was reeling.

I rehearsed what I would like to have said a thousand times over. "I think all of you are going to hell, which is what I suggest you do." No, that was too mild. I could take a gun and shoot some of them. I could take a baseball bat and beat them into a pulp and then ask, "How does that feel?" Then they would know how that black woman felt. A chill crept over me as I realized I was becoming one of them. God help me, I was losing it. Hatred took root in my heart as I kept my feelings inside. Strangely enough, every time I found myself in that state of mind, I would ask God what to do. But I knew the answer.

"Ned, say something!" God would demand.

And I would respond, "I will Lord. I am just being patient."

I walked slowly toward the parsonage. My mind was working overtime. I felt a chill that caused a shudder through my body. These attitudes were not new to me but the level of violence – a woman was beaten until she lost her baby! – was. I began to think about all the times I had been around people like that. It never ceased to amaze me how religious people, people who professed allegiance to Jesus Christ, could talk openly in a community establishment about "doing something to the niggers." What shocked me the most was the fact that some of these people were in my own church! I knew them! I know that were it any other issue they would give the shirt off their backs to help someone in need. But after thinking about it, and getting in touch with my roots, I realized that I had been hearing this kind of talk for as long as I could remember. Today it was a group of men in a café in Sandersville. Five years ago it was a group of young men on a military training exercise. Fifteen years ago it could well have been my own family members.

"That nigger got what he deserved."

"That nigger woman should nave stayed home."

It was the endless litany of my life.

As I walked along U. S. 11, I began to recall some of the times I had heard about acts of violence where some "nigger" had been taught a lesson. I tried to keep the thought from coming to the surface but I couldn't. It's funny how your mind can lock on a memory, and every detail comes back as if it had happened earlier that day. I could see in my mind the front cover of The Saturday Evening Post and an announcement of the leading article inside the magazine. Two men had confessed to the killing of a young black kid named Emmett Till. They did not have to worry about being arrested because they had already been tried and found "not guilty" and could not be charged again because of double jeopardy. Those bastards sat there and laughed about the killing of a fourteen year old kid. As I walked along I found myself actually trying to remember more of the details.

The year was 1955. I was a junior in high school, and I read the story in the study hall class of my high school. Have I mentioned that I spent most of my study hall period reading newspapers from large Southern cities? It always proved more exciting than high school algebra. There, with photos of themselves, the two men talked openly about how they killed the young black. Only in their terms it was the killing of a "young nigger."

I could recall all of the details of that article. I had read about the murder when it first happened. However, I had read about it in a Southern newspaper, and it was slanted to make the killing something less than what it was. Emmett Till was a young black boy, fourteen years of age, who made the mistake of whistling at a white woman. I was not unfamiliar with the story but the magazine article offered more information than any other source I had read. It was the first time I had read in detail about a racial killing.

My original source of information had been the Times-Picayune and the Clarion Ledger. Both wrote only the details of the killing. They reported how a young negro from Chicago had made lewd remarks to a white woman. It created a stir but it was, in the eyes of a lot of locals, just another "nigger from Chicago" finding out that Southerners do not allow for such behavior as whistling at a white woman. I recalled that while the local papers played it down, the national news called it an outrage. The people I knew shrugged it off as the outside media trying to paint Mississippi as a lawless society. We did not have a television so I can not speak to what was being reported there.

But I was an avid newspaper reader and my high school's library did subscribe to several out-of-state newspapers including the Nashville Banner, The Memphis Commercial Appeal, and The Atlanta Constitution, among others. I loved reading the different papers, with emphasis on the sports section. I did scan the news stories and when I found something about Mississippi, I usually read the whole article.

I could recall all of the stories about Till, and it was easy to see the difference in the reporting from what appeared in The Times-Picayune and the Clarion Ledger. For the first time I began to notice how some details were omitted from the Times-Picayune that were included in the other newspapers. I learned something that I had always known but not acknowledged. Reporters lose their objective when it might offend their advertisers.

After a short while, I had learned much about the lynching. In a sense, I became the resident expert on the real facts surrounding Emmett Till's death. No one ever sought my knowledge nor would they have been very receptive to it. Why that event stirred my interest so much I can not tell you. I just found it interesting and, at the same time, disturbing. For most, Till's death was a way to "teach them niggers a lesson." In reality, it was a catalyst that jump-started the aggressiveness of the civil rights issue in the South. It was a catalyst that started a revolution.

Why do I remember such things? Why can't I just rid my memory of this event? Why do I keep remembering the acts of violence? Again, I prayed that God would keep these thoughts out of my mind. They hurt. They reminded me of my inaction, of my running from the problem, that I was not doing anything about this situation. It was not new to me. I grew up around people who, when angry, would threaten their adversary, "I'll kill you." I had that remark directed to me by my own family members, and I had directed it toward others. I would never have done such a thing. It was a "figure of speech", one used without thought. I never saw anyone actually follow through and kill someone, so I thought it was an idle threat. But as I read about the Till case, it dawned on me that two men actually *killed* a fourteen year old black kid. Not only did they kill him, they bragged about it in the *Saturday Evening Post*, and were paid for their story! They said killing him was a matter of principle, but I had a hard time making sense of the killing and how these men justified it. I was in the minority. My friends and family saw it making complete sense. A "nigger" made a pass at a white woman, and he deserved to be killed. What's the big deal?

The big deal to me was that these men took a fourteen year old kid from his uncle's home, picked up some friends, drove to a deserted area, beat the young man half to death, shot him, tied a metal object to his body, and tossed him in the river.

People in my neighborhood thought no more of that than they would have someone shoot a dog. Come to think of it, they would resent the death of the dog much more than Till's death.

And now, in Sandersville, at Phillips Café and Truck Stop, men I knew were talking with the same disregard for a black man or woman's life. Reading about it happening in Till's case had been like a movie. Being in the presence of these men in the cafe was disturbing and frightening. I actually found myself trembling as I walked toward the parsonage. This was real. How in the world can I bring about change in this community? No one would side with me. It would be me against the whole community. How I wished I was still in the ivory tower of Gilbert Hall on the campus of Emory.

The Emmett Till Case

Emmett Till was from Chicago, a city that was held in contempt by most of the people I knew. It was a "northern city" that was a Mecca for blacks. Emmett and his cousin, Curtis Jones, were visiting relatives near Money situated in the northern part of the state. They were staying with Curtis' grandfather, Mose Wright. The town had just recently experienced another racial issue where a black girl had been flogged for "crowding white people" in a store.

On a Wednesday evening in August 1955, Emmett and Curtis drove Mose Wright's 1941 Ford to Bryant's Grocery and Meat Market, a country store with a big metal Coca-Cola Sign outside.

It was there that the boys met up with some friends, and Curtis began a game of checkers with a 70-year-old black man sitting by the side of the building. Outside the store, Emmett was showing off a picture of a white girl who was a friend in Chicago. He bragged that this was his girlfriend. One of the boys then dared Emmett to go inside the store and talk to a white girl. Emmett went into the store, bought some candy and, as he was leaving, said to the girl, "Bye, baby."

The old man playing checkers warned the boys that the girl would go to her car and get a gun and blow their brains out. He had lived in Mississippi long enough to know when a black man ought to keep quiet. Black men were never to talk to a white woman. If the black man was lucky, he'd get away with just a severe beating. To flirt with a white woman was to invite death.

The old man's remarks frightened the boys so they got in their car and drove away. Three days passed and the boys forgot about the incident. After midnight on Saturday, Roy Bryant, husband of the woman Emmett had spoken to, and his brother-in-law, J. W. Milam went to Wright's cabin to get that "boy who did the talking." Mose told them the boy was from up North and did not know what he was doing. Mose suggested the men give the boy a good whipping and let it go at that. The men dragged Emmett from Mose's house and then asked Mose his age.

"I'm sixty-four," Mose told the men.

"If you cause any trouble, you'll never live to be sixty-five," they told him.

They pushed Emmett into the back seat of their car and drove away. Three days later his body was found in the Tallahatchie River. The barbed wire, which had been put around his neck and tied to a cotton gin fan, had come loose. There was a bullet in the boy's skull and one eye had been gouged out. The reports were that Mose Wright could identify the boy only by an initial ring. The sheriff wanted to bury the mutilated body immediately. However, Curtis Jones called Chicago, passing word to Emmett's mother of his death and of the planned burial. Emmett's mother demanded that the body be returned to Chicago. The sheriff agreed to her demands but had the mortician sign an order that the casket would not be opened.

According to reports, the casket was opened by Emmett's mother so she could be sure it was her son. She recognized Emmett and in vengeance declared that the world would see what had been done to her son. There was to be an open-casket funeral. The body was photographed, and the photo was published in the black weekly magazine, *Jet*. All of America saw the mutilated corpse.

In retrospect, it was the Till murder that brought national focus on Mississippi and the state's racial attitudes. The more the nation raged against Mississippi, the more the people of Mississippi moved to the defensive. Tom Ethridge, a writer for the Jackson Clarion Ledger, called the condemnation of Mississippi by the Northern press a Communist Plot designed to destroy decent Southern society. Civil rights activists were frequently described as Communists or Communist sympathizers.

The two men, Milam and Bryant, had been charged with kidnapping before the corpse was discovered. They were then charged with murder. The trial came quickly because most everyone, in Mississippi as well as the nation, was outraged by what had happened. The horror was so universal that two men could not find a local white attorney to represent them. It appeared that the Mississippi establishment had turned its back on them. Negative publicity filled the newspapers.

The publicity eventually backfired. After an intense crusade of the national media to brand Mississippi as a racist state, the citizens finally pulled together. Around the country, disgust at the incident was rampant but, in Mississippi, it only fostered sympathy for the two accused. Not one, but five, prominent attorneys from the Mississippi Delta area agreed to represent Milam and Bryant. More than $10,000 was raised for the defense. The state appointed a prosecutor but he was given no budget or personnel. There was no investigation to help the prosecution.

If there was a positive note in this whole episode, it was the courage of Mose Wright and his wife, Elizabeth. In 1955, for a black man to accuse a white man of murder, was to sign his own death warrant. Mose Wright had not slept in his home since the kidnapping. He was afraid Milam and Bryant would return. He was warned to leave the state but did not.

Sixty-four year old black man, Mose Wright, testified against two white men. For the first time in memory, a black man pointed toward two white men and accused them of murdering a black. It was an act of courage unheard of in Mississippi.

And it was all for naught. The jury found them both not guilty. The twelve man, all-white jury received their charge from one of the five defense attorneys, John C. Whitten. His was a simple pitch. "Your fathers will turn over in their graves if they are found guilty, and I am sure that every last Anglo-Saxon one of you has the courage to free these men in the face of that (outside) pressure." The jury deliberated the case for a mere hour and fifteen minutes.

Two months after the trial Milam and Bryant sold the story of Till's murder to an Alabama journalist for $4,000. The story appeared in a national magazine. The two Mississippians attempted to justify the murder by claiming that they did not intend to kill Till. They just wanted to scare him but, when the young boy refused to repent or beg for mercy, they said they had to kill him.

Milam told the journalist, "He (Till) was hopeless. I'm no bully. I never hurt a nigger in my life. I like niggers in their place. I know how to work'em. But I just decided it was time a few people got put on notice."

Nothing is Perfect but Shame

That following January our high school football team went to the Senior Bowl in Mobile, Alabama. We went on the team bus and arrived well before the game started. As we stood around with our letter jackets on and feeling more macho than usual, a group of black children gathered around. They were jovial and danced and cut up with one another. After a while we began to joke with the kids. Then we wanted to show them we were a tough group.

For some reason I looked at one of the kids and asked, "Have you heard of Emmett Till?" My question was designed to scare the kid and it did. I will never forget the look of fear in his eyes. He stopped dancing and just stared at me.

Never in my life have I felt so much shame. I wanted to hug the child, and tell him that I was sorry. I did not. I just stood there wanting the world to swallow me on the spot. To my knowledge, that is the only time I have ever said anything like that to a child. To this day there is a pain in my heart that aches every time I recall the incident.

I was surprised with my feelings. Having three brothers, being a football player and living in a small town, I was no stranger to fighting and meanness. I had a lot of fights and some were vicious. There was the time I kicked dirt in my brother's eyes to get the upper hand in a fight we were having. I had witnessed times when fighting involved someone pulling a gun or a knife. My cousins knew me as someone that would fight for the fun of it. There I was, with friends standing around, feeling lower than I ever had. The look in that little black boy's eyes haunts me to this day.

Something important happened to me that day.

"Somebody's got to teach them nigras a lesson." Sitting in Phillip's restaurant I felt the pain of that little kid all over again. I visualized the pictures in the magazine of Milam and Bryant, one with a big cigar in his mouth and the other with a cigarette dangling from his lips. They represented everything I hated about bigots. Later that evening, as I sat in my study, I remembered that almost every man in the café that day was either smoking a cigarette or a cigar.

The Old Tree Comes Down

It was in late July when Dot and I noticed someone had cut down the dead tree in our backyard. I surmised they worried that it might fall on the parsonage. I did not know who had cut the tree down, nor did anyone mention having done it. The mystery tree-cutter had also cut the trunk and branches into short pieces. I was relieved it was down because the limbs had started falling every time it rained. As rain soaked into the dead wood, the weight of the water would break the limbs sending them slamming into the ground. If one hit our car, it would do serious damage. No need to worry now.

I made a mental note that I could burn blocks of wood next to the ditch without fear of the fire spreading. As soon as I could find time, I'd start the process.

The End of Summer

It was August and I had been preaching for almost two full months. I was a fixture in town by now. As a means of marketing Sandersville Methodist, I bought some paper placemats with an etching of a church and several prayers printed on them. I bought a rubber stamp with Sandersville Methodist Church imprinted on it and stamped every mat. Phillip was very happy to accept my gift and immediately placed them before every single diner that came to eat in his cafe. The members of Sandersville Methodist were impressed to see the name of their church on the placemats and my popularity grew. Everyone in town knew my name, and I was warmly greeted as I walked around the town.

An attitude also was growing in Sandersville and in all of Mississippi. The incidents of racial strife were happening with more frequency.

> August 16, 1962; Greenwood, Mississippi: Police beat a black youth with clubs and blackjacks then stripped off his clothes and continued to flog him on the floor of the police station.

It was one of many such stories and, like most, just went away.

The racial strife that covered Dixie was growing in intensity. It was not just in Mississippi. The newspapers kept the stories coming on a daily basis. The talk in Phillip's Cafe often turned away from football and focused on the events involving the "uppity nigras." It was never in debate form. No one dared to speak up for the person who had been beaten or who had their homes bombed or burned. It was always those "outside agitators" who brought this on the blacks. The general consensus among most Mississippians was that none of the violence would have occurred had it not been for the outsiders.

"We have always treated our niggers well," was a remark I must have heard a thousand times. Some even referred to slavery as good for the blacks. "I bet they wish they had the same care and feeding our forefathers gave them. Being a slave had its good side," was the feeling of some people.

An article that appeared in a black newspaper, *The Chicago Defender*, best describes the attitude of most whites in the South. It was published on Sep. 24, 1955, the same year of the Emmett Till murder. The writer was Lew Sadler, a white radio announcer in Mississippi, who broadcast on-the-spot coverage of the indictment and arraignment of Roy Bryant and J. W. Milam.

> Greenwood, Mississippi – During the middle of the week, a reporter who said he was with your paper stopped by the station here to talk to me. He said he had heard my "on the spot" report over the air from Sumner, Miss., the day Milam and Bryant were taken to Sumner for arraignment.
>
> I was busy on the mike at the time and didn't have much opportunity to talk to him. He did take two photos of me at the mike, and before I had a few off-minutes, he was gone. Now, did [he] really want to hear what I had to say, or [was he] just curious about something? Would you like to have something to run with those photos, if you use them?...
>
> All right, why are the people of the South... Mississippi in particular, being prosecuted because of all this trouble? Didn't our sheriff have the two suspects in custody long before the Till boy's body, if it was his body, was found?
>
> Does that look as if our law was slanted?
>
> It had been said by someone far more intelligent than I that "The Southern Negro is sitting in the white man's wagon, and the white man is having to do the driving."
>
> That is no secret to any white or colored person here in the South. So it's easy to see that they're on our backs, and we're not complaining. But why do

the people of the North insist that we hold them on our laps?

My wife was raised by a Negro woman, as have so many other ladies of the South. That still is the case. You can drive by our parks and yards and see how many white children are cared for by, not white nurses, but colored women.

I've seen many times the mother come home from work, and the kids would hold on to the Negro woman's legs letting themselves be dragged to the sidewalk and on into the car before letting go, because they didn't want her to leave. Does that look like we are allergic to Negroes?

The owner of this station has a brother who owns a station in Natchez, Miss., and when something needs to be done here he will send for James, a Negro who works for the Natchez station, to come here, nearly 200 miles to do it, rather than pull in someone else. Doesn't that sound like we are loyal to a good Negro?

When we need a baby-sitter at home, we have a Negro woman come in, rather than a white girl. We do not lock up the baby's bank either. Does that sound like we do not trust the Negroes?

A person does not have to drive very far through town to see Negro and white children playing together. Does that sound like we do not want our children playing and mixing with Negroes?

There are Negroes living in the town, as well as white people living in the colored section. So does that sound like we are trying to segregate the colored or whites?

I could give you many individual cases of many varieties of the help we have given the Negroes, including last winter when I gave James, the boy I was telling you about before from Natchez, my only pair of leather gloves. (By the way I've never had an extra $3 to get another pair.)

So please, as a favor to the South, while you are getting the news try to dig just a little deeper and you may come up with something that will enlighten the North to the fact that we of the South have a "good-neighbor" policy of our own.

The only line we draw is at the door of our schools. Poll the Negroes of the South and you'll find the Southern Negro feels the same. As I said before… they're on our backs, and we aren't complaining, but why do you insist they be in our lap too? (Williams, *Eyes on the Prize*, 54-55)

Mr. Sadler's views were consistent with those that I had been exposed to most of my life. When I was a small child my parents had hired a black lady named Minnie. She was special to our family and worked in our home three or four days a week. Minnie also cooked most of our meals, cleaned the house and did all the chores a maid would do. I have no idea how we afforded her but I am certain she was never paid more than a dollar a day. When she came into our home, all of the kids would rush and give her a hug. She welcomed us with open arms and would hug back and laugh and give the impression that she loved to be with us. I never heard either parent or grandparent chastise us for hugging Minnie. However, should we have hugged her out in public, I am certain there would have been consequences.

The first of the two following incidents confirm my conclusion. The second confirms my confusion.

As a child I had played with black children. They were my neighbors because we lived on the edge of the quarters. We lived on the west side of the street and less than one hundred yards to the east was a black home. The black section was called, appropriately for Mississippi, "The Quarters." (The term is a carryover from the days of slavery when all slaves lived in the "Slave Quarters".) I knew my grandmother did not like for me to play with blacks. When I reported some of the fun things I had done with them, she angrily asked if "any of the nigger rubbed off on me?" In some ways I was shocked by such statements. In other ways I was amused. But, she had not said it to be funny. White children did not play with black children no matter what the circumstances may be. And yet, I could hug Minnie, and Mama, as we called our grandmother, never asked if any "nigger rubbed off on me." Mama could be a very mean woman.

I have no memory of hearing a positive word from my grandmother pertaining to blacks. She referred to them as "niggers", and did so with a vengeance. Ironically, she made a part of her living sewing for them. I recall having black women come to our home with patterns and material for, say, a dress. My grandmother would lay out the pattern, pin and cut out the pieces, and sew up a dress. The black lady would pick up the dress and pay my grandmother for her work.

If my grandmother had worked on credit, the poor black person would catch hell until they paid. As I've mentioned, we lived very near the black section of Picayune. Most of the blacks in our area did not have automobiles. To do their shopping, or get to work, they had to walk past our home. I can recall Mamma Bennett spotting an acquaintance of one of her debtors.

"You tell that nigger I want my money," she yelled.

The unfortunate victim kept walking but muttered, "Yes ma'am, Ms. Bennett."

As I recall, several of my family members shared my grandmother's hatred for black people. One of my uncles told me years before that blacks were not like whites. God had damned them because of something they had done.

"That's why they are niggers," he would say.

Of all the relatives I have, this one uncle was the most racist of all. My brothers and I would go fishing with him on occasion. The trip to the local creek in Picayune led through the "Quarters." Once I noticed a beautiful young black girl jumping rope with some of her friends. I remarked that I thought she was beautiful. My uncle's response was almost irrational.

"Don't you ever let me hear you say that about a nigger again, do you hear me," he shouted. For the rest of that day he took pains to tell all of us how nigras were not our equals. He had little real evidence of such a thing, but he believed it with all of his heart.

As I reflect on that era in my life, I can recall several other situations where I was "taught" that blacks and whites did not go together. I recall a junior high principal pulling some of us students together to urge us to get our parents to come to a meeting about the "niggers coming to our school." It was 1954 and the Supreme Court had just outlawed school segregation.

"You boys get your mammas and daddies to come to the meeting. If they don't, then niggers will be coming to our school. You don't want that to happen, do you?"

Frankly, we had no idea what he was talking about. After some explanation we all agreed with him that we did not want that.

"Go and tell your parents that the niggers are trying to come to our school."

There were many other "lessons" taught but to relate each would take more space and time than I have. For most children, it had a profound impact. Many of my friends and relatives believed the "nigger" was a lower form of life and could be treated as such. If ever there was a truism about the South it is found in a song from *South Pacific*:

> You have to be taught to hate the people
> your parents hate, Before you are six or
> seven or eight, you have to be taught

So, while I was upset by the remarks heard in Phillip's Café, it was not the first time I had heard them. I had heard them from family, my grandmother in particular and, of course, Uncle Greg.

If there was a saving grace that summer, it came in mid-August. That was the date the high schools started football practice. Sandersville's team was supposed to be good, so every afternoon a number of the locals would gather to watch the team practice. Soon I became a part of the "sideline coach's club" made up of those locals who had played a little football and knew more than the school coach. Ned Dillard had actually been a high school coach and did know his football. He was also the most outspoken critic of the team and the coaching staff which numbered two. It was a fun thing to do, and I could visit with several of my church members at those little gatherings.

Chapter Nine

The Ole Miss Incident

Unfortunately, it was a brief respite. The newspapers continued to carry reports of racial strife. However, they were now carrying reports on the college and university football teams. Is this something new? Most of the locals focused on the sports section while only the athletically uninformed talked about the racial strife. At that time, all of the schools in Mississippi, and most of the South, were segregated. The Mississippi State Legislature had outlawed playing against blacks. All of the state schools were prohibited from playing against schools that had black players. Consequently, discussing football was a total escape from the black-white issue. The Ole Miss Rebels had gone undefeated in recent years and could very well do it again.

It is important to understand just what the University of Mississippi football team represented to the population of Mississippi. In 1959, Ole Miss lost only one game and it was to their hated rival, Louisiana State University. The second time that season they met LSU on the field was in the Sugar Bowl. This time the Rebels beat the Tigers and were declared one of the greatest teams in the history of the Southeastern Conference. To say this provided inspiration and pride for the whole state is an understatement. The University was as Southern as any institution could be. Its banner was the Confederate Flag, and its fight song was Dixie. Its mascot was Colonel Rebel, a character dressed as a plantation owner. A home game ritual was displaying the largest Confederate Flag in the world to a cheering crowd. The band would be in standard marching formation when the flag would be brought onto the field fully enveloping the band. When it finally cleared the field, the band members spelled out the word Dixie. Then they'd strike up their rendition of Dixie, and the crowd would go wild.

While Mississippi State and Southern Mississippi had fans, it was Ole Miss that represented the true Southern heritage, and it always would.

Word began to spread that a black man planned to enroll at Ole Miss in September. James Meredith was not the first black to attempt to break down the racial barriers at Mississippi schools. While I was in college, a black man had attempted to enroll at one of the state universities. He was arrested and was taken to the State Insane Asylum at Whitfield, Mississippi.

The authorities said, "He's crazy and needs to be put away. Any nigra that tries to go to a white school in Mississippi had to be crazy."

One black man had wanted to enroll at Southern Miss. The local police placed a bottle of liquor in his car and promptly arrested him for possession of alcohol. That was the way the threat was treated. Many assumed the same thing would happen to Meredith. Because of the failed attempts in the past most whites discounted Meredith's chances.

He was just another "wild, crazy nigger" as one put it, "who wants some publicity."

Another local offering his opinion said simply, "If he tries, he's a dead nigger."

But Meredith's enrollment would be different. For one thing, he had the support of Medgar Evers, the state leader of the NAACP. Evers was a well-known man throughout the state and one of the most hated. To the black population he was a hero. To the white community he was the devil reincarnated. The boys who hung out at Phillips Cafe hated the mention of Evers' name. He was the first full-time field secretary for the NAACP in Mississippi and was active in the civil rights movement. He was a man to be reckoned with. Unlike other black leaders, Medgar was not going away.

I had heard of Evers before his involvement with Meredith but knew little about him. It is important to understand Evers because he added credence to Meredith's quest to enter Ole Miss.

In the book, *Eyes on the Prize*, the author gives a brief but interesting account of Evers and his activities in Mississippi.

> When Medgar Evers came home from World War II, his brother Charlie talked him into trying to vote in their hometown of Decatur. The Evers brothers and four other blacks registered at the courthouse, but when they tried to vote on election day, they were met by a mob of whites wielding guns and knives. Years later, Medgar Evers described the experience to a reporter. "We had all seen a lot of dead people in the war," he said. "I had been on Omaha Beach. All we wanted to be was ordinary citizens. We fought during the war for America, Mississippi included. Now, after the Germans and the Japanese hadn't killed us, it looked as though the white Mississippians would... We knew we weren't going to get by this mob." The blacks left without even seeing the voting booth. (Williams 1987, 208)

Later, Evers completed his college work and went into the insurance business. In 1954 he applied to the law school at the University of Mississippi in Oxford. Ironically, it was while he waited to hear about his application to Ole Miss that the U.S. Supreme Court ruled that racially segregated schools were unconstitutional. The temper of the times was explosive. The white citizens of Mississippi were outraged. They formed the White Citizen's Council designed to prevent the integration of public schools.

The Mississippi attorney general, James P. Coleman, who later became governor of the state, invited Evers to Jackson to discuss his desire to enroll at Ole Miss. Evers was denied enrollment. The reason given was he could not supply any recommendations from Mississippi whites.

Shortly afterwards, Evers went to work for the NAACP. The attitude of most whites toward the organization was summed up by what Governor Ross Barnett defined the acronym to mean: "Niggers, Apes, Alligators, Coons and Possums."

With the support of Evers, James Meredith began his quest to enter Ole Miss. Meredith approached Evers in January of 1961. Meredith was a sophomore at all-black Jackson State but wanted to transfer to Ole Miss. Evers suggested that he write to Thurgood Marshall, the head of the NAACP Legal Defense Fund. Meredith did so, explaining that he was a native of Mississippi and had spent nine years in the military. Marshall did not want to waste money on Meredith if he did not have the academic credentials for Ole Miss. Meredith proved to have everything needed and the effort to enroll him at Ole Miss was underway.

It was in early September that a federal district court ordered the University of Mississippi to admit James Meredith. The talk of football was put aside and a call to arms was issued to all true Southerners. The gang at Phillip's thought this to be the darkest day in the South since Lee surrendered at Appomattox.

"No way that nigger will ever see the inside of a building on that campus," was the vow of one of the gang. Others voiced agreement and even committed to go to the campus of Ole Miss to personally stop Meredith from enrolling. The talk of violence whipped the men into a frenzy. Some spoke of the weapons they had and would use against anyone who tried to "get that nigger in Ole Miss." There was not a single voice of reason, but then again, it was the mob mentality that ranted and raved until they left for home. There was a mean spirit present that day. These men, and no doubt thousands of others across Mississippi, were speaking openly about taking up arms against the government, if necessary, to protect their way of life. That morning was a preview of many days of rage and plotting to keep that "nigger" out of Old Miss.

To understand just how great the threat of insurrection was, the name of Ross Barnett must be added to the equation. He was the sitting governor of Mississippi. If he was not the most bigoted governor in history, he was a close second. He was the man who claimed the NAACP stood for "Niggers, Apes, Alligators, Coons and Possums." He was a Southern Baptist and a faithful member of First Baptist Church of Jackson, one of the largest churches in the state. Barnett boasted that he had never missed his Sunday School class in the past 25 years. His view of Christianity was that God was white and blacks were not and that said something about them. He preached at gatherings all across the state that if "niggers" were allowed to attend white schools it would lead to the "mongrelization of the races." As the federal government moved to enroll Meredith in Ole Miss, Ross had his platform. He was in his element. The whole state was a powder keg and Ross was lighting the fuse.

Ross's popularity was sagging at the time and, the year before, he'd even been booed at an Ole Miss football game. "Good Ole Ross" went on statewide television to make his stand against Meredith entering Ole Miss. This, he believed, was the issue that would rebuild his popularity with the people of the state. He announced to all who watched, which included most every person in the state, that "There is no case in history where the Caucasian race has survived social integration. We must either submit to the unlawful dictate of the federal government or stand up like men and tell them, "Never." The customers at Phillip's loved Ross. The fact that a year ago they had criticized him for having gold plated bathroom faucets and suggested he be booted from office was forgotten. But that was just politics. This was about the preservation of a lifestyle. For some it was more than that. It was a life and death issue.

James Meredith and Sandersville

The Meredith issue was everywhere, including Sandersville Methodist Church. To paraphrase an old biblical saying, "where two or more Mississippians were gathered, James Meredith was the topic of conversation." It was impossible to carry on a conversation with anyone without Meredith's name being mentioned.

All the predictions were doom and gloom for Mr. Meredith: he would disappear, be sent to the state mental hospital, or be shot by the Klan. As Sunday approached, I prepared for an onslaught of statements and questions. I followed my usual routine of going to either Vossburg or Goodwater for the first service of the day. That Sunday it was Vossburg. Surprisingly, no mention was made of the crisis that faced Ole Miss and, as a result, the threat it provided to the "Southern way of life." I was a bit surprised but concluded that perhaps Vossburg hadn't gotten the news. However, as I drove into the parking area for Sandersville, it was obvious that the Sandersville church had been reading the newspapers or listening to the radio. As I exited the car every eye turned my way. My usual practice was to greet those outside the church then rush in to begin the service. I tried that but out of the crowd came the voice of Ned Dillard.

"What do you think we ought to do about that nigger wanting to attend Old Miss?"

I heard the tone of the question and reminded myself to be patient. I did not answer immediately.

"Well?" The tone sounded like a directive for me to answer.

Tired from preaching and the half hour drive, I blurted out, "They ought to let him go to school if he wants to."

Wrong answer.

Ned's face turned beet red. "What do you mean! That nigger will not go to Old Miss."

I had finally made the mistake I feared the most. I let my mouth engage before my mind could interfere. So much for patience. What do I do now? I tried to think of something I could say to defuse the moment.

"Well, they could always flunk him out," I replied. I just wanted to go inside and preach.

"Are you telling me you want a nigger to go to one of our schools?" Ned was really mad and everyone just stood around to see what would happen next.

"Listen," I said, "I know this is an important issue, but I need to get inside and start the service." With that I turned and went inside the building.

Everyone followed, including Ned. I knew I had created a problem for myself and put Ned in an awkward position. He was not used to people walking away from him without finishing the conversation. My reasoning was rational and he knew I had to move on with the service. The conversation would continue immediately following the service. That was one of my longest sermons.

The crowd left, and I had shaken every hand I could find. As I feared, Ned was the last in line.

"Now preacher, tell me again what you said about Meredith going to Ole Miss?"

"Ned, I think the United States Government will place him in Ole Miss. Maybe we ought to accept that and go on with life." Wrong answer again.

Ned turned red in the face again and, with his face just inches from mine, said menacingly, "Preacher, you better remember where you are."

If only he knew how much I did not want to be where I was. Others standing around in the church lawn, seeing the tenseness of the moment, quickly changed the subject. I concluded they did not want to see their preacher and Sunday School Superintendent came to blows. I was shaken and wondered why I had answered him at all. But I realized that by not answering, I would be giving an answer. It would have been so easy to say "I agree with you," thereby keeping the peace and not hurting the church's peace. I prayed with the question, "Lord, why did you send me here? What sin have I committed that led to this punishment? Now it was more than the gang at Phillip's or the racism throughout Mississippi. It was in my own church. Up until that moment, I had forged a tenuous relationship with Ned. Now I knew it was shaken, if not destroyed. I needed his leadership in the church, and I regretted the whole issue had come up at all. But I knew the issue was far from over, in Sandersville or the state.

Outside of Phillip's Cafe and Sandersville, not all white citizens felt so warm toward Ross Barnett. Congressman Frank Smith accused the governor of "leading the people of Mississippi down another blind alley... Whether we like it or not, the question of state vs. federal law was settled one hundred years ago." (Williams 1987, 215) It was a courageous statement. Others followed Smith's lead. Eight ministers serving near the town of Oxford, issued a statement urging everyone to "act in a manner consistent with Christian teaching concerning the value and dignity of man." (Williams 1987, 215) The Reverend Duncan M. Gray, Jr., rector of the Episcopal church, 'asked that politicians and students exercise 'the leadership necessary to assure the peaceful admission of James Meredith to the university.'" (Williams 1987, 215) Hearing these remarks gave me some hope and kept my spirits alive. It also gave my church members another target. For the moment, they were focused on larger targets than their preacher. They would get to him later.

Ross Barnett kept railing against the admission of Meredith. He spoke at a football game in Jackson telling the crowd, "I love Mississippi. I love her people, her customs! And I love and respect her heritage." (Williams 1987, 215) All the while the crowd yelled "never", over and over. What those people did not know was that Ross was negotiating with President Kennedy. Since the federal government determined that Meredith enroll at Ole Miss, Ross tried to get President Kennedy to have soldiers escort Meredith to the school and force, at gunpoint, the University to accept him. Barnett could then put the blame on the President and save face with his constituents. To the credit of John Kennedy, he refused. He threatened to tell the people of Mississippi that Barnett was negotiating with him. Ross pleaded with the President not to do that. Kennedy suggested they bring Meredith to the Ole Miss campus that evening. The President would then announce that Meredith was already at Ole Miss and thus defuse the tension. Later that evening, Meredith was flown to Oxford and placed in one of the dormitories.

Not knowing that Meredith was already on campus, more than 1,000 men gathered in a park in Hattiesburg to plan a convoy to Oxford. Every man was armed and ready to do battle. In their minds they were at war. I am confident many of the Sandersville locals made the trip to Hattiesburg and attended that meeting. It was hard for me to understand the fervor with which these people acted. Some had served in the armed forces and fought in WWII or the Korean War under the banner of the American Flag. Now they were talking about doing battle against the selfsame flag. They were a mob with a mob mentality. As much as I wanted to get away from it all, I found there was no place to go. I know what it was like to be a minority.

I had grown to accept Sandersville as my parish. I liked many of the families, including Ned and his family. But the community would never be the same again. Tension permeated everything. The racial divide had always been there but now there was a cocked trigger: a black man was enrolling in a Mississippi institution of higher learning. Had it been a local high school, the response would have set off a huge negative response. Being it was the University of Mississippi, Ole Miss, whose mascot was "Colonel Reb", no wonder it caused a statewide reaction of anger and a vow of "Never!" As the events of the Meredith episode unfolded, the community became more hostile toward blacks, and God helped those who did not agree with the establishment.

On September 30, James Meredith was secretly escorted to a room in Baxter Hall on the campus of Ole Miss. Earlier that day, over four-hundred federal marshals, patrolmen, and prison guards had moved into place at the Lyceum, the campus administration building. The Mississippi National Guard was put on alert, and the use of federal troops had been authorized by President Kennedy.

By seven that evening a full scale riot was taking place on the Ole Miss campus. Rocks were thrown and cars were overturned and windows were smashed. While some were students who would join in any activity that promised adventure and excitement, many had nothing to do with the university. They were the guardians of the South, so to speak, committed to keeping the "nigger" out of Ole Miss. The Mississippi State Highway patrol left the campus as the violence began. Governor Barnett was asked by federal officials to have the troopers return but they did not. The rowdy crowd vented their fury on the federal marshals blocking the front door of the Lyceum.

In Juan Williams' book, *Eyes on the Prize*, the events of that evening are outlined in some detail. I use this reference because the events as recorded through the local media omitted much of what was happening, particularly the negotiations of our governor with the President. According to this book and other reports, the events of that evening went as follows:

> The governor had promised the Kennedys that he would make a televised announcement of the state's compliance with Meredith's enrollment. As the campus violence raged, Barnett faced the cameras. "As governor of the State of Mississippi, I have just been informed by the attorney general of the United States that Meredith has today been placed on the campus of the University of Mississippi... ," he said. "I urge all Mississippians and instruct every state official under my command to do everything in their power to preserve peace and to avoid violence in any form."
>
> The governor then added, "Surrounded on all sides by the armed forces and oppressive power of the U.S.A., my courage and commitment do not waiver... To the officials of the federal government I say, 'Gentlemen, you are trampling on the sovereignty of this great state... You are destroying the Constitution of this great nation... May God have mercy on your souls...'"
>
> Unaware of the governor's words, President Kennedy prepared to make his own television speech to the nation. As he did so, the federal marshals on campus began firing tear gas. "Americans are free... to disagree with the law, but not to disobey it," the President said. "For in any government of laws and not of men, no man, however prominent and powerful, and no matter however unruly and boisterous, is entitled to defy a court of law... You have a new opportunity to show that you are men of patriotism and integrity. For the most effective means of upholding the law is not the state policemen or the marshals or the National Guard. It is you."
>
> On campus, the rioting was out of control. Shortly after the President finished his speech, the body of French reporter Paul Guihard was discovered. Guihard had been shot in the back at close

range. Ray Gunter, an Oxford resident who was watching the mayhem, was shot dead about 11 P.M. John McLaurin, Barnett's representative at Ole Miss, recalled that night. "If Governor Barnett had gotten on the radio and asked for people to come to Oxford to defend the state of Mississippi," he said, "I felt like the road wouldn't have carried all the people that would've come in through Mississippi, Alabama, Arkansas, Tennessee, and Louisiana."

Around 10 P.M., Deputy Attorney General Nicolas Katzenbach called the White House from Oxford to say that federal troops would be needed to squelch the rioting. Army Secretary, Cyrus Vance, ordered troops at an air station in Tennessee to move in. At 11:45, the President called Barnett again to demand that the highway patrolmen return to the scene. Barnett agreed, but by midnight the order had not been issued. The governor went on radio and declared, "I call on Mississippi to keep the faith and courage. We will never surrender." (Eyes on the Prize, pp 216-217)

In less than an hour of the arrival of federal troops, the riot was over. Two men were dead. One-hundred and sixty marshals had been injured, twenty-eight by gunfire. Three-fourths of the two-hundred arrested were not university students. The next morning James Meredith registered without incident and became the first black student at Ole Miss.

Dot and I watched the television account of the riots. It was an eerie feeling. My distaste for Governor Barnett grew as the evening passed. Based on what was reported through the one television station available to us, a station near Laurel, the State of Mississippi was being invaded by foreign troops. Having been a member of the Mississippi National Guard, I knew well that some of the troops were local young men. It seemed that Mississippi was at war with itself. We stayed up late that evening as did most people in Mississippi.

The next day at Phillip's the talk was about the "invasion". Some were gleeful over the number of marshals injured. The killing of the French journalist was "deserved" because "he had no business being there." One man reported that he and some of his friends had traveled to Hattiesburg last evening to join with several hundred others who were ready to drive to Oxford and do battle with the invaders.

"Why didn't you all go up there and help the others?"

The man was speechless for a second and then added, "We waited for a while."

I almost chuckled when I heard this report. I pictured a group of farmers and merchants driving several hundred miles to Oxford, armed with shotguns, prepared to do battle with federally trained, seasoned troops.

Asked again why they did not go, the response was, "We were waiting for Ole Ross to give the order."

"This is a sad day for the South," one person stated and most shook their heads in agreement.

The name of James Meredith had been changed to "that nigger at Ole Miss." The new prediction was that he would never live to get a diploma.

Chapter Ten

Fall: Football, Leaves and Nesting

Sandersville continued to be an unattractive town. The weather-worn buildings, the rusted Coca Cola and R C Drinks signs made it even more unattractive. I am confident that the events of the preceding days had made it uglier than I had first thought.

Maybe it was not the town, though it was run down and dirty, but the attitudes of the people that made it so unattractive. However, in the surrounding communities there was a beauty that began to awaken in the early part of fall. This was especially true in the Vossburg and Goodhope areas. The leaves were beginning to change colors and the hot, dusty weather began to turn cooler. There is something about the South and its fall season. The cooler weather, the burning of leaves and the colors make it a special place. The drive from Sandersville to Goodhope had taken on a whole new dimension. Many people in the deep South dump their garbage on the side of roads. The less traveled the road the more garbage dumped. In the hot summer months the piles of discarded automobile tires, cans and other junk stand out like a sore thumb. As the season changes, the beauty of the leaves overwhelms the ugliness of the roadside. Fall brings a freshness to the area. It also brought football.

Again, football became the savior for the community. While no one forgot James Meredith, interest in the football season pushed him from the forefront. Reports of violence, of sit-ins and bombings continued to dominate the headlines but the locals did not linger on the front page and editorials. The big question was, "How good are the three colleges in Mississippi?" Football, once again, was the main topic at Phillip's. Ole Miss was having a good year, as was Southern. Mississippi State continued to struggle.

Mississippi also had a Junior College system that allowed the sport of football. Mississippi's was one of the strongest junior college programs in the country. Jones County Junior College was in nearby Ellisville. Each year Jones fielded a strong team, and many of the locals were fans of the school. In the fall the weekends were spent watching Sandersville High School on Friday nights, watching televised college games on Saturday, and attending the Jones Junior College games on Saturday night. Some spent time watching pro games on Sunday but college and high school football were the favorites. The following Monday would be spent discussing what was done, what should have been done and who should have won each game.

Most of those who met at Phillip's had played some football. Their criticisms were not without some merit. The knowledge of the game among the "Monday morning quarterbacks" made for some very interesting discussions. The significance of football cannot be overstated. It kept the minds of many people busy and the aggressiveness of football actually served, vicariously, as an outlet for all the anger the local people felt toward the Old Miss situation. The frustration that came from the integration of Ole Miss was still present in the minds of the locals. However, it was more than they could grasp and assimilate without a lot of anguish. Football, as it usually does in the deep South, was the ideal escape mechanism.

I made it a practice to attend all of the home high school games. The largest crowd would be less than 500 but what they lacked in quantity they made up with quality. Sandersville fans were loud. Everyone in the community could be found at the stadium on Friday nights. I had developed a good relationship with the coaching staff of the high school team. The school had only two coaches. The head coach, the son of a Baptist minister, was a nice young man who genuinely liked kids. His assistant was also young but not as mature as the head coach. Often I would drop by the practices on weekday afternoons. I was not the only one who watched the practice. At times there would be up to twelve men standing around watching the team. The conversation was not about the "nigger" at Old Miss, but how well the team would do this year.

My expertise in football consisted of having played, coaching a team in Georgia and reading everything I could get my hands on that had to do with football. My reputation as a knowledgeable fan was enhanced by a fluke observation. I had noticed that the center leaned on the ball before he snapped it. Once he snapped the ball, he would fall forward leaving an open path to the quarterback. This made him less effective as a blocker and caused a poor snap exchange, which usually resulted in a fumble. The following Friday night that exact sequence took place. On Monday, during the critique of the weekend game, someone pointed out that the preacher had called it right. I was now a part of the elite who knew football. It may have boosted my prestige but it had a negative effect on the coaching staff. The only problem was that if a preacher could see the flaw, why couldn't the coach? I was careful not to say anything else.

Interestingly, I had once wanted to be a football coach. While a student at Emory, I worked with the local YMCA which provided me the opportunity to fulfill my dream of coaching a football team. My team was neither high school nor junior high but in the local Gra-Y (Gra-Youth) league consisting of ten, eleven and twelve year olds. Our teams would play every Saturday morning. The coaches took turns officiating the games as well. Our team was quite good and my quarterback, many years later, eventually became the starting quarterback at Georgia Tech.

In a conversation with one of the men watching the practices, I happened to mention that I had officiated a few games. That was another mistake. The local coach had a junior varsity game and asked if I would serve as an official. It sounded exciting so I agreed. The only problem was that I was the only official. The game was played in the afternoon after school. Most of the high school students were there along with several townspeople. The game had little real meaning except to football fans. I had great difficulty being the linesman, the backfield judge and the referee. On one occasion, the hometown quarterback dropped back for a pass. Two of the opposing linemen had him in a tight grasp and were about to throw him to the ground. I noticed that he was a target for anyone who wanted to take his head off so I blew the whistle. Just as I blew my whistle he threw the ball. As luck would have it, the pass was completed. The receiver ran into the end zone scoring what would have been a touchdown. Unfortunately, the ball was dead at the spot where the quarterback had thrown it. No one went so far as to boo the preacher even while he was wearing the stripes of an official. However, there were some icy stares from a lot of the local fans. It was not my day because the local team lost. I retired as an official that very day. I had a feeling the local coach would not ask me to officiate again anyway.

The next day I was constantly reminded that I had blown the play. As one person said to me, "You know you're a resident of Sandersville. If the game had been somewhere else the score would have counted." I made a promise to God and to myself to retire from officiating. Interestingly enough, no one tried to talk me out of it. If the people of Sandersville were serious about anything, it was football.

Football created and sustained community spirit. It also served as a gathering place for people of all denominations so the Baptist, Presbyterians and Methodists could join in a celebration. Fortunately, I was married to someone who loved attending football games, especially college games. In small towns this was the closest thing to a social event there was. People dressed in school colors for the high school games and, because of the cooler weather, the clothing was colorful and bright. While we were in college, Dot and I had attended the Southern Mississippi College games. The dress style was almost formal. The men wore jackets and ties and the ladies dressed in suits and usually wore a chrysanthemum adorned with the colors of the college. For Southern, the colors were black and gold. Dot had a brown tweed suit with a hat trimmed in fur that she wore to some of the games. She was a knockout in that outfit. She has always had a neat body and this outfit accentuated her body and her behind in particular.

But, while football offered a break from the daily pressures and an escape from the harshness of bigotry, it was not far removed from the attitudes that Southerners had toward blacks. Southern's mascot, for example, was a man dressed in a confederate soldier's uniform who carried the nickname of Nathan Bedford Forrest. This is the Nathan Bedford Forrest that founded the KKK. If that was not enough, the fraternities would harass each other with racial terms. One cheer was: "Old Black Joe, Old Black Joe was an ATO."

The beginning of fall offered a relief for me and I think for the people of Sandersville. School was in session and all of the rhetoric about integration abated somewhat. The incidents of violence continued but the talk was of school, football and getting firewood cut for the winter. Only the diehards continued to talk about the "nigger" at Ole Miss and of the invasion of outside agitators. The church services went well, and I was declared to be one of the best preachers they ever had. Harvey brought up the idea of the church withdrawing from the three-church circuit and becoming a single church appointment. The congregation loved the idea now that they had an "educated minister." No one discussed the additional cost to the church, and little concern was expressed for either Vossburg or Goodwater. When I mentioned the other two churches, I was assured they would end up with some other church.

With fall came not only football but cooler weather. It was a good time to burn the limbs of the old tree. They were an unsightly mess in the backyard. It would be a simple task. With a minimum of effort I pulled out a few of the smaller limbs and began the burning. I fantasized that the job could be done in a day or two. I'd come home and burn a few before dinner. I soon realized the project would take much longer. The first pile burned for more than two hours. I changed my plan and decided it would be a fall and winter project.

Dot and I began to think more and more about starting our family. We had been married for almost three years and people began to ask when we were going to have children. We had thought about it before at Emory but it would have been too much of a hardship.

We did have one close call, and I recall being excited looking at baby furnishings. However, it was a false alarm. We were both relieved and disappointed. It would have been very difficult to have a baby while living in a one room apartment. Besides, we both had to work to pay for school expenses.

We found a "child" in the form of a French poodle just as we were leaving Emory. We named him Pierre. So much for originality. He was almost a full blooded poodle. Pierre was more than just a dog, he was family. We now had a child. Ironically, we had a black child because Pierre was shiny black. Fortunately, Sandersville was tolerant of black dogs. Unfortunately, we only had Pierre for a short while. One day, when Dot's parents were visiting, Pierre ran out into the street and was hit by a passing car. That was one of the most distressing and painful experiences of our lives. I was personally amazed at how much we had become attached to that dog. When I was a child, I was used to dogs getting killed, some shot and some run over. I had feelings for some of the family pets but was never so attached as I was to Pierre. I think Dot's deep attachment added to my feelings. Pierre's death was the first loss we shared as a couple.

The nesting syndrome began to be a pressing issue with us, especially Dot. It was time to have a child and all contraceptive measures were stopped. Being a more organized person than I, Dot began to take careful note of her menstrual cycle. Dot was irregular with her period and picking the right time for conception required some guess work. My suggestion was that we simply have intercourse every day for a month and we could not miss it. Dot concluded that I may have had other interests in addition to making a baby. She was right. However, my desires were just a little out of reason. I still hold to the theory that by having intercourse daily the chances of conception are enhanced. Of all the tasks Dot has asked me to perform, I must confess doing my part in this endeavor was most exciting.

In the process of working to make a baby, we decided we could try the dog route again. At least we would not have to wait nine months to be "parents". We planned carefully. It would be a female because they do not run off as easily as males. Secondly, it would be a small dog. I decided that Dot could make the choice. It was more a case of acquiescing than "allowing" Dot the choice. We began to search the local newspaper for dogs. A lot of people, we discovered, sell dogs. The newspaper carried ads for all types of dogs. The most frequent ads were for hunting dogs. The last thing I wanted was a hunting dog. Almost every man in the community had a hound that was reputed to be the best hunting dog in Mississippi. But, after graduating from high school, I had given up hunting.

We wanted an indoor dog. That set us apart from most people in Sandersville. Dogs were meant to be outside. However, after discovering that one farmer in Goodwater birthed hogs inside his house, surely I could keep a dog indoors. One ad caught our eye. It was for a miniature Dachshund. The owner had listed the dogs as being purebred with papers ready for any buyer interested. All of our pets had been of the Heinz 57 variety. Pierre was the closest thing we had to a purebred. All we knew about Dachshunds was that they looked like large hotdogs. Why not get something unusual. We clipped out the ad and made our way to Laurel and the home of the owner of the Dachshunds.

The house was not at all impressive. It was a small frame house that sat on brick pillars that held it about two feet off the ground. There was a full front porch with half brick and half wood columns holding up a tin roof. The man answering the door was in his late sixties or early seventies. It was hard to tell because people always looked older than they were. We introduced ourselves and were invited into the house. It reeked of dogs. As soon as we closed the door we were literally surrounded by dachshunds of all sizes and colors. They barked and pranced joyously at our feet as if to say, "Pick me! Pick me!"

"We're selling any one of the dogs you see except the mother of the latest liter," announced our host. "The price is thirty-five dollars and they are well worth it."

We were a little taken back by the price. Thirty-five dollars was more than 10 percent of my monthly salary. I had never paid for a dog in my life. Most people begged you to take one of their puppies. The owner must have seen our look of disappointment in our faces.

"Now you did say you were a preacher, didn't you?"

"Yes sir," I responded. "I'm the new pastor of Sandersville Methodist Church."

"Well," he mused, "tell you what. I'll knock off some of the cost because you are a preacher."

My heart began to beat a little faster. Perhaps we could leave with one of the puppies that danced at our feet.

"Now I get thirty-five for each dog. What I would be willing to do is knock off two-fifty. Now let's see. That comes to thirty-two dollars and fifty cents."

That dropped the cost to about eight percent of my monthly salary. Still we wanted one of the puppies.

I had always advocated that I hated ministerial discounts. Harvey Hinton's practice of giving Dot and me a discount on our groceries was embarrassing. Announcing it so all of the community could hear was even more embarrassing. However, knocking two-dollars and fifty cents was not even 10 per cent. Dot and I told him how much we appreciated his offer but that we would like to pay the whole amount.

"Pick the one you want," he said. "They all have papers."

It was not easy deciding on one puppy. We'd pick one and then another and then another. Finally, we took a little red one with the biggest brown eyes I have ever seen on a dog that was so small. We left the white house and the strong smell and went home to make a place for our newest family member. We decided, for some reason, to name her Tracey.

Since Tracey was just a little puppy, she missed her mother at night. We gave her more attention than a dog should have but still she whined in the evenings. We longed for the time when she would sleep through the night. Watching a little puppy explore the world was entertaining. On one occasion, Tracey crawled into a gown that was on the floor. Being so small, she was able to get into one of the sleeves. Unfortunately, she could not get out and was soon trapped. We were alerted to her dilemma by the most pathetic whining I have ever heard. Extracting her from the sleeve was not at all easy. She showed her disappointment in my rescuing abilities by continuing to whine.

It was time to really get serious about having a child. Dot was back at calculating just when the ideal time would be to have intercourse. She decided we should experiment with a time span of six days. That was fine with me so we began on a Sunday night. Each evening of that week we went through our ritual of making love. The first and second nights were a loving experience. By the third evening it was a routine, and by the end of the week it was a chore. I loved every minute of it. There were times when we could have been more romantic. However, there was a task to perform and I did my best. I did my part and was ready to duplicate my efforts every month until Dot became pregnant.

Fall was settling in and it can get cold in Central Mississippi. They heated our house with space heaters that burned natural gas. As the evenings grew shorter and colder, the heaters burned longer and longer. Gas was cheap, so large utility bills did not swamp us. The churches had the same heating devices. On cold Sunday mornings the building would be getting warm just as the last service concluded. The Good Hope church was the easiest to heat because it was smaller and tighter. The Vossburg church was impossible to heat because many windows were cracked and the building was one big draft. This was not a problem because I did not stay long enough to get cold. The worst experience I had with cold was at Good Hope when the heater had broken. Only about six people were present, and I suggested we cancel church. Those people would have nothing to do with such an idea.

"We're here Preacher and you are here. Why should we cancel?" Of those present that Sunday only one was under the age of 70. The men and women wore hats and gloves throughout the service. It was the strangest service I had ever attended. I thought nothing could ever top the one-arm pianist at the Wesley Chapel church in Crossroads, but this service was the clear winner in the strange category.

Finding A Common Ground

The passage of time relaxed the intensity of the Meredith issue. It remained an issue and every time the news media would report on some event involving Meredith, whether it was a report of him walking across the campus or something more significant, tensions would rise. It remained an issue at Phillip's too but without the rancor that accompanied the earlier debate. How the local football teams, the college teams and the pros were doing seemed to capture the attention of the locals. It is interesting to note that the only pro team that could be found on television was the Washington Redskins. I was led to believe that they were favorites in the South because they did not have blacks on the team. State teams did not have blacks and, as I have mentioned, they did not play teams that had blacks.

I do know some things about football and can carry on an intelligent conversation with most anyone. This included former high school coach and general expert, Ned Dillard. I must have impressed him because the tension between us eased somewhat. On one occasion, Ned invited Dot and I to his home to watch a game. His home was out in the country. As I recall, he did not have close neighbors. We enjoyed the visit because it was a good game. A contributing factor was our decision to not discuss Meredith or race in general. I was to learn that Ned was a first cousin to Senator Richard Russell of Georgia. Obviously, he came from good stock. He not only thought of himself as being knowledgeable, he was in many subjects. Talking with him was always interesting.

I was getting along well with most of the congregation. Larry and I continued to meet regularly each morning to discuss football and other issues not related to race. When the subject arose I tried to steer it to some other topic. It was not hard to do because I think both of us were tired of all the talk. Larry and I were getting to be friends, not just in a preacher and parishioner way. He had a lovely wife and kids. Billie, Larry's wife, was a very quiet, caring person. She was one of the nicest people I knew and she simply adored Larry. She always had a kind word to say about my sermons even when I knew I was lousy.

There were others I had grown to appreciate too. The Kellys were exceptional and their son was great in the MYF. Dale and his family were good people though I would never be very close to him. People were generally receptive to my sermons and bragged about me in the community. It did not take long for me to get to know most everyone in the community. That was a blessing and a bane. Everyone knew every bit of gossip going around town. If they didn't have the facts, they improvised.

How Did I Get Where I Am?

There was a couple who were members of Sandersville Methodist. I will use the names Harold and Ethel. Harold was a very learned individual who read extensively. He had serious bouts of depression and had spent time in a psychiatric hospital. Like all other juicy gossip, everyone in town knew about Harold's illness and gossiped about him often. More than one person reminded me that one of our members was "mental," a term reserved for people who had been in the psychiatric unit of the local hospital. I really liked him and appreciated the depth of his interests and knowledge. He wrote articles for newspapers including the Ledger and the Times-Picayune. I had always fantasized about being an author so I spent some time talking with him about his writing.

In one of our conversations I shared some of my philosophy with him and he seemed interested. He was smart enough to read between the lines and knew a lot of feelings I had that I had consciously suppressed.

"You may be good for Sandersville, but is Sandersville good for you?"

I was intrigued by the question. It was his follow-up remark that really caught me off guard.

"Have you ever thought through all the experiences you've had that got you where you are now?"

"Are you asking about my decision to go into the ministry?" I asked.

"Well, have you ever really thought about all that went into making that decision?" Harold responded.

I had not. I had written a paper in seminary about my credo but it was shallow at best. I often connected some of the dots but I had not really thought about all those who made me what I was. I could not answer the question. I had never thought about the people who really influenced my thoughts and my direction. It was something to ponder. Just how did I get to this point in life?

A career in ministry was far removed from my family history. In a traditional sense I could say our family was "Christian" but to my knowledge we did not have any ministers in the family. I am sure it would have been common knowledge if we had. I have mentioned in part some of my childhood. I think it important for the kids to know that I was very different from the other members of my immediate family. I looked different from my brothers and sisters. Actually, all of my siblings were half-brothers and – sisters. Plus, I have always had a strong desire to get an education and assumed at an early age that I would go to college. That desire or drive came from somewhere, but I cannot identify any person or influence that pointed me in that direction. I can think of some people who urged me to further my education but it was nothing more than a suggestion.

My family was not really into college. My older brother dropped out of high school as did one other. Both elected to go into the military at age seventeen. As I thought about it, I realized how different I was from other family members. My mother remarried after divorcing my alleged father of birth. I use the term "alleged" because I look so different from my older brother who also carried the Kellar name. I have blue eyes, blond hair and different physical features. His eyes were brown and he was a good three inches shorter than me. I do, however, look much like my mother, and, according to Dot, have much of her characteristics. That bothers me because I was not as fond of my mother as I should have been. Our resemblance at least assured me that I was not adopted or "picked up along the way". The observation made by Dot that I sometimes act like my mother is a bone of contention. Mother was not a demonstrative sort. I cannot remember being hugged very often as a child. Granted, this was true of all her children but, since this is about me, I will speak only for me. Mother did have a good sense of humor as did I. I can imagine, knowing Grandmother, that mother did not receive very much TLC either.

Speaking about my grandmother, it is important to note that in my earliest years I lived with her. I do not remember where my mother was during those years except that she was busy having other children. I never did figure out just why I was not with her. Living with my grandmother was not an easy task. She was not an easy person to like. She had had a hard life and seemed bitter about it. She loved fishing and would take me to the local creek to waste my time while she fished. As I recall, we often did not eat the fish. She would send me into the quarters to sell the fish to any black family interested. I never feared for my safety and was always treated well as I walked through the quarters. I was a regular "peddler" of fish and blackberries in the black community.

Later in life, in my junior high years, I moved in with my mother and my stepfather. We lived in several different homes but always within the town limits of Picayune. Unlike many southern kids, I never lived on a farm, never milked a cow, and rode a horse only once. That was fine with me for I cannot stand horses except at a distance. My stepfather was an exceptional man. He had to put up with mother. He worked hard to feed his family and treated me very fairly. His name was Milton Necaise and was what many referred to as a "coonass", a semi-derogative term for a Cajun. He was a good man. The only characteristic I gained from him was a decent work ethic.

It is interesting to note that my grandmother would do sewing for black people. Yet she was as racist as anyone could be. If she wanted me to run to the nearest store, which was a black owned and operated grocery store, she would direct me to "run to the nigger store" to get milk and bread or whatever she needed. However, she detested the idea of my playing with the local black kids. When I did, which was often, she would pull me close to her, look at my hands, and repeat her old question, "Did any of the nigger rub off on you?" I did not realize it at the time but I was put in a paradoxical situation. I was asked to sell goods to the blacks, shop in their stores, and do other tasks as ordered, but I was not to like them.

I need to note too, that while my grandmother was outspoken about blacks, in a wholly negative manner, I can never remember my stepfather mentioning blacks in a negative way. He was a big man who was very strong, but he was also a very gentle man.

However, a lot of my relatives were not. My cousins and I would fight at the drop of a hat. But even they were not as negative as my grandmother. It is my uncle and third cousin that stand out in my memory as being pure racists. Previously, I mentioned my Uncle Greg who took exception when I remarked about the beauty of a black girl. My cousin, Wilton, thought anyone who spoke kindly to a Black person needed a good whipping. We fought over race issues quite often. One fight was precipitated by the simple act of my shaking hands with a black guy named Robert. Robert was my age. His mother owned the grocery store I often shopped at and I liked her. She would add a piece of candy to my purchases some of the time. Robert and I often talked about football and basketball. He once told me that his basketball team scored over one-hundred points in a single game. Our high school team would score 40 points and feel like they had accomplished a great feat. I was in awe of Robert. He was my age but had more muscle in one arm than I had on my entire body. We were buddies, a no-no in that era. The day of the fight, I saw him coming down the street. I greeted him and we shook hands. Wilton was watching and confronted me about my touching a "nigger". I found it hard to understand just why anyone would be upset because I shook hands with Robert. But I had never really liked Wilton and that may have had something to do with a willingness to fight him. It never took much to get us in a squabble.

Chapter Eleven

How Did I Become a Minister?

How did I get to where I was? Harold's question was more difficult to answer than I realized. As a child I did attend Sunday School at the First Baptist Church in Picayune, but only when mother would attend. I was to soon learn that the church gave me socialization opportunities other than those of my cousins and neighbors. Most of my time was spent playing with family and neighbors. Playing with family had positives and negatives. The positives were having someone to play with. The negatives were a different story. I had two cousins who lived in Kiln, Mississippi, a small town about twenty miles from Picayune. They were "Cajuns" and were rowdy. At least once a month they would visit our family. We spent most of Saturday playing in the woods near our house. One of our favorite games was tag. It was a matter of great pride to get your "tag" in and then escape being tagged in return. Tempers would flair and one thing led to another and, before you knew it, we were all fighting one or the other. Some of the fights were as vicious as they could be among twelve and thirteen year-olds. Blood was always spilled, sometimes mine but more often theirs. As I recall, our families did little to break up the fighting. It was a learning experience, so they thought. This was the process of dealing with cousins and other kids in the area. First we got together to play, and then we'd fight. The same process would follow the next day or the next week. Obviously, I grew up in a combative family.

Sunday School was an escape from that combative lifestyle. We did play at church but strangely enough we never fought. I liked that and liked the people I met. Most of my life had been spent with family and extended family. That was my social system. Now I began to get to know others and began to make friends outside my extended family. So, the process was simple. My cousins would visit on Saturdays and we would play hard and always end up in a fight. On Sundays, I would go to church and have a great time. It does not take a genius to figure out which was more enjoyable.

I reached a point where I would go to church even if my mother did not go. My friendship base grew and I began to look forward to going to church. Soon I was a regular.

My church friends became my school friends. I spent more time with them than I did my extended family. There remained conflicts with cousins and others but I had something else in my life. I became more and more involved in the church. I would later join the church and be baptized along with my stepfather and my older brother. The process that brought us into that baptismal pool is an interesting story in itself which I will get to soon. A dear friend and classmate of mine, James Hickman, invited me to attend a "Youth Revival" sponsored by the churches of Picayune. James Walter Hickman was a huge young man who weighed over 260 pounds. His invitation was more of a directive than a request. I hated to disappoint him so I agreed to attend. The revival was held at the football stadium. There were two speakers, evangelists, from Baylor University. One was an all-American football player and the other was one of the best preachers I have ever heard. I loved sports and having a football player as a preacher was a real attraction. On the second night of the revival I accepted Christ as my Lord and Savior. I cannot tell you that I knew just what I was doing but it felt right.

My Dad and brother also decided to join the church. I always laugh when I think about Dad's conversion. He loved football, and on Saturday afternoons he would listen to the games on the radio. All of the LSU games were played at night, and he would listen to the likes of Ole Miss and Tulane and any other game he could find. Saturday afternoons were important to him. He worked from daylight to dark at the mill and having a free day was special. The local Baptist minister would drop by and talk about religion almost weekly. It was his method of converting a Roman Catholic to the "Christian" faith.

One day Dad announced to all who could hear, "I have decided to join the Baptist church." When asked why, because he was a lifelong Catholic, he replied, "Because that god damned preacher comes by every week and interrupts my Saturday. If I join the god damned church maybe he will leave me alone." Thus is the story of Dad's conversion. He, Gordon and I were in the same pool a couple weeks later being baptized. (Dad grew to become a faithful member of the Baptist church. He died of lung cancer in his early sixties. I think he got even with the Baptists at his funeral. He wanted to limit the preacher to only ten minutes and had a Rosary set up at the coffin. I saw that as being Dad's way of telling the preacher who interrupted his Saturday afternoons, "Take that, preacher.")

I need to remind the reader that Sunday school at First Baptist was not my first contact with the church. My very first experience I recall was not very positive. I had to be under ten years of age. Mama Bennett took me to a revival meeting at Antioch Baptist Church in east Picayune. I remember the preacher shouting and warning everyone that they were going to hell unless they were "born again." He described, in frightening detail, how God was going to bring the earth to an end and good people were going to heaven and bad people were going to hell. He made it sound like the great majority were going to hell and very few were going to heaven. For an impressionistic young child it was a bit much. When we left church that night, there was a distant storm. I could see the flashes of lightning. I did not sleep much that night as I awaited the end of time and wondered if I was going to heaven. I also wondered about my family. I did not want to go to someplace other than where they were going. I gradually moved from fear of church to becoming a part of the church.

I participated in church activities and so many doors were opened for me. It was a different world. For the first time, I began to think about what I wanted to be when I grew up. A lot of careers had crossed my mind, maybe a football coach or a professional soldier. Many of my family had been in the military. Still, the church seemed to appeal to me more and more. A couple years later I dedicated my life to full-time Christian service under the preaching of John Maddox and a youth evangelist named Chester Swore. I remember Dr. Swore because he preached that a girl should not kiss a boy unless she planned to marry him. Chester was like Paul in that he had never married and, with his looks, I seriously doubted he'd had many opportunities to kiss girls. His philosophy created a lot of problems for the guys in the community. The girls seemed to take Swore's advice to heart, and it was increasingly difficult to get a girl to kiss you. While I had given my heart to the Lord, I must confess I continued to give maximum effort toward "making out" with the girls. Dr. Swore made it a little more difficult.

While Chester was the preacher when I decided to go into the ministry, it was John Maddox that had the greatest influence. He always seemed interested in me as a person and was very supportive of my wanting to be a minister. I tried not to disappoint him. I even elected to not go to the prom because there would be dancing, so I took him up on his invitation to attend a party at his home on the night of the prom.

My only guilt came when a group of teens decided to steal oranges from the trees in Brother Maddox's backyard. I shall never forget what happened. A couple of us sneaked into his yard and began picking the oranges. His backdoor opened and he called out, "Help yourselves boys. I know you are in there." I shall never forget the feeling I had. I do not know if he knew I was involved or not, but I felt enough guilt to telegraph my involvement. Every time he had an altar call, and asked if anyone wanted to rededicate his life, I was there. But John Maddox meant a lot in my life, and I shall always regard him as a primary mover in my decision to become a minister.

From then on, I knew I would become a minister. My journey led me in different directions and to different churches. I am embarrassed to say most of the influences that led to different churches came from the girls in my life. For a brief while I attended a Missionary Baptist Church because I was interested in a young lady who attended that church. An added feature was that the preacher did not preach abstinence from kissing until marriage. Once they found I had dedicated my life to full-time Christian service, they licensed me to preach. I was fifteen or sixteen at the time. I was dumbfounded that all it took to be licensed to preach was the awareness of my desire to be a preacher. That church relationship did not last very long. As the relationship with the young Baptist lady ended, so did my relationship to her church.

My dating life led me to Methodism a year later. I was dating the Methodist minister's daughter and he kept telling me about the advantages of Methodism. The girl, Joan Ennis, was a classmate of mine in high school. Joan's father, David Ennis, was pastor of the Picayune Methodist Church. David was a good preacher and had a great sense of humor. He was not near as dogmatic as the Baptists were and, besides, I liked Joan very much. I joined the Methodist Church. It was either the witness (coaxing) of David Ennis or the beauty of Joan that swayed me. David was not a verbal racist, but he did tell me that if he is watching a boxing match between a white and a black, he always pulls for the white man.

Whatever the case, I became a Methodist. Shortly afterwards I received a letter from the Baptist church that had licensed me that my license had been revoked.

As I recall, I have never been a "black and white" person. I see all shades of grey in life. Maybe it is because of my childhood experiences. I was influenced by the rigid theological thinking of a grandparent who was basically ignorant about Christianity accepting what her preacher talked about. Conversely, I was influenced by the Roman Catholic community that also had a strong presence in my family. I recall my grandmother being very angry with my stepfather because he used profanity. I can also recall her shouting, calling them "son of a bastard." The difference between the two churches had more to do with drinking and dancing in my mind than they did about theological issues. I do recall that when a local Baptist revival was held, the names of all the Catholic families living the community were passed out to visitors as "unsaved." Another thing stands out in my memory about my home community. Bias was rampant. Dad used to say you cannot say "dago" (a person of Italian decent) without saying "damn dago." Then there was the anti-Semitic who intensely believed that the Jews had killed Jesus. There were the anti-Catholics who lived near New Orleans which was predominantly Roman Catholic. The universal bias was against blacks. I either made it through all of those influential groups unable to focus my prejudice or never really developed a prejudice. I realized that I was different.

Where did all this thinking come from? Oh, yes, it was Harold's question about how I had become what I was. This was requiring more time and thought than I had anticipated. I needed to let it go but I couldn't. One thought led to another and to another. I remember someone asking a rhetorical question, "If you get where you are going, will you know where you are?" Was that my dilemma? Did I even know where I was going with this question? Was Harold trying to put me in a no-win position? But I simply could not let it go. I wanted to know just how I got where I was at this time in my life.

Harold really had me going. Wait a minute, I thought. Maybe Harold wants me to become confused and then depressed so I'll know where he is coming from. No, it was a legitimate question. And I had to find an answer. Who touched my life that led me to my present situation? What influence had led me to Sandersville?

It really seemed simple. It was Brunner Hunt, the Methodist Church, the cabinet, the bishop. It was the connectional system in the Methodist Church. Those were answers but not to the real question.

I talked about my growing up and the family that I knew. I talked about my church experience. Who and what was left to bring to mind that will stop my frustration at defining the forces that made me who I was?

I thought about some people I had met because of my planned ministry. One of my closest friends and mentor was Denson Napier. Maybe it was his influence. As I reflect on my relationship with Denson, I remember him as being a maverick in the conference. If comparing him to other Methodist ministers I would list him as the follower of "the beat of a different drummer." He could be very cynical and yet very caring. My observation of Denson led me to conclude that he could, if so inclined, tell the Bishop to "go to hell." I liked that about him. I just liked Denson. He listened to me and I was not just another Wesley Foundation member who was taking his time. Being a director of the Wesley Foundation insulated him from the usual crap facing a pastor of a local church. His "church members" were students filled with idealism and chomping at the bit to get out of school to change the world. This allowed him more liberties than enjoyed by other clergy. This is not to suggest that his office made him less a minister than any other minister. It is to say that his office and his personality fit well.

Denson's contribution to my life was in his sense of independence and willingness to go to bat for me. He helped me get into Emory. My grades were not as good as they should have been, and the administration at the school initially refused to admit me. He intercede and got me in on probation. He constantly reminded me of the importance of getting a degree from seminary. If I expressed any doubts about going on to Emory, Denson would give me hell. Between Dot's pressure and Denson's harassment, I was bound to get to Emory. I shall always be indebted to Denson for not only pushing me into Emory, but believing in me enough to make the effort. He was a liberal, politically, theologically and probably other areas of life as well.

Denson gave me a view of the ministry that was not traditional. Having served a couple of churches, I knew only too well the subtle pressures that came with ministry. Every church member has every right to criticize the pastor simply because they want to, and there is no recourse on the minister's part. If I visited Mrs. Smith on Mondays, Mrs. Jones would be offended because she was not the first person I visited that week. I have mentioned about my food likes and dislikes. I would have church members get angry with me because I would not eat meatloaf. I really envied Denson's role that eliminated such inanities. I am also indebted to Denson for participating in our wedding. He, along with Dot's brother, Buford, officiated at our wedding.

Denson was a realist and helped me understand the Methodist system and its makeup in Mississippi. He was the direct opposite of those who always said the right thing. I am speaking about those people who, as they shake your hand, are scanning the room to see who else is there and do they need to shake their hand as well. There was no B.S., no game playing with Denson. He was what you saw. He schooled me on the politics in the Mississippi Conference. Through him I learned about a lot of characters that I should look out for when I returned from Emory. It was Denson more than anyone else who made me aware of a fact that I would experience sooner or later. In some circles, ability has little to do with your appointment. It was who you knew, and how well you got along with the system as dictated by those persons. He was a strong influence in my life.

Aha! I had it. But, no, there were others.

A part of the ministry that makes it such a great job is the friendships which form over the years. No one understands the complexities of serving a church like another ministry. Wilton Carter and I had attended school together and became close friends over the years. We had some things in common, like golf and political interests. The Hattiesburg District of The Methodist Church was made up of several churches and pastors. Prior to attending Emory, I had served as a supply pastor to a couple of churches. While serving at Bonhomie and Arnold Line, I met some men who are still my friends after many years. There is a bond that is almost unbreakable, and the fellowship gained from these relationships is immeasurable. Like any collection of people, some were easy to like and friendships formed immediately.

Wilton and his wife Dolores spent a lot of time with Dot and me. Dolores and Dot related well and shared the problems that come from being a preacher's wife. When I needed the company of clergy, I always turned to Wilton.

Wilton was a sharp looking man. He was always impeccably dressed and I cannot ever recall a day when everything was not in perfect place. He was the best dressed golfer, the sharpest dressed preacher and Dolores swore he would get out of bed at night after sharing some intimacy, shower and brush his hair. Our wives grew to be best friends. If one of us attended a workshop or conference, the other was always there. We spent hours talking about appointments, as all preachers do, and mapping out our long term objectives. Suffice it to say that we were close. I particularly liked playing golf with Wilton. He was one of the few golfers I have known that looked as neat after a round as he did before the round. Wilton could hit a ball three hundred yards. I liked Wilton's philosophy too. We were in tune with each other, and it was always good to have him to talk with. Having a friend who shared my philosophy was helpful in maintaining my beliefs because I could not talk openly with anyone in my church community about many issues.

I realize something now that I had known all along but was so obvious I almost passed over it. There was one person that played a major role in my reaching this place in my life. Of course, it was Dot. A major factor, if not *the* major factor, in my growth, was Dot's family.

They were special people. I am quick to add that my liberal nature was not a product of her father. Their impact on my life was more about family values. Dot was a member of Arnold Line Methodist Church where she sometimes played the piano. I believe that her mother began to conspire to have her daughter marry a Methodist minister. I was the closest candidate at hand.

Our courtship was an interesting experience for me. I had been active in dating and, like many Southern boys, talked with several different girls about marrying. It was a shameless ploy to make advances. With most girls it worked, and we would engage in sexual behavior. With Dot, it was different. She had committed to being a virgin when she married and she remained true to her commitment. It was not because I did not try. I used every tactic I had ever learned. None worked. Her virtue was important to her, which was reflective of her family values. I may not have liked it, but I respected her decision to remain a virgin. This may seem unnecessary to add to this journal, but it was a new experience for me. My youth was spent in a promiscuous environment, and my respect for women was not what it should have been. Being with Dot helped me see the importance of respecting the values of another person. I am confident that Dot had to put on her armor every time we were alone together. Naturally, she ultimately prevailed.

Chapter Twelve

If I Get Where I'm Going, Where Will I Be?

Dot and I were engaged in May of 1959, and married on December twenty-first of that year. That, by the way, is the shortest day of the year and the longest night. I pointed this out to Dot, but she failed to see what I was getting at. (Dot has cautioned me not to talk too much about our intimacy. The innuendo here is obvious.)

Becoming part of the Dickinson family helped me grow in several ways. I learned several things about family that I had not known. I have attempted to give a brief history of my family and my experiences as a member of a dysfunctional family. While my family did not experience closeness, they knew how to party Cajun style. A large bulk of our community, and our family in particular, were heavily influenced by the Cajun culture. We partied together well but there was no closeness. I was encouraged to get an education, but it was not expected. Whatever I did, I had to do on my own. When Dot came into my life I found a source that pushed me to attain the highest I could for my life. I am confident that, without her, I would have stayed in Mississippi and never dared go to Emory. I would have accepted mediocrity and become like so many other Mississippi ministers and taken the easy way out.

Harold's question provoked much thought. I had been influenced by the church, both Baptist and Methodist, even though I switched churches because of the girl I was dating. Joan's father, though not a seminary graduate, was a successful minister and served our church well for many years. It was considered a good appointment.

Does all that answer Harold's question? Not for me.

Am I so easily influenced that all it takes is an outside force to redirect me from point A to point B? Then it occurred to me that I must have something inside me that contributed to where I am. While I was encouraged by many, I had to decide just what to do with my life. If I have learned anything it is that everything we do is by choice. I also happen to believe that God opens doors in strange ways. Is it possible that God sent these people into my life to reinforce His call? Did God place something in my heart that causes pain when I see others in pain? Did God send that old black man along the road when I was in the National Guard? Most important of all, did God send James Walter Hickman into my life and direct him to practically order me to attend that youth revival?

It dawns on me that Harold may have been asking, "How did you, Ned Kellar, come to feel what you feel and become what you have become?" It was a time for introspection. Isn't that what people who have a thinking process do? Aren't inward journeys vital to the understanding of one's self?

Oh man, here we go again. What am I really like? Not just what others see, but what I know is there. What am I like? I have always been a sensitive person. I hate to see anyone hurt unless I have a keen dislike of that person. I knew that I detested "keep off the grass" signs and what they represented. I am not a rebel but sometimes I read challenges where there are none. I know I despise bigots. How about that? I have admitted that I am bigoted against bigots. I know I have a deep internal anger toward people like the fat insurance salesman that talked about killing a black man like he would kill an animal. I wish I could be more forgiving of people like that, but sometimes I wish them ill. God forgive me.

I looked at my watch. How long had I mulled over that question? Too long, I thought. Wow, where has the time gone? Have I thought enough about the question? Have I even understood the question?

I got in my car and started to drive to visit some members. Today I will travel up to the Vossburg Church. I had time to think on the drive. Harold had jump-started my mind and I could not turn it off. My thoughts were chasing after me. It was Frances Thompson's poem "Hound of Heaven" that popped into my mind.

Is there more to me? I wish I could tell you about some cataclysmic event that turned me in one direction or the other. I cannot think of a single event. I just kind of grew into what I am. I feel sorry for people who have difficult lives. I cannot think of any time in my life when I felt superior to other people. I have never been as bigoted as were most of my friends and family. Somewhere in the process of growing up someone forgot to tell me what others were told. I did not, for example, know that I should not shake hands with blacks. I sure did not know that I should not admire the beauty of a young black girl. Most of all, I did not know that I should hate Jews. I do recall hearing Uncle Greg say he hated Jews because "they killed Jesus." My call just kind of happened. My attitude toward blacks seemed to cause me more difficulty than anything.

I began to reflect on my experience at Emory. I recall that Dot and I loaded everything we owned in the back seat and trunk of a 1950 Silver Streak Pontiac and headed to Emory University. It was my first trip to that city, and I was a bit anxious. The only city I had driven in was New Orleans. Now I was going from a small town to a big city to get a degree in theology. I recalled all the warnings I had received from those ministers who had elected not to go to seminary.

"They will poison your mind with a lot of liberal junk."

Emory had a profound impact on our lives. We spent twenty-eight months living in a one room apartment with a Murphy bed. It was on the third floor of Gilbert Hall, the student housing for married seminary students. I had just graduated from Mississippi Southern where I had accelerated my schooling so I could finish and get to Emory. I wanted to finish school, get back to Mississippi and start my career in ministry.

I learned a lot while attending classes at Candler. (Candler was the name of the Theology School.)

What I learned most was that our call was to minister to people. Emory and Candler certainly offered a much more liberal platform than Mississippi Southern. Southern was a bastion against the evils of racial harmony. Their school mascot was a student dressed as Nathan Bedford Forrest, the founder of the KKK.

There were others who did a lot to influence my growth. Arva Floyd had been a missionary to Japan prior to WWII. He often mentioned that if we had converted just two percent of the Japanese leaders prior to the war, the whole thing could have been avoided. He was one of the kindest men I have ever known.

All in all, I think much of my thinking was formed while at Emory. It is not to say that my attitude changed very much. I had many of the feelings that I now have prior to going to Emory. My experience there reinforced my attitudes. I met others who felt the same way and helped me validate my feelings

In a way, those "stay at homers" in Mississippi had been right. My mind was not poisoned, but it was opened to many new thoughts and experiences. The two and a half years spent on campus were the most enjoyable of my life to that date. I often wondered why I was in such a hurry to get out of school. I truly loved the "ivory tower" atmosphere and the freedom to say what I wanted. I loved talking about subjects that would later present such awkwardness in Mississippi. I would think about sitting in the cafeteria with other students talking about a host of topics and feeling good about the camaraderie. I have always believed in the great benefits of a degree from college or graduate school. One of the greatest was in meeting people from different areas of the country and the joy of sharing thoughts and opinions.

It was imperative that Dot and I both find jobs because our savings were small. We both applied at a Sears store on Ponce de Leon Avenue. It was a regional store and occupied a whole city block. It was not an attractive place but it provided a place to work. I was hired as a salesman in the children's department and Dot was hired as a secretary. Her employment at Sears was short-lived because she was soon hired as secretary to the Director of Library at Emory.

I worked for three months that first summer in Atlanta. I made two discoveries. Atlanta is hot in the summers, and Sears is an interesting place to work. I liked being a salesman, especially in the children's department. I was amazed at the process parents went through to purchase clothes for children. I also discovered a new patience with children that tried on clothes they did not like to thwart the parents trying to convince them the clothes were the proper wear for a child their age. I did pretty well and was the leading salesman for two months in a row.

I soon found employment in a church on weekends. I became the youth pastor at Chamblee Methodist located in northeast Atlanta. It was about five miles from the campus and an easy trip in the old Pontiac. That job was a learning process. It was the first large church I had ever been associated with and had a staff of about six people, large for that time. I also worked with a pastor that was as boring as anyone I have ever heard. He let me preach once then decided I needed to focus on the kids. Word came to me that he'd heard I was a better preacher. I guess he didn't want to expose his congregation to another preacher. I liked the man, as did most of the congregation, but he was boring.

The following year I was appointed to a student pastorate in Sugar Hill, Georgia. A classmate of mine had served the previous year and recommended me to be his successor. It was a small church that was experiencing some growth. I loved the whole experience. We would drive to Sugar Hill on Saturday and visit the members. We stayed in the parsonage, a small trailer parked next to the church. In Arnold Line and Bonhomie, I lived in a two room apartment in a large home. The living arrangement was all right until we were married and Dot moved in. The walls were paper thin, so our conversations had to be whispered as well as any expressions of passion. But Sugar Hill's parsonage suited us well. The congregation was more cosmopolitan than the Mississippi churches. We even had a Yankee in the church. Most in the church had a great sense of humor and once a month there was a church dinner. I have never seen so much food in my life, and we always brought some home.

All of these experiences were refreshing to a young couple from far away Mississippi. We made the trip to and from Hattiesburg about six or seven times while at Emory. It was always an experience to drive the four-hundred miles mostly on two lane highways. We tried different routes, finally settling on one that took us through rural Alabama. Dot loved seeing cows and pasture lands and farms. There were enough gas stations to satisfy bathroom stops. Soon we bought another car, a Studebaker Lark, that got much better gas mileage than the old Pontiac. Traveling became easier and more comfortable.

A great advantage of being in student housing were the people we met and the friendships that developed. Wilton and Dolores had the apartment next to ours. Wilton did not like a bed that dropped from the wall so he removed the springs and let the bed rest on the floor. On the day that he performed his surgery on the Murphy bed, Dolores came to our apartment and announced that the bed had fallen on Wilton's head. We rushed over and found Wilton rubbing a knot on his head but proudly displaying a bed flat on the floor. We did a lot together and often talked about getting back to Mississippi. There were other Mississippi Conference men at Emory, and we all visited together from time to time.

There was one couple in particular that we really enjoyed and spent a lot of time with. Joe and Ann White were from Arkansas. Ann was as white as any person I have ever seen. Joe was balding and a real down to earth person. He worked as a student associate at Grace Methodist, one of the best known churches in the Southeast. We had worshiped there, and at First Methodist in downtown Atlanta, before I took the job at Sugar Hill. Ann was one of the most proper people I have known. I never heard her say anything improper nor did I ever see her appear unkempt. She and Dot made good friends because both were so very proper.

One of the things I remember most about Joe was his need to get mailings into the post office before a particular date. He would work on the postcards most of the day then take them to the post office. The unusual part was he delivered the letters to the downtown

Atlanta post office just before midnight so the cards would be postmarked on that date. On more than one occasion he and Ann would drive to downtown Atlanta at 11:30 pm to make sure the post date was not a day late. For some strange reason Dot and I accompanied them on more than one trip. Atlanta was a bustling city during the day but was very quiet at midnight. We wore night clothes most of the time, and I often wondered what would have happened if we had been pulled over by a cop.

Living in a cosmopolitan city, and being on a "liberal" campus, was a great experience for me. One weekend, Dot and I made a trip with two couples from Sugar Hill to see the mountains in North Georgia. It was both exciting and frightening. I have driven all of my life in the flatlands of southern Mississippi. Well, there were two hills, one just north of Picayune and another by the Pine Hill Drive-In theatre. But the North Georgia and North Carolina mountains were real mountains. We rode on roads that were narrow and had a drop off of several hundred feet on one side. It was exciting to see hills and waterfalls. The experience would bring me back to those hills in later years.

The trip home turned into a problem. We were taking a road outside of Maryville, Tennessee and came to a detour. It took us off the paved highway onto a dirt and gravel road. It was in the middle of the mountains, and the road was extremely narrow. Our anxiety level increased by a thousand percent. The road was too narrow to turn around so we proceeded toward Copper Hill, Tennessee. On the way to the main highway we met an oncoming car. Alarm turned to panic. How do we pass another car on this narrow road? Our driver, Stanley, inched over as far as he could, and the other car did the same. We pulled up even with the car and the driver rolled his window down.

Leaning out the window, he shouted, "Turn back. The road is terrible behind us."

Jewel, one of the passengers in our car, began laughing hysterically. When asked what she was doing she replied, "I'm laughing so I won't scream.

She laughed all the way to Copper Hill.

When I first saw the terrain I thought we had crashed and were poised at the gates of Hell. The soil was a deep orange and not a single blade of grass or tree could be seen. The trip bonded our group as lifelong friends.

There were so many experiences that opened my world. Most of my life had been lived in a closed community where family and extended family made up my social world. Now we were meeting people from all over the country, and from other countries. We dealt with personalities that were open and receptive to new ideas. I kept remembering experiences and began to long for the return to those educational and cosmopolitan days. During our tenure in Atlanta, the Atlanta School System integrated peacefully. But that was in Atlanta. I was now in Mississippi.

As I approached Vossburg, I was brought back to reality. In place of tall buildings and bustling traffic, I saw dilapidated buildings and little or no traffic. How did I get here? Harold's question had occupied most of that day, and now I had to get back to work.

In the final analysis, I am where I am. Why wrestle with what brought me here? The exercise had been stimulating, but I had to get on with my job. It was fast approaching the holiday season and there was much to do. Christmas is an exciting time in churches and also very demanding. My growth in ministry continued at a steady pace. I was getting better as a preacher, and the churches seemed to appreciate what I was doing.

The Gathering of Clergy

Being the pastor of a Methodist church involves many roles. One is to administer the business activities of the church. Another is to preach. But a pastor is a part of a much larger system and each minister has a supervisor. I have spoken about Brunner Hunt, the District Superintendent of the Hattiesburg District. On a regular basis the district would meet. All ministers were expected to attend. By and large, these were fun times and a great time to meet other Methodist ministers from across the district. It had its boring moments too, such as listening to Dr. Hunt talk about the many programs and projects promoted by the conference.

There were about fifty ministers in the district with most being pastors of a two- or three-church charge. The ministers were an odd collection. The district had some large churches in the conference, and some of the smallest. Most of the ministers were not seminary graduates. At the first meeting I attended, I spent several minutes surveying the group. It did not take long for me to gain confidence. For the first time in my life, I felt superior to others. Of those present at the meeting, I was more intelligent than over half of them. At the very least, I had more education. That was a key issue in the conference and in my confidence. Denson and I had talked about education many times as we sat in his office at Southern. At Emory, there were discussions about the people who had not attended seminaries.

Having a seminary education was common ground for most of my new acquaintances. The closest comparison I can think of was of us being fraternity brothers. We talked about the changes that had taken place at Emory and reminisced about Horton's Drug Store and other campus hangouts. While this was a fun part of ministers' meetings, it was also a reminder that not all the ministers were seminary graduates. The non-graduates resented the stories being told by the grads. Some saw it as snobbery. There was always an undercurrent of resentment on both sides This was one of the major reasons for the division in the Mississippi Conference.

In Mississippi, the minister with a seminary degree was the exception. There was a clear separation between those who "had been away to school" and those who had taken a less demanding route to full ordination. It was more than a difference. There was resentment on the part of those who chose the "Course of Study" route. I had heard some remarks that the seminary just messed up a good preacher and filled his head with a lot of junk. This was a real issue because much of the leadership of the Mississippi Conference did not have seminary degrees. It was clear they looked out for their fellow clergymen who did not have a degree from seminary. I could join with either group, but I was so proud of my education I elected to side with the other graduates.

I was proud of my education, especially my degree from Emory University. Going to Emory did not promise a better appointment. As a matter of fact, I was led to believe it could even hinder getting a better appointment with the present regime in power. Most of the ministers in Mississippi could have gotten a degree from a seminary if they wanted to badly enough. I was a good example of that fact. Obviously I had some prejudice toward those who took the shortcut. I admit I did not know their reasons, and they could have had legitimate ones. I knew some of the men who did not sacrifice and go on to school. I understood that an education did not equate to being a good preacher. David Ennis, for example, did not have a seminary degree, and he was a very good speaker. The issue for me was becoming as well trained as possible. The men who irked me were the lazy ones who looked to their connections to get a good appointment.

To understand my feeling about advanced degrees, it needs mentioning that I was the first of my extended family to get a college degree. I was not encouraged to do so by my family, though they seemed proud that I did. For as long as I can remember, I had wanted to be a college graduate. I do not know where that desire came from because I was the first member of my family to even get a high school education. Most of the men in our family either quit school and got married, or joined the military forces. My older brother, Gordon, quit school in the ninth or tenth grade. At age seventeen, he joined the army and spent four years in the service. My uncles, aunts and cousins were all high school dropouts. There was little family pressure to get an education. My dad would remind each of us that we would not get far without a high school degree, but that was the extent of the pressure. Dropping out of school would have been quite easy for me.

I felt I had sacrificed to get as far as I did in school. I recall my parents paying for my first year in Junior College. It cost $10 a month to attend Pearl River Junior College. After the first year, I paid my own way thanks to the Methodist Church. I used my salary as a student preacher, borrowed from the Methodist Student Loan program and did without. I need to add if it was not for Dot and her urgings, I would not have attended Emory. So I had internal drive and then I married another one.

There were a lot of good men in the Hattiesburg District who had very successful ministries. One that I met and developed a good relationship with, was Buffkin Oliver. Buffkin was the pastor at Ellisville in Jones County. Ellisville was the county seat for Jones, or as I was reminded time and again, "The Free State of Jones." We spent a lot of time discussing the issues facing Methodism in Mississippi. He was more than laid-back. Buffkin was the easiest going guy I had ever met. If there was any turmoil in his life it was buried very deep. I never saw a hint of disorder in his life.

Denson was still at Southern which made it easy to discuss issues with him. Then there was Sam McRaney. Never have I met a slower moving person. I know I have a southern accent, but Sam had a southern drawl in the truest meaning of the word. He pastored a single church in a community nearby. It was a beautiful church, and I envied his having only one sermon on a Sunday morning. I once preached a revival for him and we never worked past noon on any day of the week. Sam would complain of being tired and we'd knock off early. I did all the preaching and really enjoyed it. Sam was a cautious person and a pack rat. He would stop on a busy highway to pick up a small piece of chain for his collection. When asked to explain why he would do that, his pat answer was, "You never know when you will need a piece of chain." The fact that it was only eight inches long did not make much difference to him.

There were others that slipped my mind. I intended to get to know everyone in the district during my first year. As circumstances would have it I never accomplished my goal.

Chapter Thirteen

Hidden Haven: The Beginning (or the End)

In the early fall I received an invitation to attend a fellowship and study group at a place called Hidden Haven. I called Wilton and found that he had been invited to the same meeting. The group included Buford, Maxine, Jerry Trigg and Jim Waites. There were others, including Sam McRaney, and others whom I had met and socialized with at meetings and conferences. These men were considered the brightest and most progressive in the Mississippi Conference. They could easily be the real leaders of the conference if given the chance. However, as long as the present regime was in power, their climb would be slow and arduous. Wilton and I agreed we were fortunate to have been included in this group. We made plans to attend and decided Wilton would drive. That was fine with me because he had a much nicer car than I did. Plus riding in Wilton's car guaranteed the best ride possible. It was, of course, spotless.

Hidden Haven is located in South Central Mississippi in the deep woods and swamplands characteristic of that area. The nearest town was Richton, a typical small southern town. The area was a part of a swamp that covered several square miles. As we turned off the main highway and made our way along the narrow dirt road, we both commented that "Hidden Haven" was an appropriate name. We drove for what seemed like twenty miles, deeper and deeper into the swamp. We began to worry that we had taken the wrong road and were hopelessly lost. It was a great relief when we first saw the little cabin just off the road. We had finally arrived at Hidden Haven and were eager to become part of the group.

Most had already arrived and were discussing the normal topic when ministers gathered: Who was in line for what appointment? Wilton and I were the youngest of the group, and we took our seats on the outer edge of the circle. As I looked about the room I recognized most of the men there. Those that I didn't know were introduced by name and the appointment they were servicing. There was one man present that was not a minister. He was Maxie Dunnam's friend, Maxie being the evening's host and leader. His friend's name was P. D. East and he was from Petal, Mississippi. Mr. East was a writer and the editor of a small newspaper in Petal. I recall that he was lying on the floor when introduced and remained there as we waved at him. He did not make a favorable impression with me, but he had Maxie's attention. Later we were to learn that Mr. East's newspaper was extremely liberal for the State of Mississippi.

The meeting began with a discussion of what would be discussed. This always took time but it usually boiled down to what Maxie, and one or two others, wanted to discuss. Regardless of the topic, the discussion usually ended up being about political issues of the Mississippi Conference. I was to discover that this always happened. Sometime in the middle of the discussion, Maxie began a side conversation with P. D. East about writing a book. I recall P. D. telling Maxie that when he wrote his book he had become so identified with his characters that when one died, he cried.

After a couple of hours the meeting broke up, and we began our long journey back to civilization. Wilton and I talked about what had transpired and concluded that we liked being a part of this gathering. I liked political discussions and talking about appointments. Every Methodist preacher could talk about church politics and the appointment process. If invited, we would attend the next meeting. This was the kind of group that we wanted to align ourselves with, even though they were not in a position to assist with better appointments. We both concluded that while these men were not in power positions today, the time would come when they would be the conference leaders.

For the next few weeks it was church as usual. The routine was becoming easier as time passed. The long trip each Sunday was not as difficult as it had been at first. My car knew the way, and I learned that I could predict just how many minutes it would take to get from one place to the other. The leaves were in full color, and then they began to disappear. The trees, which were once so beautiful, were now quite ugly. The foliage hid more than I imagined. The hillsides, once a beautiful green then colored with the golds, reds and yellows of fall, were now barren, scraggly and ugly. The missing foliage revealed the landscape which held rusty appliances, old cars and other junk that looked awful. Nature had pulled back the curtain and the scenery revealed the lifestyles of those who populated the woods of Central Mississippi. It was not a pretty sight. Vossburg, never a place of beauty, was now uglier than ever.

Though nature had turned the other cheek, there was one constant that could be counted on – racial upheaval. James Meredith was now a regular part of the University of Mississippi. The fallout had settled and there were days that his name was not mentioned at Phillip's. However, the topic merely changed names. Every day there was some article in the local newspaper that kept the racial situation alive and present.

> *October 13, Birmingham, Alabama: A white man is beaten at a KKK rally after announcing that "mob violence is no answer to anything."*
> *November 1, Pascagoula, Mississippi: Nightriders fire a shotgun blast through the window of a "liberal" newsman's office.*

The little town of Sandersville remained quiet. A few still talked about Meredith and bets were made that he would not survive to graduate. But football regained its place of importance. The local high school football team would win one week and lose the other. The Lion's Club was busy planning the annual Ladies Night. I had finally made some noticeable progress in burning the old tree. The cooler weather made it easier to stand around a hot fire. Thanksgiving was just a few days away, and that is always a great time in the South. Food was always plentiful but at Thanksgiving it was obscene. It was also family time and people were more cheerful than usual. I received a notice that a second meeting was scheduled at Hidden Haven.

The Statement

Again, Wilton and I rode together to the meeting. I think we both needed the other to make sure we did not get lost in that swamp. There was supposed to be an agenda, but neither of us could recall what it was. As we entered the house I recognized several of those present. Some I knew very well like Sam McRaney and Maxie Dunnam. I had met some of the others but knew very little about them. I do not know who convened the meeting but we soon learned its purpose-a statement that had been drafted by Maxie, Jim Waites, Jerry Trigg and Jerry Furr. Copies of the statement were passed around for others to peruse and make comments. The statement was titled *Born of Conviction*. It was brief and spoke to several issues. I remember it being attached to a blue cover, much like a petition to the courts.

Everyone read the statement in silence. At first glance it seemed rather mild, but on the other hand it spoke about some very incendiary issues. I knew enough about politics to know that some of the folk at Sandersville would find it objectionable. The statement read:

Born of Conviction

> Confronted with the grave crisis precipitated by racial discord within our state in recent months, and the genuine dilemma facing persons of Christian conscience, we are compelled to voice our convictions publicly. Indeed, as Christian ministers and as native Mississippians, sharing the anguish of all our people,

we have a particular obligation to speak. Thus understanding our mutual involvement in these issues, bind ourselves together in this expression of our Christian commitment. We speak only for ourselves, though mindful that many others share these affirmations.

Born of the deep conviction of our souls as to what is morally right, we have been driven to seek the foundations of such convictions in the expressed witness of our Church. We, therefore, at the outset of this new year affirm the following:

The Church is the instrument of God's purpose. This is His Church. It is ours only as stewards under His Lordship. Effective practice of this stewardship for the ministry clearly requires freedom of the pulpit. It demands for every man an atmosphere for responsible belief and free expression.

We affirm our faith in the official position of the Methodist Church on race as set forth in paragraph 2026 of the 1960 Discipline: "Our Lord Jesus Christ teaches that all men are brothers. He permits no discrimination because of race, color or creed. 'In Christ Jesus, you are all sons of God, through faith....' (Galatians 3:26)

The position of the Methodist Church, long held and frequently declared, is an amplification of our Lord's teaching: "We believe that God is Father, that Jesus Christ is His Son, that all men are brothers, and that man is of infinite worth as a child of God." (The Social Creed, Paragraph 2020)

We affirm our belief that our public school system is the most effective means of providing common education for all our children. We hold that it is an institution essential to the preservation and development of our true democracy. The Methodist Church is officially committed to the system of public school education and we concur. We are unalterably opposed to the closing of public schools on any level or to the diversion of tax funds to the support of private or sectarian schools.

In these conflicting times, the issues of race and Communism are frequently confused. Let there be no mistake. We affirm an unflinching opposition to Communism. We publicly concur in the Methodist Council of Bishops' statement on November 16, 1962, which declares:

The basic commitment of a Methodist minister is to Jesus Christ as Lord and Savior. This sets him in permanent opposition to Communism. He cannot be a Christian and a communist. In obedience to his Lord and in support of the prayer, "Thy kingdom come, Thy will be done, on earth as it is in heaven," he champions justice, mercy, freedom, brotherhood and peace. He defends the underprivileged, oppressed, and forsaken. He challenges the status quo, calling for repentance and change wherever the behavior of men falls short of the standards of Jesus Christ. We believe that this is our task and calling as Christian ministers.

Finding authority in the official position of our Church, and believing it to be in harmony with Scripture and good Christian conscience, we publicly declare ourselves in these matters and agree to stand together in support of these principles.

The statement had been written as a petition with lines at the bottom of the document for signatures. After reading my copy, I waited for others to finish. As I recall, there was not a lot of conversation about the statement. It was obvious that some had seen the statement in advance and spent time discussing it. Some had already signed the official copy and there were spaces for others to sign if they wished. I do not know how many signed the statement that evening. I meant to sign but we soon got off on another discussion and I forgot to follow through. It was getting late and Wilton and

I decided to leave. Neither of us wanted to be driving through the woods after dark.

On the way back to Sandersville we talked about the contents of the statement, and both of us agreed we would sign. Reading between the lines it could be perceived as a very powerful document. On the surface it was not spectacular but, then again, this was Mississippi where any comment that even vaguely referred to a positive attitude towards blacks would be perceived as radical. Who would care if we signed it anyway? With that, our conversation changed to other issues such as golf and how things were going at Lawrence and Sandersville.

Wilton dropped me off at home then left to get to his own home before it grew too late. I was only home for a moment when Sam McRaney and his wife stopped by to visit. Sam was a nervous sort in some ways, and he was particularly nervous that evening.

"Did you sign the statement?" he asked.

It dawned on me that I had not. "Were we supposed to sign it today?" I asked.

"Well, I am not going to sign it, and I advise you not to either. Those who put their names to that statement will wish they had their nickel back."

I had never seen Sam so upset. Dot asked about the statement.

"It's a statement advocating integration. That's what it is," reported Sam. "It will stir up a hornet's nest," he continued.

Dot asked me if I had signed, and I told her not yet but I was going to sign it. I assured her that there was nothing to it. The next day I sent a postcard to Maxie asking him to add my signature. For some reason I sent two cards requesting the addition of my signature to the statement.

Within the next few days I had forgotten the whole issue. I had forgotten when Maxie said it was going to be published. He had mentioned that the plan was to let the Mississippi Methodist, the official newspaper of the Mississippi Methodist Conference, first publish the statement. The editor of the Methodist was a good friend of Maxie's and had championed change in the conference for several years. The publication of the statement was something I would think about another day. We had Christmas to plan for in three churches. Most of my time was spent keeping up with the issues of my community. It wasn't too demanding because few issues developed in Sandersville.

One Sandersville issue was Harold's hospitalization in the mental health hospital even though it had happened several months earlier. I guess when you are in an area with little to do, you hold onto an issue until another comes about. I had noticed that depressed people always look depressed. All anyone had to do was look at Harold to recall his hospitalization. The locals had labeled him as being "funny," which was a kind word for crazy. He was fully aware of the community's attitude and remained out of the public arena most of the time. When he did venture out, people would stare at him as if he were a novelty. His wife was a very nice lady but avoided contact with the outside world. I would see him at times, and we always had a pleasant conversation. He seemed genuinely interested in me, and I never left his presence without some positive feelings.

Harold was also a writer. He visited my church and, as I got to know him, I better understood why the locals steered clear of him. He was very intelligent, well read and knowledgeable about most subjects. Most were intimidated by his intellect and kept him at arm's length. I really liked him and enjoyed our visits. He would borrow some of my theology books and, after reading them, we would discuss the contents. He was a deep thinker. He was a refreshing person for me. I had not talked with anyone since leaving Emory on a level that characterized my discussions with Harold.

People noticed our visits and some would comment, "Been with the crazy man, I hear."

Harold knew of the gossip and tried hard to ignore it. "I know what people are saying," he said as we talked about the community. "It's the price we pay for living in a small town like Sandersville."

I knew it hurt him to be the center of gossip and fear. Harold's feelings could be seen in his eyes and heard in his voice.

"If I had cancer," he once remarked, "people would feel sorry for me and bring food to my wife. As it is, they shun her and me. They're afraid of anything they do not understand."

"These people profess to be good Christians, but they will turn on anyone who does something they do not like. They love to have someone or something to talk about." There was a trace of bitterness in Harold's voice.

I dismissed his remarks as not being relevant to me. I was not the topic of conversation around the community, so what did I have to worry about?

Other than Harold's constant battle with depression and the resulting gossip, the town was quiet. The holiday season was fast approaching. Everyone was in a festive mood. The weather was much colder now and keeping the church warm was difficult. The crowds increased at Sandersville but remained static at Vossburg and Goodwater. The prospects for new members were practically non-existent at any of the churches. The battle with the mimeograph machine continued, and I was always the loser. Every Saturday I would come home covered with black ink. Initially I had counted on success in ministry as having one church and a salary in excess of $5,000. I amended that to include a church secretary and a new mimeograph machine. That would be real happiness.

Christmas has always been a special time for me. For as long as I could remember the Christmas season held special feelings. This one was no different. It was my first at Sandersville, and I had many small tasks to get done before Christmas Sunday. Dot and I planned holiday visits with family, Christmas Eve in Picayune and Christmas Day on the farm. All of Dot's family would be home on the farm, including her sister Nell who lived in Houston. There would be tons of food. Ella Ruth would prepare a Japanese Fruit cake which had five layers and was covered with everything that I liked. Christmas with the Dickinsons was a far cry from what I experienced as a child.

Christmas was a good time. My Dad cooked a pork roast with sweet potatoes and a generous amount of garlic. Dad was a Cajun and cooking was an art that involved a lot of hot pepper. He also made delicious pies. Later in his life, Dad worked as a cook on an oil rig in the Gulf. His crew numbered over 100. After cooking for so many Dad forgot how to do small dishes. That included pies. The problem was that Dad didn't know how to make one pie. He was used to baking about ten pies every day while on the rig. When he came home he made ten pies! There was never a shortage of pies in our home. Even our extended family had difficulty eating all the pies. Dot participated in my family's special times. I don't think she understood my family, but she tried.

It was easy for me to participate in the Dickinson family Christmas. They were a close family but went out of their way to make the "in-laws" feel welcome. The Dickinson family always had some task to perform. If it wasn't the septic tank, it was the well. This held true at Christmas. Mr. Homer was a man who believed that every waking hour was a working hour. The only time he ever rested was on Sunday. He never missed church nor a meal. The man could easily out eat any member of the family. He did this, according to his report, with only half a stomach. Years before he had surgery and a portion of his stomach had been removed. I was reminded of that surgery time and time again.

"I wish I could eat as much as you can, Preacher," was a remark I heard many times.

On Monday, New Year's Day, Dot and I were invited to the Dillards for lunch and to watch the bowl games. It was football-watching day and that is what we did. From the Parade of Roses to the Rose Bowl, we watched football. It was more than just watching. Every man there would get worked up about this team or that team and often shouted advice to the coaches on the television screen. The Dillards were gracious hosts. I saw a side of Ned that I had not seen before. We had a delightful time.

Chapter Fourteen

The Bomb Drops

(Note: The following paragraphs contain dates that could be inaccurate in that my memory about specific days is a little fuzzy. However, the events listed are accurate. I recall the experiences and remember the statements and remarks with amazing clarity. Either this all began on Wednesday or Thursday, January 3, or very close to that date.)

The holidays passed and it was a typical Wednesday morning, January 3, 1963. I got up and got dressed and started out for the morning paper, coffee and a rehash of the bowl games. For some reason, I elected to visit the post office before the usual routine of picking up the newspaper and having coffee at the café. When I arrived at the post office it was empty. It was the first time I had ever seen it empty. Usually it was crowded with the locals picking up their mail and sharing bits of gossip. I was the only one in the post office. Usually I found Miss Hinton ready to discuss the events of the community but she was nowhere to be found. I thought I heard a movement in the mailroom but no one came out to greet me. It was a mixed blessing. Miss Hinton could tie me up for several minutes with her stories of what was happening in the community. At least I could get back to the café and shoot the bull with my friends.

I opened my box and found the usual array of junk mail and information from the Mississippi Conference. I threw away the fliers advertising the latest sales in Laurel. In the bottom of the box was my copy of the Mississippi Methodist Advocate. I took it out, glanced at it and then put it under my arm as I sorted through the other pieces of mail. Something caught my eye when I glanced at the Advocate. I put the mail down on the counter and re-opened the paper. My heart quickened as I read the lead article. It was the "statement." I remember seeing the words "Born of Conviction". I had almost forgotten I had signed the thing. There it was with a long list of names at the bottom. Skipping over the content of the statement I looked for my name. There it was. Ned Kellar had signed the statement, "Born of Conviction." It amazed me how my name stood out. My heart rate increased and my breathing was shallow.

I tried to read the article but my mind was now racing. I saw words like "bold" and "courageous." For a fleeting moment I felt some pride but the concerns about fallout overcame those feelings. I had learned just how hostile this area could become when the Ole Miss incident occurred. Oxford was a far distance away. This was local. It was in Sandersville. How many times had I been reminded that Sandersville was in the heart of the "Free State of Jones County." I had a sinking feeling about this.

As I stood in the lobby of the Sandersville Post Office my thoughts were going wild. "Wait a minute," I reminded myself. "I should have expected this. I had been so adamant about signing the thing." But still I felt uneasy. I looked around the empty lobby now happy it was empty. Maybe no one else had seen the publication. But who was I kidding? It was common knowledge that Miss Hinton took liberties reading every newspaper and magazine that came to her post office. I folded the paper into a small package, and stuffed it in the middle of my other pieces of mail. No one would recognize it as a newspaper.

I made my way toward the café. I picked up a copy of the Clarion Ledger, fearful that the headline would have the statement along with my name. I quickly scanned the paper and there was not any mention of the statement. The same was true of the Times-Picayune. If those two papers did not write about it then who would know? At least no one in the café would know because the Advocate only went to Methodists and the only Methodist I knew who attended the café each morning was Larry Hosey. I bought a copy of each paper just in case the statement was buried somewhere in the depths of the papers. I would read every word of each paper when I got home.

As I stood at the door of Phillips Café I thought about Harold, or as he was known, "Crazy Harold." He had told me that the people of Sandersville are nice people. But, if you ever cross them, or do something they do not like, they will turn on you in the bat of an eye. As I gripped the door to the café I thought, "Well, I'll soon find out."

I entered the café with a forced smile on my face. I was one of the better known personalities in the town and was usually greeted warmly by most everyone. I expected the usual, "Morning Preacher." Instead, I was greeted with a thunderous silence. At first every eye in the café was directed toward me. I stopped and just looked at the people. They began to turn and look in the other direction. No one spoke a word to me as I made my way to a booth. It was one of the most uncomfortable and confusing times in my life. I scanned the room for Larry but he was not there. Now I really felt alone. I buried my face in the paper waiting for the waitress to deliver my coffee. She did not even look my way. I did catch the eye of the owner. I had heard him talk about kicking the crap out of any nigger who tried to enter his café. I was not sure just where I stood in his eyes. I sat there for several minutes. Did they know about the statement? How did they find out so quickly? I knew that news travels fast in this small town but this would set a record. After sitting there for what seemed like an hour, I glanced at my watch. I had been there less than five minutes. I stood up and walked out.

Harold was right. These people will turn on you quicker than the bat of an eye.

I walked out of the restaurant not knowing where to go. Larry Hosey had not been in the restaurant so I decided to walk across the tracks to the depot. We had spent many hours together, and I knew I could count on him to at least talk with me. I opened the door of the depot. Larry was doing paperwork. He did not say a word. I asked if he had enjoyed the bowl games.

"I'm busy right now." He never looked up from his desk. The message was clear. He was my best friend among all the residents of the area, and he would not even look at me. I felt the deep pain of complete rejection. It was a first for me. All of the charm and ability to defuse a situation that I had developed into a fine art failed me. There was nothing I could do or say that would defuse this situation. I turned and left for the relative safety of my home. I needed to get home and tell Dot what had happened.

As I walked down the street I had the feeling that every person driving by knew that I was one of the "twenty-eight." It was a foolish thought because most of the people who drove past were not the least bit interested in Sandersville, nor the State of Mississippi for that matter. They just continued to drive north or south, probably wondering who in the world would live in such an ugly town. I had seen the same physical ugliness, but now I was seeing a different kind of ugliness, and it was directed toward me.

Dot was shocked at the article but immediately realized there was more to the statement than I had thought. How could anyone be so upset about a statement so innocuous as the one we had signed? In my heart though, I knew that what we had stated would upset people. I just did not believe it would turn friends against me. The telephone began to ring.

I answered and a voice on the other end said, "I hear you boys had a big meeting up in Jackson."

"Who is this?" I asked.

The speaker continued without identifying himself. "You boys are gonna be in a lot of trouble because of this. You shouldn't have listened to those people."

"I don't know what you are talking about." I was getting angry and shouted, "Who is this? If you don't tell me who you are, I'm going to hang up!"

"You boys are gonna be sorry you ever signed that nigger-loving paper." With that he hung up.

There were other calls throughout the day. Most of the people just hung up when I answered. Our phone was on a party line, and at least four other families had access to our calls, just as I had access to theirs. My line was a single ring. Others may have two or three rings. Every time I picked up my receiver I could hear others lift theirs. If the community had not read or heard about the article in the newspaper, they would know through the most effective communication system in Sandersville: the party line.

The television station reported on the statement in their news program. It was treated as if it was the biggest event in recent history. All I could hear were the words, "Young, white Methodist Ministers." What gave the news even more impact was the fact that it was something local boys had done – not outside agitators, but local boys, born and reared in Mississippi. By noon, the national news services picked up the story. Not only did the residents of Mississippi know about the "twenty-eight young, white Methodist Ministers," but now the whole nation knew. I phoned Wilton to see if anything had happened up that way.

"All hell's broken loose. There's a meeting planned at the church tonight." Wilton reported that he, too, had been receiving phone calls. No one had called and offered any encouragement.

"I guess my friends are too frightened to say anything," Wilton said. "We're on a party line and anyone who calls would be talking to a group of busybodies. I don't blame anyone for not revealing any information on my line."

I told him I was in the same situation.

"I've had only one threat," Wilton reported, "Some guy called about a meeting in Jackson."

I told him that I had received the same call. Evidently, the same man had been calling every member of the "twenty-eight" with the same accusation and the same threat.

"We have to get together as soon as possible."

I agreed and we decided on Friday as the day for the meeting.

That afternoon I drove to the nearest newspaper vending machine to pick up a copy of the Jackson Daily News. The same headline from the Clarion Ledger graced the front of the News. As I thumbed through the paper, I came to the editorial page and found that the lead editorial was about the "twenty-eight." It read in part:

> Actually, Christianity is the most phenomenal of the many religions that have helped carry mankind from the dark caves of stone to the bright ones of marble, glass and aluminum. Its directness lifts thy empty heart as no other. Its message, often beautiful and sometimes painful, is couched in such striking phrases that interpretations and opinions, chiseled a thousand times over, have failed to hide the wonder of its hope, and the scope of its spirit…
>
> Perhaps the twenty-eight young Mississippi Methodist ministers were aware of such wonder when they signed a pledge or resolution or something of that nature wherein they said more emphasis should be placed on the "brotherhood of man" in this world.
>
> And perhaps they were aware that such publicly avowed sentiment at this time might cause a rustling of feathers within their congregations. And in the press, and among politicians. Well it has…

If what I had experienced this day was any indication of "rustled feathers" the editorial was an understatement. Opening the Mississippi Methodist Advocate, I read in detail the statement and all the names listed. It was then that I remembered Maxie and Jim Waites had promised the editor of the Methodist the chance to be the first to print the statement. "Born of Conviction" covered the front page. Unlike what the other papers had editorialized, the Methodist was very supportive. As I read the article, and accompanying editorial, I felt much better. At least someone was supportive.

I wondered what Dr. Floyd was thinking now. Did he approve of the Statement? Dr. Floyd was a reserved man. He never advocated we should write a statement and publish it. What must he be thinking as he read about what has happened? We had asked what could be done to ease the racial tension. As I thought about it, I concluded he would never have advocated a statement. He had suggested we take our time, and be nice to all the blacks we met. Well, we just accelerated the process. Or maybe set it back another hundred years. Had we done the right thing? It had seemed right at the time. It had seemed to be in keeping with what I knew the church should be. I thought too about those ministers whom I knew had advocated the pulpit to be a voice of change, of preaching a Gospel that talked about God loving all people and expecting us to do the same. Dr. Dow Kirkpatrick, a minister I admired, spoke about these issues every Sunday and no one, to my knowledge, threatened his life or tried to run him out of town. I wondered what the others were going through as the news reached their communities. Maybe Sam was right. Maybe we would all wish we had our nickel back. In the heat of the moment, I began to question the wisdom of my action. Maybe it had been too soon to act? Originally, I had not wanted to come to Sandersville, but I had settled in and it no longer seemed like such a bad place.

Now I worked to convince myself that the action I took was the right thing to do. I just needed to toughen up and take the redneck taunts in stride. Yes, that's what I will do. Maybe if I kept telling myself that, some of my anguish would disappear. Besides, I had seen integration working in Atlanta and wasn't that the Deep South? I had played with blacks for most of my childhood, and nothing bad had happened to me. Yes, by God, it was the right thing! I must have carried on that internal conversation for an hour or more. Just as I would fire myself up, back came the nagging doubts, the questions and the anxiety. If it was so right, why did so many react so strongly? It was a silly question for me to be asking. Hadn't I seen the acting out against blacks? Didn't I hear old Red threaten a poor old black man and anyone who sided with him? Had I not heard my family talk about "niggers" as if they were worthless? Many talked about killing a "nigger" much like they would kill a mangy dog. I began to chastise myself for denying the reality of the situation. Like the man said on the phone, I was in deep trouble. What concerned and frightened me the most was I had put Dot in the middle of my troubles.

I took a short drive to the church to prepare for Sunday worship. When I returned home, Dot reported a phone call from Dale, a man who was only marginally active in the church. However, his wife was very active, as were his sons. I knew her as having a perpetual smile and speaking in a slow Southern drawl that stood out among Southern drawls. Dale had left a strange message which Dot did not understand. Dale wanted me to come to his house and help him hold up his car. After a few moments of interpreting his message, Dale called back to tell me that he wanted me under his car. He explained to Dot that he did not have a jack and wanted to use me instead. It was a veiled death threat. Hearing some nut on the phone talk about killing you is scary. To have someone you know, someone you dined with, someone in your church, saying he wanted you dead is more than disquieting – it is frightening. It also made me angry. I did not want to believe it was as it sounded. Maybe Dale let his temper get the better of him. He did that sometimes. He was also a staunch segregationist. The very idea of his minister advocating anything removed from his belief system was obviously more than he could take.

Then, as I thought about it, I became angry. He had called my wife and threatened me through her. Her naivety had spared her some of the shock and pain. She had concluded he needed help and had asked for mine. Any gesture on the part of any person in Sandersville would have been a relief from the constant harassment. I was not going to let anyone get away with threatening me without some response. I picked up the phone and called his home number. His wife answered and the moment I told her who I was there was a pause.

"I would like to talk with Dale," I announced.

She paused again then said Dale was out and would not be back for a while.

"Please tell him that I am home, and if he wants to see me let me know," I announced. "I understand he was looking for me." It was not the brightest thing I had ever done, but I had had enough. Or so I thought.

That evening, just after dark, there was a knock at my door. It was a bit scary in light of all the phone calls I had been receiving. I took a deep breath and opened the door. It was Ned Dillard and Harvey Hinton., two of the staunchest members of the church.

"We need to talk," Ned said in a voice filled with anger.

Harvey was more polite and asked if they could come in and talk about the newspaper article. I invited them in.

"You have yourself in a lot of trouble and don't expect any support from the church. We will be lucky if they don't burn the church and the parsonage," Ned ranted.

It was clear that his concern was not his preacher, but the church buildings. Harvey sat silently as Ned continued his rage.

"I thought of you as a friend. Goddamn, I even had you as a guest in our home. Now look what you've done."

At first I found myself reeling from the verbal blows, but then my anger returned.

"If stating my beliefs keeps us from being friends then it was not much of a friendship to begin with." I was shouting. Ned and I were standing face to face. Harvey interceded and possibly prevented us from getting into a physical brawl.

"I'm still your friend, but I wish you had not signed that paper," said Harvey. "Understand that we are concerned about the church as well as you. There are some people who feel very strongly about this race thing and you set them off. We have to do something to keep this thing from blowing up." Harvey was speaking calmly but his concern was obvious.

"I'll tell you what he can do to help," interrupted Ned. "He can recant his damn statement."

Looking him straight in the eye, I said calmly, "I have no intention of taking back anything I have said or signed."

"Preacher," Ned said much calmer now, "this thing can really blow up. I'm mad as hell at you right now, but I don't want anything to happen to you or to the church."

With that we sat down and began to talk about a course of action that would keep the lid on the situation. Two things happened that evening in our home. A certain amount of healing took place between the three of us. Harvey was the calming influence. The second thing that happened was with Ned. He accepted the fact that I could believe differently than he did, and we could still respect one another. Ned agreed that the best plan was to have a meeting of the congregation and talk about what happened. Not only did Ned agree to that plan, but he agreed to take the lead in the meeting. He and Harvey told me that they would do everything possible to keep anyone from damaging the parsonage or the church. The two left after two hours of heated debate mixed with some healing and then searching for a solution. It had been quite a night. It was not over. I couldn't forget what both had said about someone burning the parsonage or the church. I stayed up much of the night watching each car that passed the house, half expecting someone to jump out with a torch and set fire to the house. It was a long night.

As I lay in bed that evening, a thousand thoughts rushed through my mind. I revisited my internal conversation about the appropriateness of what I had done. I thought about how naive I must have been. I knew that the statement would cause concern on the part of some people, but I never realized it would cause such a furor. My experiences with bigotry had taught me that many people hated black people, but this was the first time I had experienced such hatred directed toward me. That day I became painfully aware of blind hatred. The greatest pain was where the anger was coming from. A member of my church had actually threatened my life. It was not the first time I had been threatened, but it was the first time a friend had threatened me. And over what? A statement of conviction that simply stated something I believed. I came to my senses and reminded myself that I was expecting rational people to do rational things. But racial issues were not dealt with rationally in this section of the country. That evening, my life changed. I began to lose an innocence that had been a part of my life, and an idealism that I had about the ministry.

Chapter Fifteen

Threats and Letters, Letters and Threats

The next morning I arose early. I really did not feel like getting up but I did. Dot and I were both exhausted from the lack of sleep. It was Friday and, if I followed my routine, I would be at Phillip's restaurant by eight a.m. There was a part of me that wanted to go, but I decided to stay home. There were things that needed my attention so I would stay home and complete some tasks.

The old oak tree that had been cut down lay beside my driveway. I could move it or, better yet, burn it. I began what was to become almost a daily ritual. I began burning the old tree that had been sawed into pieces. I piled up a few of the limbs and set them on fire. Because the pieces were large, it would take more than an hour to burn a single piece. I stood and watched the fire slowly consume one limb after another. I found myself thinking how wonderful it would be if I could burn my problems like I was burning the tree. Each limb would be a painful remark someone had made, or a threatening phone call, or something else that had caused distress. As I finished my first burn, I realized I felt some relief. Burning the tree was cathartic in a lot of ways. I could daydream as I watched the fire. Better yet, I could think about the sermon I was going to preach on

Sunday. What was I going to preach about? I certainly knew that a lot of my congregation was wondering the same thing. What could I expect? Do I try and assuage the congregation? Do I pretend that the 5,000 pound elephant was not in the room? This was the week I went to Vossburg. I had not heard a single word from either of the other two churches. What was happening with them? Was I in for another confrontation like the one with Ned? What would the reaction be? Would anyone be present? I shuddered as I stoked the fire.

There were disturbing reports coming from communities where members of the "twenty-eight" served churches. One minister had his tires slashed. Another had to leave his home in the middle of the night in fear for his life. Wilton reported that his church was in an uproar. The same was true of Buford. Each report of violence, or the threat of violence, added to our anxieties and our fears. I do not know how many cars I watched drive by our home each evening. I am sure many were simply people going home or going to work. What if? I kept thinking. I switched on the back porch light and left it on all evening. If someone was going to break into our home they would have to pass through the light, as if that would stop anyone.

The telephone continued to ring. There were crank calls, veiled threats and the people who just hung up when we answered. Later that day, the Kellys came over and told us that they still liked us.

"We just can't come out and say that we agree with you because this is a small town and people just wouldn't understand."

I realized that I was not the only one hurt. Others were hurt that their friend, the preacher, did not believe as they did. While I felt some hurt from those who had turned on me, my real anger was toward those who did not have the courage to face me but hid behind the telephone. Harvey called that evening and told me he had talked to Larry Hosey. Larry no longer considered me a friend. I had already gathered as much by his response the previous day. Having a fear that someone does not like you is one thing, but to be told bluntly that he no longer desires to be a friend, deepened the hurt. Of all the pain I had felt to that point, knowing that Larry no longer wanted me as a friend was the worst. I tried to rationalize it all but it just plain hurt. I feared that most of the people who had reached out to me since I arrived in Sandersville would feel the same. In my own thoughts it struck me that, for a guy who did not want to serve Sandersville, I was now offended that they did not want me.

The next day I was determined to return to my regular routine. It may have been that I wished this was all a bad dream, and I would receive the same warm greeting I had experienced in the past. It may have been that I just wanted to prove to the town that I could stand tall, regardless of what others thought. At least that was the image I wanted to project. On the inside I was teetering on the edge of collapse. I felt totally and completely rejected. I walked to Phillip's, picked up my newspaper, stepped inside and sat in my usual place. Opening the paper to the sports page, I buried myself in the news of the sports world. A cup of coffee was placed in front of me but, when I looked up, the waitress was walking away. She did not say a single word, but at least I received service. Then Larry came in and sat at another table. He did not speak nor look my way. I had hoped that he would not come by, but I should have known better. It is easier to deal with hurt if you do not have to face the one causing the pain. I sat there with ambivalent feelings. On the one hand, I was hurt because of the rejection. On the other hand, I was angry. Damn, I thought, can't I have an opinion without it destroying a friendship? I knew the answer but did not want to admit it. My heart broke. I felt tears come to my eyes. I lifted the paper so that no one could see until I regained my composure. I did not stay very long that day. The news still talked about the "twenty-eight" and their "Born of Conviction" statement. It felt strange to be the outcast when I had been the center of most conversations in the past. It was obvious that it would take more than a little time for this to blow over.

I learned from the few who would talk to me that the talk in the town was that there would be a killing before this thing ended. I was surprised to find that a good number of people were convinced that the parsonage would be bombed. It did not take a genius to figure out who they were talking about. As I passed people on the street some would nod hello, but no one stopped to talk with me. The whole community was tense, and I was the topic of conversation wherever two or more people were gathered.

The telephone calls continued. Many of the callers referred to me and "comrades," a not so veiled suggestion that I must be a communist. To one I was a communist dupe, and to another I was solely responsible for every attempt at breaking down the barriers to integration. It seems the only evil I was not responsible for was letting Meredith into Ole Miss. Others mentioned the mysterious meeting held in Jackson and the known commies who attended. My sense of humor came to my rescue by reminding me that at least I was providing some relief for Harold. No one talked about him now. They had a "real" nut in their presence. In my fantasy, I could see all the people on my party line waiting for the phone to sound that one long, single ring. I had, no doubt, replaced all the soap operas as the source of entertainment. I knew no one would dare use the phone lest they missed my calls. If there was a saving grace, it was that most people in Sandersville went to bed early, and there were few late night calls.

It was Saturday and tomorrow was Sunday. I was reminded by Ned that the meeting of the congregation was scheduled for Sunday evening.

"I'll keep it under control," he said. "You just make sure you come ready to defend yourself."

Every time I thought about the meeting, I grew anxious. I wished someone would call to tell me it was cancelled. I stayed in direct communication with my prayer life. I wondered if God ever gets tired of hearing the same prayer. I did not know what I was going to say, nor did I know what to expect from the crowd.

I read the statement in the Mississippi Methodist Advocate several times over. As I did so, I found another article titled "Freedom of the Pulpit". As I read the article, I began to see it as a reaffirmation of those who signed the Born of Conviction statement. At least I read it that way. The article talked about Methodists believing in the freedom of the pulpit, that is to say preaching what God placed on their hearts. Aha, I thought, that is what this statement is all about. The editor then quoted a District Superintendent from the North Mississippi Conference.

> These critical days through which we are passing demand dedication, self-denial and sacrifice in preaching the whole Gospel without any reservation whatsoever, with the fear of God in our hearts and without prejudice toward any man – We affirm the freedom of the pulpit. We have utmost confidence in our ministers and support them in the preaching of the whole Gospel in the spirit of Christ.

The editor then added a rather pointed statement. He wrote:

> We know that all must stand at the judgment bar of God and give an account of the deeds done in the body. This includes ministers who will have to give an account of their preaching.

It was more reinforcement. I thought I had done the will of God by adding my name to this document. Thus far it had fallen on a few receptive ears.

I thought about what I had read and what the writer was saying. I had never been advised on a sermon subject. I preached what I thought God wanted me to preach. I had never, and have never, entered any pulpit without uttering the same prayer: God help me to say what you would have me say. (Someone else will have to be the judge of whether I reached my desired goal of being who God wanted me to be.)

Some good things that happened on Saturday came in the form of two letters. They lifted my spirits. To date, the only encouragement I had received came from Wilton and Buffkin Oliver. The first letter was from The Board of Lay Activities and was written by J. P. Stafford, conference Lay Leader. The letter was dated January 3, 1963, the day the statement was printed.

Sandersville

Cary, Mississippi   January, 3, 1963

Dear Brothers:

Welcome to the fold of those who are willing to stand up and be counted. There is still plenty of room left for others, and we hope many will join you. For our part we will not feel so lonesome any more.
In the future, there will be an answer for those who ask – Where are the Pastors of the Mississippi Conference? We can say there are, at least "7000" (twenty-eight) who have not bowed the knee to Baal. Our grateful appreciation for your courage, conviction and determination. You will have our support, prayers and best efforts in the days ahead.
Having assumed the role of prophets, the pressure will be much greater as you try to live up to the demands this role places on you. When the shooting starts and you are far apart, maybe it will help to know that hundreds of consecrated laymen will applaud you, and countless others will wish you well in secret-that lack the courage or fortitude to come out into the open.
Blessings on you,

                                    J. P. Stafford

The second letter was from J. R. Rush, the Lay Leader of the Lake Methodist Church, where Wilton served. He wrote:

Route 1
Lake, Mississippi   January 3, 1963

Rev. Ned T. Kellar
Sandersville, Mississippi

Dear Brother Kellar:

I am delighted and encouraged that a group of our ministers have publicly affirmed their position on vital issues of Christian concerns. My prayer is that the laymen of our Conference will, by the grace of God and under the leadership of the Holy Spirit, follow your Christian example and make the Methodist Church in Mississippi more truly the body of Christ. I am proud of you and will pray that you, and all of us, will have the vision, courage, and faith to speak the truth in love and make our Christian witness in these troubled times.

Blessings on you,

J. R. Rush,
Lay Leader

Both J. P. Stafford and J. R. Rush was very liberal for Mississippi Methodist laymen. J. R. Rush's son James had also signed the statement. I had met both men and Wilton always spoke highly of Mr. Rush. I thought about how good it must be to have a man like J. R. in your church. I was not so fortunate. Both letters raised my spirits considerably. It is strange how easier conflict is when you know you are not the only one fighting the battle. Having Wilton and the signers on the same team meant a great deal, but to have laymen on a conference leadership level was significant. The letters were morale boosters. They helped reinforce my resolve. For a while I was ready. Bring on all your weapons! At least that was my bravado.

The Meeting

Sunday finally came. I had carefully printed the bulletins on Saturday evening, folded them and was ready for Sunday morning worship. I arose early and began the drive to Vossburg. I tried to anticipate what would happen when I arrived. Would they even let me out of the car? Would I be in any danger? Many thoughts crossed my mind. As I approached the church I did not see any hooded characters, nor did I see anything faintly resembling a lynch mob. Everything appeared normal. The crowds had dwindled a little since the District Superintendent had announced that Sandersville was leaving the charge. But good old Woody was there and gave his usual greeting. The service went without a hitch. It surprised me. I wondered if the news had not made it to Vossburg. Maybe there was a time warp here after all. Whatever the reason, I accepted the handshakes following the service and began the drive to Sandersville.

I usually make the trip in less than thirty minutes. Today it took forty minutes. I did not want to make it to the church until everyone had entered the sanctuary. Only one or two stood outside to greet me. "Greet" may be a misnomer. They were there to make sure I made it to the sanctuary. Willard began with the opening hymn, I had a prayer and we took care of the usual announcements. Ned announced the church meeting for that evening. It was a simple announcement, nothing more. This was followed by another hymn, the offering and then time for the sermon. I always pray before I preach but today I prayed as never before. I read my scripture then looked at the congregation. I certainly had everyone's attention. Every eye was focused on me. I cannot remember what I preached but I gave it my best. I have always been a topical preacher and spoke to the issues of the day and how we could fit these into the gospel. Whatever I said, it seemed to be received fairly well. I do not know what the group thought I was going to talk about, but I did what I usually did. I purposely did not speak to any of the issues contained in the "Born of Conviction" statement. That may have disappointed some, especially those who wanted to take issue with its content. The only difference for me was I was alone. Dot did not attend either service. That was planned by both of us. She can be very direct at times and it was best that we leave things alone.

The service ended in its usual manner. There was an invitation to join the church then a couple of verses of a hymn and the service was over. It was the tradition for the preacher to rush to the back door and shake hands with each person who attended. Some unusual things happened that day. The people who usually held my hand and talked long and hard about some issue, simply touched my hand and left.

Two people not only shook my hand warmly, but also whispered a few encouraging words to me. The first was Rose, a diminutive lady, with curly hair and a quiet voice. She held my hand and whispered, "I appreciate you. I think you did the right thing."

I almost lost it. Those few words did more for me than I could ever express. She was followed by Billie Hosey who was smiling as she took my hand.

"You need to know that we love you."

The morning had not gone as badly as I had thought it would.

Ned shook my hand and reminded me of the meeting. "You need to be there a little early. Now you say what you want to say, and I'll take over from there. I'll ask you to leave after your remarks. Don't worry, I'll run the meeting."

His suggestion that I not worry fell on deaf ears. All I could do was worry.

The meeting was scheduled at seven, but I arrived at 6:30. The church was nearly filled already. People crowded into the pews. I sat in the front pew with Ned and Harvey nearby. There was a lot of conversation among the attendees prior to the beginning of the meeting. Most of it was the usual visiting that takes place at a church meeting. I didn't hear anyone mention the cause of the meeting but voices were hushed.

The wait for the start of the meeting was excruciating. I felt everyone's eyes centered on the back of my head.

Sandersville

Someone said, "Haven't seen you here in a long time." People seemed surprised that so many were present. By seven it was an overflow crowd. I halfway expected to turn and see people in white robes and masks with a KKK emblem stamped on their costume. However, there were no burning crosses in the church yard and no men dressed in white sheets. Ned had said he would take care of the meeting, and he had done his homework. At exactly seven o'clock he called the meeting to order. There was a brief prayer then Ned took over.

"I'm gonna ask the preacher to make a statement. He can say whatever he wants to say. I don't want anyone to say a word until he is finished. Then you can ask your questions. All right preacher, let's hear what you have to say."

I had been sitting there reciting to myself over and over, "I can do all things through Christ who strengthens me…" I stood and faced the crowd. There were no white sheets with hoods, just the usual folks I saw often in the church or in town. I had thought about what to say but had not written anything on paper. I did not know what to write. I actually thanked everyone for coming, just as I would if it was a worship service. I briefly thought of a few cute things to say but decided against them all.

"I know you have come to hear my response to the questions you have about the statement I and others signed. I can only tell you what I believe the statement said, and what it means. Like anything written on paper for thousands to see, many interpretations can be made, some accurate and some inaccurate. I thought a lot about what I was signing and frankly did not see it being as inflammatory as it turned out to be. Some have decided it was an avocation to integrate the schools of Mississippi, but it was not."

I had everyone's attention. I looked around at the crowd. Some met my eyes while others looked away. I tried to size up the group as I usually do with any group to whom I am speaking. The anger was obvious with some. Dale and his entire family were there, as was Larry and his wife Billie. I said a quick, silent prayer and continued.

"I know many of you are angry, and some of you confused, about what happened this past week. It has been a difficult time for all of us, and I regret that something I did upset you. I signed the statement after reading it without a full awareness that it would upset some of you. The degree to which some of you have reacted has surprised me, and caused me some personal hurt. No one of us likes that kind of hurt, but sometimes hurt happens. You need to know that I believe what the statement says, and if I had it to do over again, I would do the same thing. I do not say that to rub salt into a wound, but to let you know that this was a very personal decision, not meant to cause pain to anyone. I knew the issue addressed in the statement to be volatile. As I have said, and will say many times tonight, I did not expect it to be as volatile as it turned out to be."

There was some restlessness and it was obvious some wanted to say something. Ned literally starred them into submission. I continued.

"Some of you have asked me to recant my position so that it would not hurt the church. I can no more do that than you would if you were in my place. I am no martyr, nor am I a hero. Neither am I a bad guy, and I'm certainly not a communist. You people know that. I am the same person I was last week when we sang together and prayed together and worshipped together. I am the same person who sat at your dinner table with you and your families. You have learned something about me that you did not know. If you stop and think about the sermons I have preached, you will remember that I have spoken often about brotherhood and loving your neighbor. You have received what I have preached, shook my hand when you were leaving and said, 'good sermon, preacher'."

Some of the restlessness died down. I could still see some were chomping at the bit to say something. They were waiting for a pause, but I kept on talking. I hoped I was making sense. I would like to report that all the tension left me but that's not true. I would get though this moment. At least I thought I would.

"I have visited with many of you in your homes, at church and at dinners. We have laughed together, prayed together, and just hung out. We see each other most every Sunday. We see each other at football games, and some of you see me at the Lion's Club. I have not changed nor have I fooled you into believing something about me that is not true. If there has been a change, it has been my growth in loving this church and you as my congregation. You may not want me any more. That's your right. However, I have no intention of going to the bishop or district superintendent and asking to be moved. You may want to ask that I be moved, but this will not cause me to ask to be moved.

"Let me say this about the statement I signed. When I first saw it, I thought it to be innocuous. It did not appear to me as a revolutionary document designed to change the world. Later, after reading each paragraph over and over again, I began to see the potential volatility contained in the words. If I made a mistake, it was not reading the temper of the times. Evidently, we in this state and in the South, are so on edge that the least thing sets us off. We are quick to turn on one another, even our closest friends. Why? Have we allowed ourselves to become so stirred up by those who hate that we react by hating everyone who does not believe as we believe?

"I realize that I am close to preaching to you. I only want to make the point that I have not changed. I am the same person you knew last week. My intent was not to preach a sermon, but to speak to the statement Born of Conviction. I have done that to the best of my ability. You may want more, and I will attempt to answer any question you may have."

I stood to one side awaiting the first question.

Ned stood and said, "I think the preacher has said all he needs to say. I'm going to ask him to leave and allow us to talk with one another."

I assured him that I did not mind answering questions.

"Preacher," he said, "I told you I would take care of this matter. I think you ought to leave now."

No one said a word. As I walked out of the church, I felt both relieved and nervous. I wondered if I was simply following Ned's directive, or if I was running from the crowd.

I went home and waited. Dot wanted to know what happened, and I tried to relate the sequence as I could recall them.

"No one said anything?" she asked.

"Only Ned, who told everyone to shut up."

The greatest irony was that I never wanted to be sent to Sandersville, and now I was defending myself and declaring I wouldn't ask to be moved. I longed for Emory and the camaraderie of people who thought and believed as I did. What I missed the most were the debates held in hallways and in classrooms, where issues were discussed and debated with no one being threatened with harm or death. I missed a lot of things. I dreamed of another place and another time. However, reality was, I was pastor of Sandersville. At least for the next few minutes.

Chapter Sixteen

Expected and Unexpected Conflicts

Later that evening, Ned and Harvey came by to report on the rest of the meeting.

"The only person who had anything to say was Dale who wanted you to explain your position on integration," said Ned. "I told him that was not our business as long as you don't preach about it. Now preacher, I am not sure I believe what I said, but I said it." Ned continued as if he was letting me know his position. "You know damn well that the schools of Mississippi are not going to be integrated."

Harvey brought up making Sandersville a single church charge. "I believed you were the one who could do it. This whole issue may have changed that. We'll have to wait and see. Time will heal this matter. It will be rough for a while."

Ned added, "Look at it this way, preacher. The parsonage is still standing. The church has not been bombed, and no one has been killed. I think the people will agree that they want you to stay. I say we did a good job."

We all shook hands and the two of them left. All three of us were exhausted. It had been a very trying day. Dot and I both slept better that evening.

I had weathered the storm, at least for the present. Not all of the "twenty-eight" had fared so well. I began to read, and hear via the grapevine, that some had suffered far more than I had. There was an article in the newspaper that reported a minister having to leave his home on very short notice. His name was Bill Lampton who just happened to have been my barber while I was at Emory. Bill was a very likeable person, one who got along with everyone. I had heard about his problem and then I read the "details" in the newspaper.

Methodist Minister Says Feared Violence

Columbia (UPI) – A young minister who signed a statement opposing racial discrimination said Tuesday he left his church because of the possibility of resulting violence.

"It looked like I had another Ole Miss on my hands," said the Rev. Bill Lampton, 27, pastor of the Methodist church at Pisgah. He referred to the Sept. 30 integration riot at the University of Mississippi.

Lampson was one of twenty-eight young Methodist ministers who released the statement last Wednesday.

He said two tires on his car were slashed Friday night and the next day some leading members of his congregation expressed fear that violence might erupt.

"They came to me to advise me of the fact that they were fearful for church property," said Lampton. "And that there were rumors of group action."

Lampton, who was contacted at a relative's home here, (Columbia) said if violence developed at Pisgah he feared it would have spread and "many parties could have been hurt."

Saturday afternoon, Lampton left Pisgah with his wife and child. No church service was held Sunday at his church.

Lampton said he did not know whether they would return to Pisgah. He will officially remain the church's pastor until the next meeting of the Mississippi Annual Conference unless Bishop Franklin and the Conference's six District Superintendents hold a special meeting and transfer him.

The statement, which Lampton signed, opposed discrimination, called for a "freedom of the pulpit" under which preachers might express their convictions and urged that public schools remain open. State law permits the closure of public schools to prevent racial integration.

Stewards of the Pisgah Church, four miles west of McComb, met last Thursday night to discuss the meeting.

Lampson and the Rev. Norman Boone of Brookhaven, District Superintendent, attended the session, which was described as a "lively affair."

At a regular meeting of the stewards Sunday night a committee was appointed to investigate possible conflicts between Lampson's position and that of his congregation.

There was another minister who had to leave his church as well. His name was Jim Rush, the son of J. R. Rush, who had written one of my first letters of support. Jim served the Philadelphia Circuit in Neshoba County. Jim had learned that a meeting was being held at his church by District Superintendent Jim Slay. When he got to the church, the door was locked because the members did not want him at the meeting. After banging on the door, he was let in only to be asked to recant to the congregation and publicly have his name removed from the statement. Jim refused and the members voted overwhelmingly to remove him as their pastor. Jim and his wife had to leave the parsonage and move in with his parents at Lake which was on the circuit served by Wilton.

A third signer of the statement, Jim Nicholson, was also relieved of his pastorate. His District Superintendent was Willard Leggett, the leader of one of the conference's political factions. Leggett decided the situation was irreconcilable and removed him from his pastorate. Jim had already been in trouble with his church because he had preached a sermon about the Old Miss situation that rankled many in his church.

As far as I knew every one of the "twenty-eight" was called before their official boards to speak about the statement.

As I read about Lampton, Rush and Nicholson, I realized that I was more fortunate than I had thought. At least I was still at my church. I knew the storm was far from over, and those who did not want me to stay could continue to work toward removing me. If the parsonage had not been bombed by now, it was probably safe. I still slept with one eye open.

Time to Visit Family

Even though the storm had waned some, I continued to listen for cars slowing in front of the house. There were more and more reports of violence across the state and across the south. The situation was worsening by the day. It was time to get away for a few days. We thought about visiting Wilton and Dolores but had not met with Dot's parents since the statement became public. It had to be done sooner than later.

The first of the week, we drove the short distance to Hattiesburg to visit with her parents. While it was good to get away from Sandersville and all of the tension present in the community, the visit to the farm had its own tension. Dot's dad was an outspoken segregationist. He did not espouse violence, but he verbally attacked anyone who challenged the policy of segregation. The closer we got to Hattiesburg, the more nervous I became. Verbal confrontation was not so difficult with the people in Sandersville. I did not relish confrontation with Mr. Homer Dickinson. I did have one thing going for me. Homer's son was just as involved as I was. As a matter of fact, Buford was far more involved than I. The second thing I had going for me was Dot. Mr. Homer's children could do little wrong. This is not to say that he accepted his sons-in-law as equals to his daughters. I knew the stories about his reaction to his eldest daughter Nell's marriage, and it caused some fear on my part. Allegedly, he went after his gun when Nell's husband-to-be announced that he was going to marry his daughter. While I did not fear being shot, at least not by Mr. Homer, there were some anxious moments. Dot was much less worried about her dad than I was. Ella Ruth, Dot's mom, was much more open than Mr. Homer. I anticipated that she would have some concerns, but that at least we would be welcome.

As we drove up the gravel road toward their home, Ella Ruth was the first person to greet us at the door. There were the usual hugs and the always warm welcome. Ella Ruth did not say a word about the crisis involving her son and son-in-law. After a few moments, Mr. Homer arrived home from work. Dot and I were sitting in the "fireplace room," a spare bedroom cum family room. It was the gathering room on any cold day. As he entered the room, he removed his hat and looked at me.

"You boys are going to end up in Parchman," he said as seriously as he had ever said anything to me. Parchman is the state prison for Mississippi. Neither Dot nor I said a word. That was the total conversation we had about the issue. It was easy to see he was upset. Had I not been a member of the family, I am confident I would have been asked to leave his home. Knowing him as well as I did, I was convinced that he was angry more about my having put his daughter at peril than anything having to do with the statement. I know, too, that he was worried about his son. Mr. Homer was torn from within. His well known and often stated hatred for blacks warred with his devotion and love for his children. He was well aware of what was happening in the South, and of the dangers that awaited anyone who espoused social change.

Ella Ruth's reaction to any crisis or any unusual event, was to cry. It pained me to see her cry and know that I was the cause of her worry. That was a time I wished I did not have anyone in my life so my actions would cause pain only to me. The thought never set roots because I did not know how I would have made it through this ordeal without Dot. She could have sat back and said, "I told you so," but she did not. There were times when we argued over the whole issue, but she always supported me. Knowing I was putting Dot through a difficult time, and that I had contributed to her family's distress, was the only time I regretted getting involved in the whole issue. When I first signed the statement, I had been thinking only about myself. But I had unwittingly dragged others into the conflict. I had put at risk the people I loved the most. For the first time in several days, I began to think of the others who were involved. I had been thinking only of myself, and what I had to do to survive the crisis. It was Dot, I realized, who answered most of the phone calls from the nuts. She had been a target for those who wanted to punish me for my actions. She had faced the same rejection and hatred that I had faced. I was embarrassed that I had been so self-centered. I knew all along that Dot was a strong person and that I leaned on her. One thing I discovered in this crisis was that Dot keeps her cool. She was, and is, the glue that keeps me together.

Being in conflict with Dot's family did not sit well with me. They were my adopted family and I loved them all. I had declared the Dickinson's as my own family, whether they wanted me or not. As mentioned previously, my own family experience as a child was not as I had wanted it to be. There was always some conflict between family members. Frequently, violence was just a word away. My grandmother was given verbal explosions. Her favorite angry words were "son of a bastard." I heard her yell that many times toward in-laws and anyone else who crossed her. I mention this again because, with Homer and Ella Ruth, there was no combativeness. Theirs was a close-knit family, and I had envied being a part of that. I was always treated well.

Now, being part of a problem for them caused me great pain. I felt like the outsider who had disrupted a family that I loved. Usually, visiting Dickinson was a rewarding time. This day's visit was filled with tension. I wondered if things would ever be the same. At the moment, my professional future was uncertain at best. There was reason to believe that my future in general was a bit uncertain. That part did not bother me so much. What did bother me was the possibility that this family would not hold me in the positive light that had characterized our relationship in the past.

Getting through the rest of that day was a chore. I cannot recall what we did to pass time. Watching the news on the television was not one of the things we considered. Every time we turned on the TV, the news was about the "twenty-eight white Methodist ministers." We had hoped to escape the turmoil for a little while, but it was clear that that was not possible. There was no sanctuary. Even if there had been, my paranoia level was so high that I would have perceived people singling me out and commenting on the "nigger-loving" Methodist. That evening, as we had dinner, there was a silence in place of the usual lively discussion.

It was also the time, as I think about it, that I decided that being tough was the only way I could be sure of not being hurt. Being a tough guy had spared me pain before, and I could fall back on that role. I had a mean side, something I learned in my early life. However, meanness did not fit very well with ministry so I had worked hard at being a nice guy. Smiling and shaking hands with people is second nature for a minister, and I worked to master that skill. But now I need to be tough to survive mentally. I would be tough with the issues and nice to the people. That was my plan, and I was sticking with it.

In the days that followed, I grew more and more aware of feelings of uneasiness. I was depressed. And I was angry. Some mean things had been said about me, and I had not fought back as much as I had wanted. Ministry removes privacy and imposes diplomacy. I was always cautious about my remarks lest I offend someone. If I did offend a person, they may stop worshipping at my church, and I would lose their support, and on and on.

But now I had to do something with my anger. I began a conversation with myself. My naiveté told me that I could believe anything I wanted, and it was no one's business. How dare anyone not like me because of my beliefs? How dare people not speak to me after all I had done for them! Had I not always been there when a death occurred? Didn't I make trip after trip to Laurel to visit someone in the hospital? At that moment in time I felt that all the people of those three small churches could go to hell. Damn them for reminding me of past pain! Damn them for upsetting my family.

The next day we left Homer and Ella Ruth to return to Sandersville. The trip to Hattiesburg was meant to be an escape, a retreat from all the hassle and pressure. For Dot it may well have worked. For me it was a reminder of past pain and present fears of what I dreaded the most – not being accepted by my adopted family. I again questioned what I had done. Had I really screwed up? There was little joy in our lives at that time. But I put on my tough guy persona and moved on with life.

For some reason, probably to bolster my tough guy image, I continued to make my daily trip to Phillip's Cafe. I followed the same routine I had always followed. It was not an act of courage as much as it having something to do. The reception remained cool, though one or two people would speak to me. No one ever sat with me as they used to, nor did anyone say more than, "Morning, preacher." Some stared, others looked away. But worst of all were those that looked right through me, as if I wasn't there. I was surprised and hurt by that. I had settled with the church and my in-laws. Why was I continually treated as an outcast? While no one really talked to me, I later learned that they constantly talked about me. I also learned later that it was peer pressure that kept them from me. They feared that if they talked with me, others would assume they felt and believed as I felt and believed. I have found that true in the South. If you are different, people will keep you at a distance. Perhaps that's true everywhere, I don't know. But I knew it to be true where I lived. The temper of the times was so volatile that people would maintain distance lest they be associated with the "enemy." It made for some lonely moments at Phillip's. One saving grace still left to me was dropping by Harvey's store.

The monthly meeting of the Lions Club arrived, but I had no intention of attending. I had resolved my differences with the congregation and that was the extent of my responsibility. I had not resolved much with the local community at large. I assumed many were upset with me but had no allegiance to me as the church members did. Besides, if they did not like me, that was their problem. I had enough problems of my own. I would not go to the meeting and considered dropping out of the group altogether.

However, about an hour before the meeting was to begin, Harvey and Earl came by and said they wanted me to go with them. I agreed so I wouldn't offend them and we drove the four or five miles to the Lion's Club. As I entered, normal conversation stopped. It would have been better if someone had said, "There's that nigger-loving s.o.b." At least I would have something to be angry about, but the silence left me defenseless. Just as quickly as the talking stopped, it started again. Only I was not a part of it. I realized how courageous Harvey and Earl were for bringing me to that meeting. Being friendly toward me was not accepted behavior in Sandersville. It must have been hard on those present that I had been friends with prior to the "statement". We used to joke and kid with one another.

We ate the usual meal of country fried steak and gravy. All the while, different members of the club held the attention of the group and the usual jokes were told. Yet there was something different tonight. After a joke was told, and the laughter subsided, there was silence – an awkward silence.

Finally, Ted, a younger member of the club asked, "Preacher, how have you been doing?"

For a moment I was speechless. Then, for some reason I responded, "Things have been better."

He roared with laughter and said "I bet they have."

A couple others began to laugh and finally the entire club was laughing.

"I bet you've slept better too, haven't you?" It was the New Yorker, the Yankee who had been the butt of more jokes than all the other club members combined.

I did not know whether they were laughing at me, or with me.

Harvey retorted to the group, in a soft voice with that twinkle in his eye, "Now you boys leave my preacher alone."

Ted was on a roll. "Hell Harvey, we like your preacher. We can't say that we like everything he says, but we like him. Hell, he ain't half bad. Maybe a third bad, but not half."

With that remark, Ted's laughter increased by ten decibels. Maybe it was wishful thinking on my part, but that evening I felt some of the separation with the town began to heal. It was not going to be a quick healing, but this was a start. The rest of that evening, I was a part of the group, at least that part of the group who knew me best.

The same character who had stared at me so coldly in Phillip's restaurant, was a member of the club. His cold stare was just as disquieting as it had been the first time I saw it. Few, if any, present that evening would have harmed me physically. This man was clearly the exception. No doubt he wanted me to know that, while others were willing to accept me, he would continue to hate me for what I had done. While I had relaxed some I still felt his chilling stare.

On the way home, Harvey asked me how I felt. I told him how relieved I was that most were willing to accept me as they had in the past. I noted the one man who had made me feel so uneasy, and Harvey warned me to stay clear of him.

"He is dead set on keeping colored people out of our schools and could well harm anyone who tries to do anything to promote integration." In so many words, Harvey warned me that this man and his friends were the type to burn down the parsonage or the church. With the preacher inside.

Chapter Seventeen

Expected and Unexpected Support

The next morning I began my usual routine, remembering the Lion's Club meeting and the little bit of healing that had taken place. Unfortunately, the healing had not made it to Phillip's Cafe. There were the same cold glares and poor service. Nothing was said but that had become the "usual" manner of dealing with the enemy. Try as I would, I could not stop the silent treatment from hurting. I sat through the cup of coffee and newspaper reading. It was easy for me to lose myself in the paper. The only problem was that the newspapers did not require much reading. I could read the entire paper, including the want ads, in about half an hour.

Finishing the paper, I began the second leg of my daily journey which took me to the post office. After the letters from J. P. Stafford and J. R. Rush, I looked forward to picking up my mail.

Miss Hinton gave her usual greeting. Then added, "Preacher, you have been getting a lot of mail."

A lot of mail in Sandersville was a couple of letters a month, not including junk mail. I had three letters in my box, along with the usual stuff from the Methodist Publishing House. I recognized the return address on two of the letters. One was from Emory University's

Candler School of Theology. I recognized Dr. Ted Runyon's name on the return address label. I was excited to get a letter from Emory and especially Dr. Runyon. He had been my theology professor and was a dynamic young man. (I qualify that description by saying "as dynamic as a theology professor could be.") I had always been treated well by Ted and loved chatting with him. I wish I could say that theology was my best subject, but my transcript would label me a liar.

It was a lengthy letter. I read it hurriedly then reread it. Many people sent me notes expressing their sympathy, but this one said it best. The only note of empathy I had received from the congregation was Rose's passing remark that first Sunday after the statement was published and at the meeting. No one else had said a single word that could be interpreted as supportive. I read Dr. Runyon's letter again to make sure I understood what he was saying.

> Dear Ned:
>
> Already news of the results of your action has reached Georgia, and no doubt at this moment you feel very much "on the spot" with many of the persons in your congregation. Part of the price involved is the pain of misunderstanding between yourself and those who mean a great deal to you, and without it you may find yourself in a rather lonely position in your community. You wouldn't be human if at moments you did not wonder whether it was worth it, whether it would not have been better to work quietly toward the same objectives, carefully avoiding any crisis. How effective can one be in this ordinary, everyday ministry, having gone so far out on a limb on this one issue?
>
> I cannot help but feel, however, that the stand you have taken will be one of the most significant acts of your ministry, a ministry directed to and for the very people who may now feel that you have somehow betrayed them. It is for them that you have done this. For you know that a church, which simply says what we want to hear, is of no more use to a man than

it is to God. Every Christian knows that what God has to say to us always comes as a "hard saying," as the demand for justice and racial righteousness as well as the offer of mercy, forgiveness and love. To be sure, it is possible to find false prophets who will speak only smooth and comforting words. But who wants to be ministered to by a false prophet? No, the pulpit must be free though it be always unpopular, for from it we must be able to receive the clear word of judgment of God upon which our salvation depends as surely as it depends upon his word of Grace.

I want you to know that we here at Emory are proud of you.

May God sustain you in hope and joy as you serve him faithfully and confidently in his Kingdom which is forever!

Sincerely,

Ted Runyon

It was a gift from God. I needed the affirmation.

Someone once said that real contact is "when a soul touches a soul." That is what Dr. Runyon did with his letter. It did more for me than I can explain. He knew me, my personality, my gifts and my graces, and he also knew me as a struggling student seeking to understand my search for personal meaning.

"Is it good news or bad?" Miss Hinton had been watching me read the letter.

"Miss Hinton, it is great news."

"Well," she responded, "I guess you could use some. Lord knows that there hasn't been any around here for the past few days."

I thought I detected a note of empathy in her voice, but was afraid to pursue it. I thought it better to read the next letter outside where there was a little more privacy.

The second letter had a return address that looked very official. The return address indicated that it came from the United States

Congress. The author of the letter was United States Congressman Frank Smith, from the great state of Mississippi. Even though I had been away from the political scene in Mississippi, I did recognize Congressman Smith's name. The last thing I expected was a letter from any politician, much less a U.S. Congressman. It was a short note of support. It read:

> Dear Brother Kellar:
>
> I want to express my appreciation for the fine statement made by you and other Mississippi Methodist ministers. As a Mississippian and a Methodist, I appreciate it very much. The tragic divisions in our State today are going to be resolved only when more of our leaders accept their responsibilities. Your action will help to point out the responsibility that our religious leaders must assume.
>
> Cordially,
>
> Frank E. Smith

It was a good mail day. I received two letters from two people who openly supported what I had done. If the day had ended there, I would have celebrated for a long time.

The third letter was from a young minister, just starting out in the ministry, and serving the same church that I had served while at Southern Mississippi. It was the Dickinson's church, Arnold Line. His name was Harold Beasley, and I had met him when he did a funeral for my sister-in-law's infant who had died shortly after birth. All I could remember was a short, fat man, about twenty-five years of age. His letter had been read from the pulpit of Arnold Line Methodist, and I thought about how it must have affected Dot's parents. He openly attacked the signers of the Born of Conviction statement. That, of course, meant he had attacked me, the son-in-law, and Buford, the pride and joy of the Dickinsons. I know how much that must have hurt them. I cursed him as I read the letter.

Sandersville

January 9, 1963

To the editor of the Mississippi Methodist Advocate and the preachers that expressed their feelings in the Advocate in the form of the article "Born of Conviction."

This article is doubtless one the most disgracing blows the Methodist Church has experienced in the past several years. I would like to say very emphatically, that if this article expresses the conviction of the majority of the ministers of our Conference, something is wrong somewhere. It is certainly not my feelings. I stand for segregation 100% because peace can be better maintained through segregation. The Bible says, "Follow peace with all men, and Holiness, without which no man shall see the Lord." This letter is just inviting integration, confusion, turmoil and ill feelings in our Church. I can't believe your conviction can be of God because it cannot bring glory to Christ. You and I, as ministers of the Gospel of Christ, should confine ourselves to preaching the Good News of Salvation. Any time we wander away from this purpose we invite disaster, and that is exactly what this article is doing. The article is very evidently a fruit of liberalism, which throughout the past several years has modernized and conformed our great Church of Methodism until it is no longer the radiant fiery Church that it used to be.

I believe that if we do not grieve the Holy Spirit of God and let him lead us into God's will, God could straighten things out by Himself without you or me trying to do it for Him.

I believe that you are wrong in what you said and what you are trying to do, and I will fight it with every chance I get and with every ounce of strength I can muster, for Christ's sake.

> A Friend in Christ Jesus
> Herbert W. Beasley, Pastor
> Soule's Chapel and Arnold Line

For several moments I compared Mr. Beasley's letter to that of Dr. Runyon. Ted saw the ministry as a matter of God working through men and women to accomplish His goal. Mr. Beasley left the work up to God and thought we should not interfere. In the mind of one, preaching the Gospel was to take up the cross and present it to all people. For the other, it was to preach the good news as long as we did not apply it to any social situation.

After reading Beasley's letter, a strange thought crossed my mind. Mr. Homer would agree with what Beasley said in his letter, at least in principle. I wondered just how he would accept the criticism of his son. It never entered my mind that he might resent what was being said about his son-in-law.

Somehow, the letter from Beasley did not bother me except that it must have hurt Dot's family. Maybe it was because I did not know the man well, and did not like the little I knew of him. There was resentment on my part. He had read the letter at church in the presence of Ella Ruth and Mr. Homer. I vowed then to make sure I never crossed paths with the Beasleys of the world. All I had to do was reread Runyon's letter to set my spirits on a higher plane.

It was a courageous move for a man who represented a section of a state that took pride in keeping the white race pure. It was courageous in another way, too. Runyon was doing this out of a deep conviction and at considerable political risk. It was not a move to gain votes because most blacks could not vote in Mississippi. When I considered the risk taken by this man to try and comfort a preacher who, by the way, did not live in his district, I was deeply moved and certainly impressed.

Up to this point I hated visiting the post office because it was another place where I experienced resentment. In the small town of Sandersville, people did certain things at a certain time. The same group could be found at the local restaurant at a given hour. So it was with the post office. Miss Hinton was always very pleasant, but those who seemed to hang out in her lobby each morning were not. Nothing was ever said, but the stares and body language said plenty. Now, as a result of the letters I had received, I looked forward to my next visit.

The daily newspapers continued to carry stories about incidents where some black had been beaten or some churches burned. It was an inflammatory time. Try as hard as I could, I could not separate my congregational duties from events reported in the newspapers. Added to daily newspaper reports were the rumors that ran rampant across the state. Sandersville had their fair share. I never knew just what to believe. But I knew the history of Mississippi and its manner of dealing with blacks. Over 45% of Mississippi's population was black, a higher percentage than any other state in the union. Mississippi also led the nation in beatings, lynching and mysterious disappearances. As one man put it, "If a nigger didn't need to be found, he never would be found." I would have questioned that conclusion had I not known about an incident that occurred when I was in high school. That had been my first experience with Mississippi justice as administered by police in my hometown. A relative of mine drove for a local taxi company. The fleet of taxis numbered two. Late one evening a young black man got in the cab and asked to be taken to a particular destination. After taking his fare to the named site, the young black man got out and said he was not going to pay. When my relative told him he was going to call the local town policeman, a man named Lott, the black said, "Fuck Mr. Lott!"

Later that evening, the young man was arrested. My relative said the policeman asked him twice just what the man had said. As if he couldn't believe it. The policeman led the black man away – never to be seen again. My taxi driving relative loved to remind everyone of the event.

"That's what happens to a smart talking nigger," he reminded anyone within earshot.

The sad part of this story is that the family of the young man never knew if he was alive or dead. They were afraid to press the issue lest they end up the same way.

I had a good friend in high school whose father was the county sheriff. My mother praised him to high heavens.

"That is one sheriff who will keep the niggers in line."

Justice for blacks often ended in a fatality, something my family approved of.

One other incident comes to mind. While sitting around with a group of friends one evening, the oldest person present told about a cousin of his. The cousin worked for the National Guard and confiscated a .30 Caliber machine gun one evening. He took the gun and drove toward the "quarters." He loaded the weapon the fired 700 rounds into the houses. The story excited most of the group and they all wanted to do the same thing. Did the man actually fire a machine gun into houses of blacks? I do not know, but I knew that if these young men had access to a weapon that evening, they would have done the same. As I have stated, there was a lack of respect for a black man's life. That was the state of mind that prevailed in the 1950's and 1960's.

Sandersville was spared from the headlines. That could be attributed to the smallness of the town, and that it was not on the regular beat of any newspaper. Another reason was that nothing happened in Sandersville. If it did, it never made the newspapers. I am confident that there were Klan members in the area, but there were no bombings, nor lynchings, nor any overt acts of violence that I knew of. I suspected some of the people from the Sandersville area may have been involved in activities involving the Klan, or other groups who felt compelled to "save" the South. The only hint of Klan activity was a remark one of the ladies from our church made when I was critical of the Klan in her presence. She quickly reminded me that the Klan had done many good things.

"The niggers are afraid of the Klan. They know the Klan will come after them if they get out of line."

Other than that one remark, the Klan was something that lived somewhere else. If they lived near, they never bothered me. For that I was happy. What would have happened to me if there was a local Klan group? They would surely have acted out if only to save face with the locals. I honestly tried not to think about it too much. I imagined how things would go if I lived in an isolated area where the news media could not find me or my congregation. I probably would have done well with the race issue. I even think I could have brought some around to my point of view. There were those who gave me some hope. Rose, for example, who thought as I thought. How many other Roses were there in the community? How could I ever find out when the populace was constantly stirred by the media? Why didn't my "supporters" come out and speak up for me? I knew the answer to my question even as I asked it. There was too great a risk. I would move on in a few months. These people had to live there most likely for the rest of their lives. Changing the community under the present circumstances was a fantasy. I lived in a world of television, of daily newspapers and of the dreaded telephone. The world kept invading my parish leaving a wake of anger and frustration. I was ready to let go of the issue if the issue would let go of me. It was not to be.

The Laurel-Leader Call, the local newspaper, printed an article regarding a statement made by Dr. Selah, pastor of Galloway Memorial Methodist Church. In the article, Dr. Selah was reported to have said that, "there can be no color bar in a Christian church." He went on to call for voluntary desegregation of all public institutions. The article read in part:

> Dr. W. B. Selah, of Galloway Memorial Methodist Church in Jackson wrote the statement in response to questions from the Associated Press, prompted by a "no discrimination" stand by twenty-eight Methodist ministers last Wednesday. Dr. Selah said "to discriminate against a man because of his color or creed is contrary to the will of God.
>
> "Forced segregation is wrong. We should voluntarily desegregate all public facilities. We should treat men not on the basis of color, but on the basis of conduct."
>
> "It is not sinful for white people to prefer to worship with white people or for colored people to worship with colored people. The sin comes when a church seems to erect a color bar before the Cross of Christ.
>
> "As Christians, we cannot say to anyone, 'you cannot come into the house of God.' No conference, no preacher, no official board can put up a color bar

in the church. The House of God is a house of prayer for all people, black or white," he said.

His prominence and tenure at 17 years, the longest of any Methodist church in the state, stirred strong reaction and interest. As his statement was made public on Sunday, ministers, Citizens Council leaders and others hurried to find what had been said.

"Race prejudice is a denial of Christian brotherhood. Any kind of prejudice – racial or religious – weakens the nation by dividing it into hostile groups," he said.

The statement seemed to endorse the twenty-eight's original statement printed in last week's Mississippi Methodist Advocate. Later that week, twenty-three ministers under District Superintendent W. L. Robinson of Tupelo, voted to endorse the statement of the twenty-eight at a regular district meeting. Dr. Robinson said there were no dissenting votes, although six ministers abstained. It was good news and further validated our actions. On one hand, everything was happening so fast, but on the other hand, it seemed to stand still. Nothing really changed. The hatred was still there and the violence continued. There were now fifty-one Methodist ministers in Mississippi who had made or confirmed a statement that was contrary to the majority opinion of Mississippians. Hopefully it would grow, and the church would be the catalyst that brought the terrible sin of discrimination to its knees.

That thought was short-lived. While a small part of the North Mississippi Conference joined the cause, there were individual ministers in the Mississippi Conference that condemned the statement. Herbert Beasley was small-time and did not hold much, if any, influence in the conference. However, there were reports that some well-established Methodist clergy were speaking out publicly against the statement. Ironically, the pastor of my hometown church in Picayune read a statement to his congregation condemning the content of the Born of Conviction statement as being out of touch with the laymen and citizens of Mississippi. There were others who did the same thing. For some, it saved a failing ministry. For others, it was a deep personal conviction and they were exercising their right. I was to receive letters of support from across the nation, but not one single letter came from fellow ministers in Mississippi. I understood how some would conclude we had disrupted the calm and peace of the conference, and they resented us for that. But from the perspective of a "newcomer" to the conference, I failed to see the very peace they wanted to protect. The two factions in the conference had been fighting for years. It would continue for a while.

The events in my world began to accelerate. Letters continued to arrive, along with lengthy statements of support or condemnation. The Tuesday after the release of the statement, Dot received a letter from Billie Hosey, the wife of the man with whom I had spent many hours talking about football. He was my friend, or at least he had been. I was glad the letter was written to Dot because I feared the contents would be negative, and I just did not want to deal with the pain.

It was a hand written note on small lined paper not unlike that found in a tablet.

Tuesday, January 8, 1963

Dear Dot,

For some dumb reason I have used all my large envelopes that came in this box of greeting cards, so please excuse the folded card.

We missed you in church Sunday and hope you will be well soon. Would like to see you with us at WSCS tonight. We all love you and Ned and, as soon as time has been given its opportunity for everyone to realize and weigh all the many things you all have done for us, against the publicity of Ned's own private conviction, then everything should be back to normal.

We need both of you to help us with the work that must go in the Lord's house. I pray and shall pray that this all shall soon be forgotten. I must tell you this, I have never admired anyone so much as I did Ned when he preached two sermons Sunday, he did a good job of preaching and that was courageous to me. I am not any good at expressing my thoughts but they were mostly from my heart. There is a prayer in the Upper Room for you yesterday, Monday, January 7.

Show us, Lord, that hate and enmity can lead only to violence. Fill our minds with the thoughts of goodwill toward men. Help us to know that we can find the answer to the vexing problems of Life as we seek to know Thy will for us. In the name of Christ, our Strength, Amen.

May God be with us all.

Love, Billie Hosey

This was the first letter directed to Dot. My involvement with the issue had brought pain to Dot. Billie's letter reminded me of that. I was lost in my own survival and sometimes would forget that the slings and arrows came Dot's way as well mine.

Billie's letter was an opening for me to visit with her husband who now appeared to be my former friend, Larry. Billie called and asked if I would drop by and talk with her and Larry. She was working hard to be the calm voice of reason. I agreed with some fear and trepidation. I agreed to meet with them the following weekend, Saturday morning, the 12th. Larry wanted to meet in the morning so he could watch the football games.

My visits to the post office brought more letters. I know Ms. Hinton wanted to know the contents of each letter. She often hinted about wanting to know why people were writing me personal letters. I received two more letters that week. One was from Mrs. Nell Hearn, Director of the Wesley Foundation at Jones Junior College. She wrote:

Dear Reverend Kellar:

I want to express my appreciation to you for the statement issued by you and twenty-seven other Methodist ministers stressing freedom of the pulpit and supporting an official "no discrimination" church position. I am grateful that we have ministers in the Mississippi Conference who are willing to stand up and be counted – to voice publicly their convictions. Let us pray that thousands of other Mississippians, both ministers and laymen, will feel compelled to take this stand and speak their convictions during these next few months.

Please know that my prayers are with you and yours. May this year prove to be your greatest thus far in God's service.

Your friend in Christ,

Mrs. Nell M. Hearn, Director
The Wesley Foundation
Jones County Junior College

This letter stood out because it came from Jones County, right in the heart of the "Free State of Jones." I never did learn what happened to Mrs. Hearn as a result of writing this letter. Jones County Junior College was a part of the state of Mississippi public school system. It must have been difficult for her after her superiors found out that she had written a sympathetic letter to those misguided ministers. I deeply appreciated her letter. Mrs. Hearn knew the area and must have understood that this letter would result in her being placed in harm's way, at least professionally. It felt good to discover that there were others from the area that actually sympathized with the "radicals", and were willing to risk their support being made public. It was Mrs. Hearn's letter, the whispered support of Rose, the letters that came daily, and fellowship with the other radicals that I was able to maintain my sanity. No one, to my knowledge, understood the terrible anxiety I felt, but just knowing that someone cared made it easier to accept the hatred. I had a gut feeling that many people in the state of Mississippi supported our cause. They just did not do it publically. Few had the courage to express the caring. Being there for me made a big difference.

The other letter came from Scarritt College For Christian Workers in Nashville, Tennessee.

> Dear Mr. Kellar,
>
> I have read in the Mississippi Advocate the statement the twenty-eight young ministers of the Mississippi Conference who have chosen to take the stand for Christianity in the racial issue.
>
> I want you to know that the eyes of all of us in this part of the world are upon you and our hearts and prayers are with you. Surely God will bless your actions.
>
> Sincerely,
>
> Alice Cobb

It is hard for me to express the feelings I would get as I read letters like these two. Not only did they cheer me up, but they reinforced my resolve to continue my work. The task grew more difficult though. It appeared that the news media would not let a single issue pass without mentioning the "twenty-eight young, white Methodist ministers." I have always believed that God has his hands in everything good that happens. It was more than a coincidence.

Just when I hit bottom emotionally, someone would come along and, verbally or in the form of a letter, say or write something that lifted my spirits to great heights.

It never failed to happen. This is not to say that I lived on cloud nine. I fretted sometimes, got very angry at times, felt alone and misunderstood and mistreated. I doubted myself and my actions more times than I want to admit. But invariably something would happen to restore my faith and sense of well being.

On the other side there were those who took pieces of the statement and used them to condemn our stand. More than one person reminded me that if "you boys" were not influenced by the Communists, then why did you mention not being a Communist? It was their way of saying "thou dost protest too much." While the reasoning lacked logic for the accused, it made all the sense in the world to the accuser. No one wanted to believe that any one of those signing the statement did so out of a deep sense of Christian conviction. Either we were dupes of communism, or outright Communists, or we had been brainwashed by liberal professors in seminary. It seemed to be the only rationale that made sense to those who held so dearly to the "ways and customs" of the South. Why else would local boys, born and bred in the South, turn against what they had been taught? Some critics were crass and mean and referred to us as "nigger loving liberals". The only thing they could not say about us was that we were outsiders. We were their cousins, brothers, sisters, classmates and good friends.

On Thursday of that week, the Jackson Times, an independent weekly newspaper, led its front page with a headline in half inch type:

MORAL BLOCKBUSTER IGNITED BY CLERGY
Jim Crow Eyed By Methodists

The article read in part:

> Christianity (Methodism) and segregation collided in Mississippi during this past week.
> Reverberations were heard from Rankin County to Chicago. It began when twenty-eight young Methodist ministers signed a statement that said this:

"Jesus teaches that all men are brothers. He permits no discrimination because of race, color, or creed."

Reactions to the remarks were expected to be forthcoming from political circles, some congregations and a segment of the press.

It was an interesting article and, as I read it, I found comfort and understanding. I even thought it was supportive of our stand. I was also intrigued by the editorial printed on the front page next to the article I have quoted from. It was titled:

Preachers Should Always Speak Out

The editorial reads in part:

> There are many church people who believe that a preacher's business is behind the pulpit, serving up an hour and a half of salvation Sunday mornings and evenings. They believe he should tell them what they want to hear, and if he doesn't he should get a call to go elsewhere.
>
> But were Jesus Christ and the men in his immediate circle of the ilk that strayed not from their text to step into the street?
>
> Certainly not. There are over 1900 years of evidence to the contrary. The founder of the Christian religion was not the pathetic figure of some artistic conceptions. Indications are that he was most vigorous about his purpose on this planet, and did not hesitate to take his doctrine into the social climate of his time. Indeed, if it thrives not there, it thrives not at all.
>
> Thus, we believe that preachers are right in speaking publicly about the social problems of our day. In doing so they indicate that their calling is not one for

the shallow water mark, but for the troubled water off from the shore.

Perhaps more influence from the pulpit, and less from politicians and the press is what we need.

If the editor of the Jackson Times had asked me what preaching was all about, I could not have said it better. I filed that article away and will keep it for as long as I live.

Chapter Eighteen

Saturday Morning Meeting with Larry Hosey

I found myself facing a meeting that I wanted to attend, and was yet very uneasy. That was me on Saturday, January 11, 1963. I had genuinely missed talking with Larry about all the subjects in the newspaper, football in particular. I just liked being with him and wanted the friendship to be rekindled. However, I was not sure Larry would want to be friends again. He was obviously into the separation of the races and was the first to tell me about the "Free State of Jones County."

We had planned to meet early but several things came up that delayed my visit to his home. I drove down the dirt road arriving at about noon. Larry's home was across a small dirt road from the railroad tracks. The road was dusty and the homes bordering the road were yellowish from all the dust. They were all small houses, some in good repair and some not. All had screen doors and a small porch. I thought about how loud the trains were from the parsonage. From across the street, they must have been extremely loud. I wondered that the building would hold together with the strong vibrations from the trains that passed by both day and night.

When I pulled in front of his house, I got out and walked to the door. Billie and the kids met me and greeted me warmly. Larry was sitting in his easy chair in front of the television. Billie invited me inside. The front room of the home was the living room. In the corner of the room was a small television set showing the lineup for today's football game. Larry kept his eyes glued to the screen as Billie announced my presence.

"I will leave the room so you two can have some privacy," Billie said in her quiet voice.

I remained standing, waiting for Larry to acknowledge my presence, and invite me to sit down. I stood there for several seconds. My awkwardness was obvious. Then Larry asked me to sit down. We both sat there for a while, neither speaking to the other.

Finally, Larry said, "You know Preacher, I was really hurt by your article in the newspaper. You know a lot of people don't agree with you, and some are really mad at you. All of my life I have been told that niggers and whites should not mix. Now you have gone on record as saying that they should."

I waited until I was sure he had finished what he was going to say.

"Larry," I began, "I know you do not agree with me on that issue. If I hurt you with that statement, I am sorry. However, it is a personal belief of mine, and I do not ask that anyone else agree with it."

Before I could go on Larry interjected, "Well, a lot of people around here will not agree with it. I've told you that we take pride in living in the "Free State of Jones County". People do not want to see niggers and whites in the same schools. No one wants integration in Jones County. Look at what happened at Ole Miss."

"I know that," I acknowledged to Larry.

"Then why did you do that?" interrupted Larry. "You knew it was going to make a lot of people mad."

I tried to explain my purpose. "Larry, my signing that statement reflected my own views. No one has to agree with me. But I reserve the right to share my views. I know it upsets you and I feel bad about that."

"I thought we were friends," Larry said. "I enjoyed meeting with you for coffee," he continued. "Few people know as much about football as you do, and I thought we enjoyed meeting and talking."

I realized that Larry had taken my position as being a slap in his face. I know he must have heard some talk about his preacher being a "nigger lover" that put him in a real conflict. How could he save face with his friends without withdrawing and directing his anger toward me for betraying his trust?

"Larry, I did what I did out of personal conviction. I am genuinely sorry for any hurt it caused you. I have told you that," I explained. "It is not personal."

For a while we just sat there. I began to fret that we were not going to solve anything and I prepared to leave.

"Where are you going? Why don't you stay and watch some of the game with me?" Larry asked.

It was Larry's way of saying the issue was closed. He had held his beliefs for all of his life, and I was not going to change them on a single Saturday afternoon. We had resolved that we could watch a game together though our philosophies were very different.

I stayed for a couple of hours and we hooted and hollered when our team scored and groaned when the other team scored.

When I had to leave he called after me, "See you Monday morning."

That was that. Somehow we had resolved our conflict without either of us backing down. I drove home, reported to Dot, changed clothes so I could go to the church and print the bulletins. I had lost so many fights with that damn mimeograph machine I had given up and just resigned myself to having ink spots on my hands and clothes. But, I had watched football with my old friend Larry.

Church as Usual

It was January 13 and it seemed the "Born of Conviction" issue had been around a lifetime. This would be the first time to visit Goodwater since the statement had hit the press. At least this would be the last time to have to deal with this in one of my churches. I was not as uneasy with Goodwater as I had been with the other two. I am not sure why but I wasn't. Sure enough, the church had the usual crowd, and no one said a single thing. We had the service and one of the laymen reminded me that we had our revival in the Spring and we needed to prepare for it soon. I gave them assurance that I would find someone to preach for us.

"Well, Brother Kellar, we would like for you to preach."

I was very flattered until he reminded me that the church could not afford to bring someone in to preach. At least they were pleased enough with my preaching to have me as the speaker. I chose to look at it that way as opposed to me being the only one they could afford.

The service at Sandersville went as well as could be expected. I had a very attentive group. I wondered just how many people came to hear the next chapter in the saga of the great debate on the race issue. As the group filed out following the service, everyone shook my hand except Willard. Rose held my hand for a while and winked at me. Billie and Larry were present and greeted me warmly. Ned asked if I had signed anything recently. I laughed and he responded with a slight grin.

Dot and I went to lunch with Harvey and Jewel at Phillip's. Harvey talked about a new grocery store that had opened up down the street from his store.

"Preacher, be sure and come by tomorrow. I am going into a pricing war with him."

I had met the man who opened the store but did not know him well. Harvey had had sole possession of the grocery market in Sandersville for many years. Now someone was intruding into his territory and he was going to teach them a lesson. I could not wait to see just how "cutthroat" the competition was going to get.

As I anxiously awaited the great sale, I spent most of Sunday afternoon doing two things. One, I reread the copy of the Jackson Times article about the "blockbuster" let loose on the good citizens of Mississippi. I had recalled reading Dow Kirkpatrick's name in the article. I read it carefully this time and, sure enough, there was Dow's name and a quote from him. How I had missed this in my first reading, I do not know. In the interview, Dow began with these words:

> I think the race problem will be solved in the South before it is in the North. Why? Primarily because Southern people have a warm person-to-person relationship with Negroes that I do not find in the North."

How in the world had I missed that remark? My hero spoke those words. I kept trying to make sense of what he was saying. What did he mean? Was he saying that the southern community felt warmer toward "negroes" than the northern part of the country did?

I failed to understand just what Dow was trying to say. I knew he supported our position because I had heard him preach on the importance of brotherhood while I was in Atlanta. The interpretation of his quote by some suggested that he was really on the other side of the issue. After reading the article, the one thing most saw was the statement that the North had a bigger problem than the South. It reminded me of a conversation I had had with one of the ladies in our church at Sandersville. The subject of the Ku Klux Klan came up in our conversation.

"You know, Brother Kellar, we in the South have been good to our nigras. Even when we had slavery the nigras were cared for and well fed. No one of them was ever harmed unless they got uppity or sassy."

I will give the benefit of doubt to Dow. But if he was saying that the South treated their blacks better than other areas, he was wrong. Blacks were treated as being less than human in the years of slavery and, frankly, conditions had not improved a lot in the years following emancipation. The black person could not vote and, if they tried, they could end up dead. Dow could not have been reading the same articles I had been reading for the past six months. I had kept a list:

> March 22, Jackson, Mississippi: Jesse Harris, a black man, is sentenced to thirty days in jail for sitting on the "white" side of a courtroom. He is beaten once by deputies and twice by prison guards.

April 9, Taylorsville, Mississippi: A black soldier, Roman Ducksworth, is shot to death by a white policeman for refusing to sit in the back of the bus.

April 24, Shreveport, Louisiana: A black Masonic Temple is bombed.

May, Philadelphia, Mississippi: Willie Nash a black epileptic, is riddled with bullets while handcuffed and in police custody.

June 20, Jackson, Mississippi: The editor of a black newspaper is beaten by police en route to Forest, Mississippi, to investigate reports of a black man killed by whites.

The list is just a sampling of what was happening to blacks in the Deep South. Where does that kind of viciousness come from? I do not have an answer. However, I can share an experience with you that may speak to the cause. When I was in high school in Picayune in the 50's, there was a game some played. They would take little green oranges, hop in the back of a pickup and drive through the black community. If they saw a "nigger" they would try to hit him in the head with an orange. I have heard a number of reports from the various night riders. They would drive up to the root beer stand and shout, "Got me a nigger."

If Dow Kirkpatrick is saying we in the South are kinder to our blacks, God help those who live in other areas. The personal relationship, from my perspective, was akin to that of master and slave. If a black person stayed in his/her place, they were well cared for and appreciated. If not, they posed a danger to the peace and tranquility of the community.

Some Good Things Happen

The next several days and weeks were an emotional roller coaster. One day would bring a letter of support that encouraged me to stay the course. Other days there would be a remark, a critical column in the papers or a letter to the editor criticizing all those who signed the statement. However, Larry and I resumed our morning meetings to discuss the important issue of who would win Saturday's football game. Harvey revealed his plan of competing with the new grocery store. He announced he would sell bread at ten cents a loaf. That was a 30 per cent drop in cost. The other store owner dropped his to a dime then Harvey dropped his to a nickel. It was a heated competition according to Harvey. As it turned out, Harvey continued to sell to the same people he had always had as customers, and the new store picked up what was left.

Since things were quiet, I checked with Wilton about his situation. Apparently, he was receiving the same mail I was receiving. We decided we needed a round of golf. We made plans to meet later in the week. Dot and Dolores could spend some time together as we played a round at the Forest Mississippi Golf Course. Dot and I drove up to Forest to meet with the Carters. The course did not cost but a couple of bucks. It was much more expensive than the course we played in Atlanta. That one charged theology students $.82 cents for 18 holes, or $.42 cents for nine holes.

To an avid golfer, being on a golf course is to allow all the problems of the world to disappear. That's what we hoped for. However, as soon as we teed off, both of us turned our attention to the strife facing us daily. Wilton had had a difficult time and talked about transferring to another conference. We kicked the idea around a bit and finally began to concentrate on our golf game. After a short while, the conversation returned to the controversy that stemmed from the statement.

I asked, "Wilton, do you ever feel you are being watched?" I was uneasy asking the question because it sounded so paranoid.

"Listen," he said, "We may well be being watched right now."

I laughed. "That will really help my game."

Later that afternoon we sat in Carter's home and talked about the real possibility of moving to another conference. We concluded it would serve two purposes. One, it would take us away from the racially charged State of Mississippi and, two, it would free us from the Mississippi Conference politics. It sounded great to both of us, and we began to fantasize about being in a conference where we could preach without worrying about everything we said.

"And," Wilton added, "we could serve just one church instead of a charge."

"Right," I chimed in, "and we could make maybe $5,000 a year."

We spent the next several minutes talking about all we could gain by leaving the Mississippi Conference. The time came when Dot and I had to begin our trip back to Sandersville. We both relaxed while in Forest. Now, the thought of going back to Sandersville, brought back the tension we had been living with for the past couple weeks.

On the drive home Dot and I talked a little about transferring to another Conference. I would go back to North Georgia in a heartbeat. Some of the twenty-eight talked about moving to Southern California and Arizona. That seemed a little far for Dot to be from her family. We did have friends in South Carolina so we could move east. Then it dawned on us that South Carolina was a southern state as well, and the racial attitudes would be similar to those in Mississippi. The only saving grace would be the absence of politics in the churches. It was something to think about. Minister's week was coming in mid-January so I could explore the opportunities then. That ended the discussion.

We were now in our third week since the statement had been printed. Things were relatively quiet in Sandersville as well as the other two churches. Plans were progressing for the revival at Goodwater. We had not had a crank call in three days and it was time to celebrate. I went to the post office.

I had reached the point of being Ms. Hinton's favorite visitor. Everyday I went to the post office to pick up my mail. I had mail everyday. Being a Methodist minister guaranteed I would get every mailing from the Methodist Publishing House. If I ever felt unloved, I could always count on the Publishing House mail. At least somebody up there loved me. They even addressed it to me personally... and to the "box holder." Ms. Hinton eliminated my need to open my box. She handed the mail to me personally.

"I see you got some today from Ole Miss, from Kentucky, from Duke University and, look, here is another one from Old Miss. You sure are popular." At least she did not ask to see the letters.

One of the letters was from Dr. James Silver, a professor at Ole Miss.

His letter read in part:

> Dear Mr. Keller:
>
> I am writing to you as one who was greatly heartened by the "Born of Conviction" statement in the January 2 issue of the Mississippi Methodist Advance. This resolution was another bit of evidence that there is still some chance for Mississippi to follow the right course, although, frankly, I see no reason for optimism for the near future.

I was immediately aware of two things. One is that he did not know me because he spelled my name with "er" not "ar". He referred to the newspaper that carried the article as the Mississippi Methodist Advance, not the Advocate. While I did not feel optimistic about the near future, I thought I would try denial for a while.

As I read more of the letter I learned that Dr. Silver was looking for information about the abuse I and other signers of the statement had encountered from our churches. He was going to make a formal presentation to the Southern Historical Association and needed reports from the signers of the statement. I found it interesting that he said he would not use our names unless they had been used in the newspapers. Our names had been used in every newspaper in the state and on every television station. I filed his letter with every intention of getting back with him.

A second letter was from Louisville, Kentucky.

> Dear Brother Keller:
>
> The Methodist minister of the Louisville East and West District of the Louisville Conference, Southeastern Jurisdiction and the Lexington Conference, Central

Jurisdiction, met in regular session January 14, 1963 at Kenwood Methodist Church, 7032 Southside Drive, Louisville, Kentucky.

At this meeting, Dr. William James, pastor of Memorial Methodist Church, Elizabethton, Kentucky, read the statement, "Born of Conviction" printed in the January 2, 1963 issue of "The Mississippi Methodist Advocate" and spoke briefly regarding the matter. A motion was unanimously adopted that a letter be sent to each of the twenty-eight ministers subscribing to this statement and that a copy of said letter be sent to Bishop Marvin A. Franklin, Dr. W. B. Selah and Dr. Sam Ashmore.

The motion included that words of appreciation be expressed to you for the clear and reasonable statement relating to the position of the Methodist minister in the current racial crisis in Mississippi and for the courage manifested by you in your stand.

Sincerely yours,

Vernon W. Chandler

This letter coming from the Central Jurisdiction (The Black Jurisdiction for Methodism) had a special meaning to me. I had never understood why the black churches had to have a separate jurisdiction but now I understood it was a way of keeping the churches separate, even though we were all Methodists. That is another issue to be covered at another time.

A third letter came from Duke University Divinity School.

Dear Rev. Keller:

In these tension-filled days, it is often difficult to determine what stand to take on various issues, but worst of all would be to take no stand at all. Therefore, we offer you our support and prayers for the Christian position you affirmed in the January 2, 1963 issue of

the Mississippi Methodist Advocate entitled, "Born of Conviction."
We join you in praying and working that the time may come when the Church will indeed be the instrument of God's purpose, and when all men indeed will be brothers.

Sincerely,

John Rush
Harold E. Wright

The fourth letter was from the University Minister of Old Miss.

Dear Ned,

Welcome to the clan of the misunderstood!
I personally appreciate your endorsement of our Methodist position concerning race relations. Furthermore it is foolish to make our children suffer the consequences which would follow the closing of our public schools. Maybe someday people will come to appreciate one another as fellow human beings of infinite worth.
A person stands to be misunderstood on any attempt at constructive thought in this area.
God grants you the love, strength, understanding and patience you will need during this trying time.

Sincerely,

Donald H. Anderson
University Minister

P. S. I have recently become acquainted with the type of mail which you are probably receiving.

The personal mail was overwhelmingly favorable and supportive. It was the mail that kept me together. Had it not been for people, most of whom I did not know, writing letters of support, I think I would have had even greater difficulty. In a way, the jury was still out on my ministry at Sandersville. I was accepted but kept at arm's length.

Chapter Nineteen

To the Ivory Tower then Back to Reality

It was now mid January and the weather grew colder. I continued my tree burning at least twice a week. It all depended on my stress level. Some days I could have spent hours burning that tree. It continued to be cathartic even though I came inside smelling of smoke.

Dot and I had been working at getting her pregnant for a month or more. Thus far we had not succeeded though I enjoyed the efforts. We both wanted a child. Tracey, the dog just did not cut it. She was a delight but still only a dog. We went about the process with some passion at first. Then it became a scientific process with temperatures being taken, trying to find the right day with someone who was irregular. We took every opportunity, checked on all the conditions needed for pregnancy and waited. I was willing to do everything I could. For me, the male, it was a joyful task. How does the saying go? "If at first you don't succeed, try, try again." "Try and try again" we did.

Perhaps the stress we were under had something to do with her not getting pregnant right away. Lying awake at night to see if a car stopped in front of your home would make anyone nervous. We had been married four years and in the Deep South that signaled a problem. If we were asked once, we were asked a thousand times, "When are you two going to have children?" I wanted to tell them that we were trying diligently but no luck so far.

Then it happened. Dot missed her cycle in January. We were pregnant! We were excited to finally begin planning for our first child. Somehow the thought of having a child made all our other problems seem insignificant. There were some issues to deal with regarding a physician. The only doctor in Sandersville was Dr. Black who had an office next to Harvey's store. There were at least two problems with Dr. Black. First, he was in his nineties, and secondly, his office looked like Harvey's store. It was unpainted and looked as if it might collapse. We decided that Dot would go to either Laurel or Hattiesburg to get treatment.

We began to give more thought to where we wanted to spend our lives. Sandersville had settled down some and we felt a little more at ease. That is not to say that all was well, for it was not. Wilton had brought up the possibility of moving to another conference. The impending birth of our first child needed to be taken into consideration.

Minister's Week at Emory

Wilton and I decided to go to Minister's Week at Emory. It would be fun to return to the campus. I certainly had great memories of Candler, and looked forward to returning. It would also provide a chance to talk with friends and recent grads of the school. I planned to see Dr. Runyan and personally thank him for his letter of support. Buford also planned to attend, and I knew others of the "twenty-eight" would also be there. There never had been a formal gathering of those who signed the statement. Some of the signers were at Hidden Haven but not very many. I had not had a chance to talk with anyone other than Wilton and Buford since the statement was published. There were several reasons to go back to Atlanta.

While it was not a major factor for making the trip, the thought of leaving Mississippi was in the back of my mind. Dot's pregnancy exacerbated the issue. The question was, for us, did we want our children to grow up in a setting that was so prejudiced? But Mississippi was home for both Dot and me. It was a tough question.

The Minister's Week was everything I wanted it to be except it was brutally cold. I recall ice forming on the inside of our dorm room where steam from the radiator froze. Fortunately, I still had my overcoat and winter wear. I needed it. I saw a lot of friends, and most asked about the upheaval caused by the signing of the statement. Everybody wanted to know exactly what had happened. Had I been in danger? Did I have to leave in the middle of the night? How was Dot? Dot had elected to stay with her parents while I was at Emory. All in all, it was a fun time and a relief from the stress of being in Sandersville.

Wilton shared with some of our friends that we were thinking about leaving Mississippi. The response was immediate, from friends and ministers I didn't even know. A few were looking for an associate and wanted to talk with me. I talked with two ministers from South Carolina, two from Georgia, and one from Tennessee. All had openings for an associate and invited me to visit their churches. I took their cards and promised to give it serious thought. I was flattered, but also a little nervous about making it obvious I wanted to leave Mississippi. I was not ready to burn any bridges. Plus, I was getting along well with my congregation.

Wilton and I talked about the contacts he had made, and he mentioned he had talked with some people from Florida. I had not considered going to Florida because I had never been to the state. I knew several men from the Florida Conference while at Candler, but knew little about the conference. Besides, Florida seemed so far away except for the Panhandle, and that was a part of the Alabama/Florida Conference. I could not see Alabama being any more open to me than Mississippi.

I also discovered that a number of the "twenty-eight" was interested in going to the Southern California/Arizona Conference. If Florida was too far, California was out of the question. How would I get Dot home to see her parents? I discounted, for the moment, both

Florida and California. Besides, rumor had it that everybody wanted to go to Florida. It was very difficult to get into that conference.

As we drove back to Mississippi, Wilton and I talked about our opportunities to move. I told him about the South Carolina contacts and he told me about Florida. We exchanged fantasies about the different areas. The appeal of Florida, Wilton reminded me, was that they did not have very many charges. Most of their appointments are single churches. And, he added, they pay much more than Mississippi churches. Those were two strong selling points, but we would have to wait and see. At least things looked a little better.

A Return to Sandersville, to Letters Good and Not So Good

It was good to see Dot and get settled back into the parsonage. We discovered the cold had caused the pipes to freeze, and the toilet bowl was completely iced over. I called Harvey to let him know. He sent someone out to repair the plumbing. Too late I remembered when you leave a house in the middle of winter, the heater should be left on. But Dot and I had to pay the utilities and could not afford to leave a heater burning for several days. I was left with the impression that the damage to the plumbing cost the church. It was not the first time I had been led to believe that the parsonage was dear to the church. I recalled how worried the church leaders were that someone would burn the parsonage. While they may have had some concern about the occupants of the parsonage, the house came first.

The first thing I did was go outside, build a fire and burn parts of the old tree. I was becoming obsessed with that process. It had indeed become my therapy.

In the meantime, more letters came. Ms. Hinton wondered where I had been. The box was full. Of course, she had all my mail in her hand the moment I walked in. One letter came from a Unitarian minister named Charles White McGhee. In the letter he wrote:

> ...The reaction to your views on true brotherhood, and the real Good Neighbor, may bring you temporary reverses. But immediate history will bear you right.

I hoped he was right. The only pressing question I had was, how immediate?

In his last paragraph he wrote these words:

> More important than this, your conscience will be at peace with your daily life.

That was true. My conscience was clear. I knew I had done the right thing, the thing God expected me to do. That felt good. However, as I recalled the price that had been paid, it did not feel like an even trade.

Ted Hightower, the pastor of St. Paul Methodist Church in Louisville, Kentucky wrote:

> As a native of Alabama, I am aware of the pressures under which you labor and I assure you of not only my personal admiration but of my earnest prayers for your safety, for your courage and for your future…
>
> Please extend to the members of your family our prayerful support and our deep appreciation of their willingness to walk with you through these fiery days.

This is one of the few letters where the writer spoke about my family. I would get a lump in my throat every time someone mentioned how much Dot must have gone through. I do not know if Dot would have chosen the path I was on, but I know she walked it with me. I shall always treasure that thought.

The following letter is from Dot Hubbard, a Methodist Missionary in Korea, originally from Mississippi. She wrote the letter in longhand, filling the page from top to bottom. I understand she wrote every single minister a letter.

> Dear Rev. Kellar:
>
> I have just received the names and addresses of your twenty-eight young ministers who signed the "Born of Conviction" statement. So I am eager to write to

you and express to you my deep thanks for the stand you have taken. I was filled with real hope when I read your statement in our Mississippi Advocate. (I am also from Mississippi.) Surely it was the spirit of God that guided you to take such a stand of dedication to the principles of Christ, which is the purpose of our church.

I am so deeply grateful to you for your courage to be true to your convictions in this time of challenge. I am enclosing a typed copy of a prayer that I found in a youth prayer book. It was an inspiration to me, and perhaps it will be inspiring to you also, as you continue to serve during these days of challenge.

Since our people in Mississippi are confused as to what is "Communism", a dedicated voice such as yours is needed to help our people see what is right in the light of the basic principles of Christianity. I am truly grateful that God's spirit in you has helped God's church in Mississippi to see His truth stated in an honest and dedicated way during these important days.

It is my prayer that God will continue to be very near you, to give you His strength, wisdom, and grace, as you continue to serve in the center of His plan.

In His Love,

Dot Hubbard

What a blessing. Here is a woman serving in a country just a few years after a terrible war, making do with much less than I, and she is cheering me on. Dot and I were on the way to having our first child, I was getting support from all corners of the world, and there was calm and peace in Sandersville. I would live those few good days over considering what had been transpiring recently.

Every letter I had received was a blessing excepting the one from Beasley. Two letters held special meaning. The one from Ted Runyan was quoted earlier. A second letter had come from Emory as well.

It had been written by Dr. E. Clinton Gardner, also a professor of mine. He wrote in part:

> Dear Ned:
>
> I want to take this means of expressing my deep admiration of the courage displayed by you and the other twenty seven ministers who signed the statement which appeared in the Mississippi Methodist Advocate, January 2, 1963, opposing racial discrimination. I have been most distressed to learn of the opposition which you have encountered among the laity and the lack of support which you have received from the officials of the Church.
>
> Within the past few days I have procured a copy of this statement. It is frank, courageous, and well-worded. Unless the freedom to make such witness as this is preserved both in the pulpit and through the Church publications, the Church certainly cannot maintain its integrity.

In late January, I received a copy of a resolution from the faculty of Millsaps College that was addressed to Bishop Marvin Franklin, Bishop of the Mississippi Conference. For the past several days a huge amount of criticism was directed toward Bishop Franklin. My only gripe with the Bishop was his unwillingness or inability to curb the political nature of the conference. Now that the "twenty-eight" had presented their statement, Bishop Franklin's every word, action and, more importantly, inaction, added to the criticism directed toward his administration and toward Bishops in particular. The letter read:

Sandersville

Bishop Marvin A. Franklin
The Methodist Building
Jackson, Mississippi

Dear Bishop Franklin:

At a meeting of the Millsaps College Faculty on January 24, 1963, the following resolution was adopted by a majority vote:
The faculty of Millsaps College view with great concern certain events of recent weeks which indicate that the freedom of the Methodist pulpit in Mississippi is in jeopardy. Ministers – whose welfare we are particularly concerned because many of them are former students at Millsaps College – have been subject to various forms of harassment and intimidation, threats of reprisals, removal from their charges, and even acts of damage to property because they have chosen to speak their convictions.
We are concerned, first, that encroachment upon the liberties of ministers to speak freely their sincere interpretations of the Christian gospel constitute but one manifestation of those evil tendencies which would deny men freedom in every sphere. Such tendencies are a constant threat, not only to a free and valid church, but also to a democratic society.
We are concerned, in the second instance, that a climate of harassment and intimidation may continue to drive an increasing number of conscientious ministers from the churches of their region. This concern is accentuated by the fact that we are already aware that the number of able men entering the ministry is decreasing. The outlook for leadership is grim indeed if the good men we help to train are driven from the area.
Given the current situation of controversy in Mississippi, it should perhaps be emphasized that it is not a matter of agreement or disagreement with the interpretations and conviction expressed that is

at issue here; our concerns over the right and duty of free men – particularly Christian ministers – to express their convictions without fear of intimidation or reprisal. Some individuals and some churches throughout the state have openly defended this right and this duty of their minister. You spoke eloquently of this right and duty in your column in the Mississippi Methodist Advocate of October, 1961:

> The church has the right to expect her ministers to be a voice in the pulpit, declaring what he believes God would have him say. What he says may not always please all who hear, but the congregation must insist that he be a prophet of God and not a panderer of meaningless platitudes. He must not be a thermostat registering prevailing temperatures, but a thermometer, who finding the average temperature lower than the eternal truth and righteousness God requires, sets forth to point the way to the mind, the will, and the purpose of God.

We happily endorse this splendid statement.
In the light of this forthright stand, we find it particularly disappointing that the public statement recently made by you and the cabinet of the Mississippi Conference contains no reference to this crucial issue. We sincerely believe that the prevailing mood of our state would be greatly improved if it were more generally known both within the church and in society at large that you have the need for a free pulpit in a free society.
Thus we strongly urge that these men who have spoken out, and any others who in full Christian conscience, should express their sincere views on any side of controversial issues receive full support from you and your high office both by means of public statement and private attention to their welfare. We

further urge that such men be personally encouraged by you to remain in the churches in Mississippi.

As secretary of the faculty, I have been instructed by that body to forward also a copy of this resolution to the members of your Cabinet and to the twenty-eight ministers who published a statement recently in the Mississippi Methodist Advocate.

The above resolution is not to be released to the press.

Very truly yours,

Paul D. Hardin
Secretary, Millsaps College Faculty

It was good to get a copy of the resolution. The faculty was careful to add that the statement was not to be released to the press. I cannot believe that someone had not leaked the statement, but I do not recall seeing it in the paper. I know I appreciated what they had to say whether anyone else ever saw it or not.

There were others who would come forth in support of the statement. P. D. East, the same author who met with us at Hidden Haven, published his support in the Petal Paper. In a style that he reveled in, P. D. East praised the "twenty-eight", as did a couple other newspaper editors. I did receive a copy of P.D.'s newspaper and thoroughly enjoyed his "tongue in cheek" response to the statement.

But with the good comes the bad. The ratio of letters in favor of the statement outnumbered the criticism about fifteen to one in my case. However, the criticisms were harsh.

Some of the harshest came from, of all places, Methodist ministers and laymen from around the state. Only one letter addressed to me directly contained any negative criticism, and that came from Homer and Ella Ruth's minister. I was to learn that others wrote letters to newspapers and copies were sent to me. P. D. East had printed a letter directed to Sam Ashmore, editor of the Mississippi Methodist Advocate, that was particularly critical. The letter was written by a supply pastor, Bertise C. Rouse. Mr. Rouse was pastor of Dixie Methodist Church, located just west of Hattiesburg.

I think it necessary to share the full content of the letter to understand its message.

Dear Brother Ashmore:

In the January 2, 1963 issue of the Mississippi Methodist Advocate, I read the article entitled "Born of Conviction" in which twenty-eight ministers of the Mississippi Conference have boldly endorsed integration. As a minister of the Gospel of Jesus Christ, I feel that I too am "Born of Conviction" that integration is "unalterably opposed" and contrary to the teachings of the Bible, especially in the Old Testament (Deut. 7:1-3, Joshua 23:12-13, and Ezra 9:12). Jesus was a champion on the Old Testament scriptures and He didn't come to change but to fulfill.

I do not know who wrote the introduction to the article but I readily questioned the statement that, "They represent some of the best trained and most promising ministers." What do we judge a preacher's training by? Do we say that they are well trained because they have had seminary training? God could offer the baptism of the Holy Ghost. I really wonder if they are "our best trained ministers." Men led by the Holy Spirit are in accordance with God's will.

We cannot have much more conformity than "blind leaders of the blind." We need men of vision, or the Methodist Church "will fall into the ditch" like the mixed races of the past. (What happened to the Edomites?)

Bro. Ashmore, I believe that you are a man "Born of Conviction" and ask that you print this comment from an approved supply pastor who some day wants to be a member of a conference that stands on a solid foundation – "If the foundation be destroyed, what can the righteous do?" (Psalms 11:3.)

> Yours in His Service,
> Bertise C. Rouse, Pastor
> Dixie Methodist Church
> Route 3
> Hattiesburg, Mississippi

P. D. added:

And that my friends is the way a good, solid Mississippi preacher ought to sound-whether he can read or not.

While dismissing the letter of a Bertise Rouse or a Hebert Beasley, there were well trained and completely closed people who disagreed vehemently with the statement. One was an acquaintance of mine named Roy Wesley Wolfe. Roy had worked in my home church and played softball in the local softball league. I remember Roy because he had the fastest pitch I have seen in softball. Roy was also hot-headed and proclaimed himself as the wisest person around. He wrote a letter of great length criticizing the signers of the statement. To quote the entire letter would require more space than I wish to give to him. I will quote a few of his remarks so the reader can get the gist of what Roy felt about the statement and its signers. The letter is written to Sam Ashmore as well.

> Though the statement does not advocate full-scale integration, it is obvious that it supports that side of the heated controversy… . Therefore, I will write in favor of segregation.

And he did for the next fourteen paragraphs. He questioned the signers as being a majority and asked why others had not signed.

> Surely every conference member is willing to take his stand for his convictions in this and other matters.

The answer is, "not everyone was asked." Rev. Wolfe continues:

> I did not take a vow to uphold integration as inserted in the "1960 Discipline." Christians who believe in segregation, do believe in brotherly love (though otherwise accused). I do not believe that any person will ever become a citizen of the New Jerusalem with hatred in his heart toward any person (red, yellow, black, or white).

Rev. Wolfe continued his argument by relating an experience he had. He was working side-by-side with a black man shoveling dirt. Out of curiosity, Roy asked him if he was in favor of integration. The black man assured him he was not. The first image that came to my mind, when I read that, was the old man walking by my National Guard unit saying, "God bless you" time and time again, meaning quite the opposite. If any of us had asked him if he believed in integration, what would he have said? What black man in his right mind, working with a group of white men in the Deep South, would own up to wanting integration?

Mr. Wolfe continues:

> Not only do I object to the socialistic theory of One World Race today, but through Amalgamation as advocated by most Methodist publications today, but I object to our other two: (1)One world church through the Ecumenical Movement and (2)ONE World Government through the United Nations. I would never be a part of uniting with Rome and the United Nations in an unscriptural organization...

All races need their own church and together can make this present world what God wants it to be.

Mr. Wolfe closes his letter thusly:

> Yours for a Christian and Conservative USA.

While I have quoted only parts of the letter, I think the reader can surmise what the message Mr. Wolfe wanted to convey.

I was disturbed by Mr. Wolfe's letter only because it represented a group of ministers in the Mississippi Conference. Add to that attitude, the behavior of the District Superintendent of the Meridian District, James Slay, who actually planned a meeting with a pastor's congregation without informing the pastor and then telling the pastor he had to leave immediately. J. Willard Leggett allowed a church to force out Jim Nicholson. What disturbed me most was the pressure I felt from within the Methodist Conference. How in God's name could I ever expect a decent appointment with these men calling the shots? I was becoming more depressed about my future.

I began to get printed materials that did cause me concern. One such document came from Knox Broom, a layman from Jackson. It was a lengthy article and came as an addendum to a letter quoted earlier in this book. It was titled, "Cover Pulling" and the subtitle was, "Teams: Neglect of responsibility-vs.-Indoctrinated products". The article reads in part:

> Recent evidence of cover-pulling by twenty-eight neophyte Methodist ministers, and some of the leadership of the church, would be amusing but for the potentially shameful damage to the basic cause for which the Articles of Religion of the church stands.
>
> Mere castigation, or even ostracism, of those young twenty-eight Resolutors seeking attention, and appearance of sophistication by the ill-advised and immature resolve could hardly be calculated to do the cause of Soul-Saving much good. By their act they stand convicted of either seeking an education in a church-supported institution under false pretenses – if their pronouncement represents their conviction at the time they applied for admission; or by not exercising the courage of the founding fathers of Methodism by withdrawing – if their express convictions were the result of instruction and influences encountered in the Institution.

I interpreted the entire text as a way of placing blame for our activities on the teaching and publishing institutions of the church. The twenty-eight had strayed from the church's purpose of soul-winning. Mr. Broom goes on to talk about Methodist publications and other issues that upset him. The paragraph quoted sums up the attitude several had about the statement and the immature signers.

But I found time and again that, just when the skies grew the darkest, a letter would come and lift my sagging spirits. One such letter came from Dean M. Kelley who wrote from the National Council of Churches of Christ. When I first saw the envelope, I was not sure just what to do. The NCC was one of the most detested groups in the eyes of many Mississippians. Some blamed them for every "liberal" idea that came to the churches. I just hoped that Ms. Hinton did not know about the National Council of Church's reputation. Mr. Kelley wrote:

> Dear Brother Kellar;
>
> Your recent act of courage in signing the statement "Born of Conviction" in the Mississippi Methodist Advocate of January 2, 1963, is an encouragement to real Christians everywhere. It makes one proud to be a Christian, proud to be a Methodist. You have given moral leadership at a great risk where it counts most, and bishops will be judged by how readily they follow you.
> It is ironic that it should require courage to repeat the teachings of the Methodist Church, but the subsequent events have shown you are indeed in the front lines of Christian witness where those words are still prophetic. If our Lord lives and acts for men's redemption in our time, it is thanks to men like you who risk their careers and their security to do His will.
>
> Yours sincerely,
>
> Dean Kelley

Mr. Kelley, in another part of his letter, offered to help. But he knew his support would likely hinder more than help because of the attitude held by most in the South, that the NCC was an arm of "all that was evil." They were the hated One World, One Church group that Wolfe railed against.

Not long after receiving the National Council mail, I received a letter from the Houston Council of Human Relations. It read in part:

> Dear Mr. Kellar:
>
> We are deeply moved here at The Council on Human Relations by your courageous statement. This act deserves all the encouragement that every person of faith and goodwill can express.
> When you risk the welfare of your families and yourself by boldly aligning yourselves on the side of truth and of justice our words seem puny indeed…
>
> Sincerely yours,
>
> Mr. Charles Kelly

The Diocese of Galveston-Houston wrote:

> With delight I have related to many fellow Catholics the story of your courage and that of the other Methodist ministers who signed the statement, "Born of Conviction."
> I requested that they pray for all of you, and I offer my own prayers for the harmonious settlement of the many problems concomitant with the erasure of racial segregation.
> Rev. William Pickard, J.C.D.

I wondered just what Mr. Wolfe would think about a Roman Catholic praying for us?

Settling Into a Routine

My life as pastor of the Sandersville Charge had not changed much. It seemed, on the surface at least, that the community wanted to move on, which was good. I continued burning the old tree. It was taking far longer than I had anticipated, which was true of much in my life at that time. I could only burn. There was a wood- and brush-covered lot behind the parsonage, and I had to be careful not to let the fire spread. But burning a few limbs at a time was time well-spent.

I heard that other signers of the statement were considering leaving Mississippi. I gave a lot of thought to doing the same, even though the church was treating me well. But things had changed. We were cautious with one another. I lived with the tension of always being on guard. Nothing was ever said, but the feeling lingered.

To my surprise and pleasure, the crowds grew a little. Growth in Sandersville would mean a couple more in attendance on a given Sunday.

Wilton and I still spent a lot of time together and would invariably talk about transferring to another conference. I had received some letters from the pastor I had met at Emory Minister's week about getting me to come to South Carolina. Some still talked about transferring to California or Arizona. Even Wilton had communicated with some church leaders in those areas. I had not made up my mind about what I wanted to do. Most of the talk was just that – talk. It did take our minds off the local churches. We discussed the abundance of golf courses out west which made the wild west seem more attractive. My fantasy was a church that was void of racial conflict, located in a community where people accepted people, regardless of race. In my mind, I knew there probably was no such place, but dreaming kept me upbeat. Most of the time I fantasized about such places while I burned the limbs from the old tree.

Chapter Twenty

The Decision to Leave

Every time I returned to burning the tree, I had a feeling of something ending in my life. Was it all an omen? My feelings were ambivalent because some of the anger from the community was abating and fewer and fewer people talked about the Born of Conviction statement. I wondered if the passage of time made the community feel less threatened by it, or did they keep silent so I wouldn't mention it. It was like, "I won't talk if you don't talk about it." Larry and I would see each other two or three times each week, and we never mentioned anything about "Born of Conviction," nor did we talk about politics, or any subject that may cause disagreement. I felt we were guarding against saying anything that may offend the other. It made for some very shallow conversations.

However, there were some who made snide remarks or gave the impression they were watching to see if I would say anything about race or integration or to see if I would mention anything about blacks or race in general. There was constant pressure on me to make sure I didn't give my adversaries any ammunition. The only problem was I could not be sure just who my adversaries were. I learned to be cautious with everyone. On occasion I would see Bear at the restaurant and get the same stares I had always gotten from him. He did not seem the threat he once did, but I did not want to cross him or give him reason to act out. He never said a word to me, but if looks could kill I would be dead a hundred times over. That man scared me just sitting on a stool at the counter of the café.

I was sure of one thing: I did not want to spend the rest of my ministry worrying about what I said lest I offend someone. I realized I was tired, not physically but mentally. This whole experience had exacted a toll. In a time when I should have been on top of the world because we were going to have a child, I was depressed. I was tired of seeing people pass by on the other side of the church aisle without speaking or looking in my direction. To be sure, I was thankful for those who did speak, and speak warmly. There seemed to be more who gave the impression that they agreed with me, but would never speak out. I stood there taking the burning limbs into a pile as they dissolved into ashes. I was cold and the heat felt good. I played a mind game. Each limb represented some issue and, as it disappeared into ash, the issue would disappear with it. Unfortunately, the game worked only momentarily because the issue reappeared as soon as I finished the day's burning. How simple it would be, I thought, if I could just pile up my troubles and turn them into ashes. Permanently.

The idea of leaving was a constant thought. I have always been a reactive person. Now I had to give a lot of thought about a decision that would have a lasting impact on my life, on my marriage, and on our yet to be born child. A decision like this demanded a lot of thinking and planning. The first thing I needed to decide was, "Why leave?"

Was it the Sandersville church? After all, I had not wanted to serve Sandersville. I recalled how bad I felt when Brunner Hunt said I was going to Sandersville. Hadn't I told Dot a hundred times that I would leave the ministry if I was sent to Sandersville? The congregation was upset with me after the statement was published. I had been threatened, cussed at, and rejected. I had a strong case for seeking a transfer. But that same church, at least some of the congregation, accepted that I had "betrayed" them but continued to accept me. I had not lost any members because of my actions. Well maybe one or two. Could I serve Sandersville for another year? I could, but did I want to? I found that my answer to that question varied depending on how I was treated on Sundays. I would need to talk with Dot about it. But, if the church was not standing out as a reason to leave, why did I keep toying with the idea?

Was it the political climate? Ross Barnett was still governor, and I could not think of a single man I detested as much as him. The whole mess with Ole Miss was exacerbated by the rioting and the subsequent deaths. Mississippi was the Deep South, and most of her citizens took great pride in standing against anything, including the United States Army, to keep their beloved way of life intact. It amazed me how strong the allegiance was to that way of life. What amazed me most was the fact that Mississippi was the poorest state in the union. Our schools were poor, our teachers had the lowest salaries, and our brightest young people were leaving for more fertile fields.

What in the name of heaven was there that kept these people from leaving en masse? I knew the answer. This was their home. I recalled a story Wilton had told me about a member of his church in the Lake community. He visited the man on his farm and, as the man sat in his rocking chair on his front porch, he remarked that he stayed home. Always.

"In fact," he told Wilton, "I have not been in Lawrence (the closest town to his farm) in four years." Like many Mississippians, that was his place, and he planned on staying right there until God called him home. So it was with others. "I was born in Mississippi and, by God, I will die in Mississippi."

The Civil Rights issue brought a lot of hate groups to the surface. The Klan continued to beat blacks, bomb churches, and spread fear far and wide. But there was another group more sinister than the Klan. It was an organization called the "Mississippi White Citizens Council." It was formed in 1954 and elected Robert Patterson as its leader. It was made up of plantation owners, doctors, lawyers, legislators, bankers, teachers, and merchants. This group sought to prevent integration. The group (some estimated it had 90,000 members) publicly denounced violence. Nevertheless, its actions often encouraged violence. And yet the organization yielded political and economic clout. It brought to bear economic reprisals against anyone or group who supported desegregation. Effectively delaying integration for more than ten years, its clout was more subtle than the Klan, but just as destructive. The "Born of Conviction" statement was directly opposed to what the WCC stood for.

The State of Mississippi also created a tax-supported agency for the "interposition resolution", a resolution that defended Mississippi against the "illegal encroachment" of the federal government. The agency was the Sovereignty Commission. Its bottom line was to preserve and protect racial segregation in Mississippi. It was designed to keep the NAACP and Progressive Voters' League under surveillance. In effect, it spied on Mississippians, keeping files on individuals and groups who were thought to be a threat to the Southern Way of Life. It reached its heyday under the administration of Ross Barnett.

The White Citizens Council, the Mississippi Sovereignty Commission, and the general mood of state government, made it hard to live in Mississippi. It was ironic that the commission would accuse so many of being communist because of their racial views while using the very tools normally attributed to communists. It was obvious that Mississippi would rather destroy its educational system than let it be integrated. This spoke volumes about the attitude toward education in Mississippi. Was this a place where I wanted my child to grow up?

While the State of Mississippi was obsessed with preventing blacks from entering the white schools, there was a situation I faced as a resident of the state. In Jones County, "The Free State of Jones County", a grand jury called for statewide screening of school and library books to eliminate those critical of the southern way of life. The Mississippi Sovereignty Commission forced the two major newspapers in Mississippi to kill news stories about desegregation. It was an obvious plot to control what children read in the public schools and libraries. If this policy continued, my son or daughter would never know the full story, only what some organization wanted him or her to know.

As I considered all of the pros and cons of staying in Mississippi, I recalled my own experience with Mississippi history as taught by my high school teacher. It was slanted at best. This was in the early and mid-1950's. The Civil War was caused not by issues over slavery, but because the Yankees wanted to keep the southerners oppressed.

As I learned more about the history of Mississippi, I was amazed that it was not as I had been taught. With books selected by those who wanted to keep Mississippi segregated, how was anyone going to learn the truth?

Earlier, I alluded to the politics of the Mississippi Conference. Of all the negatives about Mississippi, this was the most significant to me. The conference was run by forces under the leadership of J. Willard Liggett, District Superintendent. Some church leaders told the Bishop and Cabinet that they would not receive any of those who had signed "Born of Conviction". By virtue of signing the statement, I had limited the churches I could serve. What kind of future did I realistically have in Mississippi?

As I debated the issue, I realized I was finding all the reasons why I should leave. I needed to try and find some reason to stay. It was my home. I had spent all of my life in Mississippi. I lived near Louisiana, but Mississippi was home. It was also Dot's home, and she loved being near her parents. Our child's grandparents could watch him grow up. I knew that would be especially true for Dot's parents. That was it. I could not think of any other reason to stay.

I then concluded the obvious. There were far more reasons to leave then there were to stay. If that was the case, what kept me from making the move to relocate? Why wasn't I writing to every conference in Methodism asking if they would take me? Obviously there was some reason why I was not actively seeking to move. As I stoked the embers of the fire, I accepted the fact that I should leave. Now all I had to do was convince Dot.

The only inquiries I had made to date were the conversations I had with my friend Tom from South Carolina. I had met a Reverend Chandler who offered me a position on his staff. That was a start. I knew I would move to another southern state. If memory serves me right, South Carolina was the first state to secede from the union, and Mississippi was the second. The racial crisis seemed as much an issue in South Carolina as it was in Mississippi. But, I rationalized the Methodist Church in South Carolina could not be as corrupt as in Mississippi. I chose to believe that the state government was not run by Ross Barnett. There could be only one Barnett, or so I prayed.

I worked out a plan. I would follow up on the offer from South Carolina, and hedge my bet by writing to other conferences. But I had still not seriously discussed the plan to move with Dot. Up until now, our discussions about moving had been idle talk. I felt guilty about going as far as I did with my thought processes without consulting with her. I had been frustrated and discouraged enough at times to consider moving anywhere to get away from the pressures and the politics. But, if she said no, I would make the best of my ministry in Mississippi.

I went inside to ask her about moving to another conference. The first question she asked was where. I mentioned South Carolina and she asked how far away it was.

"Further east than Atlanta," I answered.

"I mean how long will it take to drive to South Carolina?"

I guessed about ten hours. That got her attention. "We don't have to move to South Carolina," I quickly added. I was hoping she wouldn't ask what our other options were. The only other place I was considering was a two or three day drive. "First, let's decide if we even want to move," I suggested.

That was the first step of a process that would take time and considerable thought and prayer. At least we were on the same page. I suggested we make a trip to South Carolina to look at the opportunity. We would go in the spring and use it as a chance to get away. Dot's parents could keep our dog, and we could visit Tom and his family. I left it with Dot to plan a time. I then contacted Reverend Chandler and told him we wanted to visit. He was receptive to the visit and seemed anxious to show me his church.

We met with Dolores and Wilton to talk seriously about leaving Mississippi. I told them about South Carolina. Wilton had already made inquiries. He outlined the areas where he had contacted and suggested we try to get into the same conference. It would be easier to adjust to a new place if we made the trek together. After a long discussion, Dot and I agreed to look into other areas too. In a way, we got caught up in the excitement of going somewhere new. But where?

The first thing we had to do was get the word out that we were interested in relocating, not just to South Carolina but other areas as well. However, we had to be discreet. We did not want the local churches to know what we were planning and certainly didn't want the Mississippi Conference to know. And just how was I to accomplish that when my postmistress's brother was my leading layman?

Dot and I spent a lot of hours talking about where we wanted to go to continue ministry. Atlanta sounded good. After all, some of our happier moments came while at Emory. If there was prejudice, it was not as obvious as in Mississippi. Wasn't Atlanta where we could go out to dinner in style? Phillip's Café didn't compare. Then there was Lenox Square, one of the largest shopping malls in the South. I could try Atlanta or the North Georgia Conference.

The excitement of moving held appeal. Planning is more fun than actually completing the chore. It is kind of like a fantasy where you can make the outcome as happy as you like. It was easy to talk about leaving, but making concrete plans was hard.

Then, reality struck. Both of us had lived in the South our entire lives. We understood southerners. And how would her parents feel? Especially with her being pregnant. Being near her mother was important. Considering family did not affect me as much as it affected Dot. But remaining in Mississippi had a very high price tag attached. Ironically, things were settling down in Sandersville, and it was becoming clear we could stay. However, there was more to staying than just the congregation at the churches.

The first order of business was to make the planned trip to South Carolina. That one opportunity appealed to us more than the others because one of our best friends, Thomas Rogers, served a church in Greenwood, in the South Carolina Conference. His home would be open to us, and we could save money on hotels. The salary paid by Sandersville did not allow for luxuries such as hotels. Tom's home would serve as a "base of operations" as we explored the different possibilities in the state. Finally, we set a date and contacted the churches in South Carolina we wanted to visit. We received three responses and all three wanted to interview us for a position with their church. Plans were completed. It would be the longest trip Dot and I had made since our marriage. With some trepidation, we packed the car and set out on our journey.

We decided to leave for South Carolina on March 10th and stay until the 14th. The spring storms were starting with a big one forecast for our departure day. It was a dark and windy morning we started out on the trip that would cover more miles than any we had ever driven. The winds were coming from the southwest. I recalled what the folks of Goodwater had told me about bad weather always coming from the southwest. Based on radio reports, we were staying just ahead of the front. When we stopped for the night, the storm caught up with us with its rain and lightning and high winds. If I didn't know any better, I would have thought God was saying, "Don't leave Mississippi." I rationalized that if God was talking to me He was saying," Don't leave Mississippi for South Carolina."

It was a long, hard drive. We had driven back and forth between Hattiesburg and Atlanta several times, so the highway was not new to us. However, Greenwood was much further than Atlanta, and the weather made driving difficult. Still, being away from the tension in Sandersville made the trip bearable. Even as we crossed the state line, I felt a lessening of my stress level. This trip was an escape from controversy, and a flight into something that promised a better ministry. That thought kept us on the road.

We arose early the next morning and set out to complete our journey. It was midday when we finally arrived in Greenwood. Following the directions given us by Tom, and a thirty minute search, we arrived at his home. Dot and I made our way to the front door and knocked.

Janis opened the door. "We've been trying to get in touch with you but didn't know where to call. Our child has the measles, and I know you are expecting. It's not safe for you to stay here."

Our hearts sank. I had to rethink the bad luck vs. a message from God about leaving Mississippi. Was this a message from God, or just bad luck? Whatever the reason, we cut our trip short. Two very disappointed people returned to Sandersville. I decided that if God was sending a message I would have been more open to the direction He wanted me to take. Obviously it was not South Carolina.

Chapter Twenty-one

The Final Straw

I began to pray earnestly for some kind of sign. I didn't have to wait long. It came in the form of a mailing from a group that I had heard of but did not know much about. The group called itself "The Mississippi Association of Methodist Ministers and Laymen". There were no names attached. However, its message was clear. It read:

> Whereas, The Mississippi Association of Methodist Ministers and Laymen in official meeting, duly called and organized, at Jackson, Mississippi on the twenty-first Day of March, in the year of our Lord 1963, and through its only authorized officers and members, in its love for and its desire to preserve The Methodist Church, has resolved, dedicated, and committed itself to the following:
>
> To respect and maintain racial customs in churches, schools, conferences and jurisdictions.
>
> To combat the efforts of those organizations and persons who seek to use The Methodist Church, its name, or its program as vehicles to impair or destroy the private enterprise system and substituting a socialist or communist state.

> To insure that the Commandments of God, the teachings of Our Lord and Savior, Jesus Christ, and the Apostle's Creed be adhered to without equivocation by our publications, our teaching literature, our ministerial colleges, our clergy, and our accepted lay leadership; and,
>
> Whereas, only through the preservation of these Christian principles will we be able to preserve the whole body of our beloved Methodist Church, while defeat of these principles would inevitably result in integrated, improvised local churches in our neighborhoods, built with our money, teaching doctrines alien to the ministry of Christ, and unable to maintain the educational and economic standards essential to the continuance of a qualified clergy.
>
> Now, therefore, be it resolved by the Mississippi Association of Methodist Ministers and Laymen in Session Duly Organized, that every church, charge, official body, minister. Official board, board of stewards, Woman Society of Christian Service, Methodist Men's Club, Quarterly Conference, and other body, committee, or group whatsoever that is an official part of the Methodist Church or any of its local churches, by resolution or other formal action place itself on record as to the position on the above Christian Principles; and,
>
> Be it further resolved, that every Methodist in the State of Mississippi rededicate himself to daily prayer, to daily study of the Bible, and to his greatest activity in promoting these principles and seeing that officers, delegates, and spokesmen for such church groups and, particularly, official lay leaders and delegates to Annual Conference and to the General Conference, be openly committed to work toward these goals.

Although the mailing itself was not much different than some I had received previously, but its timing could not have been worse. I had just reconciled my fate and was moving toward staying in

Sandersville

Sandersville. It was not set in concrete, but I was thinking about staying. I read the name of the group claiming credit for the mailing: Mississippi Association of Methodist Minister and Laymen. Who were they? What ministers and what laymen? What role did these people play in the Mississippi Conference? Could they affect my next move? Would I have any place that would accept me? My God, I thought, I'm right back where I was a couple weeks ago.

I read the resolution again. While I wondered who the laymen were, they did not really matter that much to me. What really bugged me were the ministers referred to in the mailing. Which ministers? Were they part of the power group in Mississippi? Were they Leggett's men? I knew that some ministers had criticized the signers of the statement. Now there was a group working with laymen to openly criticize us. One thing was for sure, there would be no peace in the lives of the twenty-eight. My dream of being a minister in the Mississippi Conference was fast turning into a nightmare.

I again headed to the backyard to burn limbs. I had to search to gather enough to start a fire. I laughed at myself when I thought about having to leave soon because the old tree was almost gone.

As I stirred the fire, I realized how much of my thoughts I had kept from everyone else, especially Dot. I was the one standing outside burning limbs and mulling over my future alone. Dot and I had talked about moving but I hadn't shared my internal turmoil. But then I had never shared very much of myself with Dot or anyone. I did not want Dot to know about the wrestling match going in my soul. I kept telling myself I was protecting her, but it was me I was protecting. I had chosen not to open up to her because it might make me look undecided, weak. It was my choice, but, in retrospect, it would have been better if I had opened up to her. But I had created the problem. I needed to solve it. Like most people in this state of mind, I prayed that all of this would simply go away. But here I was, watching hot fire consume decayed limbs, knowing I had little future in my home state. I also had a pregnant wife. Intellectually, I knew what had to be done, but those damn emotions kept me off kilter. I looked around to gather more limbs and saw there were very few left.

Maybe this was the sign I had been waiting for. I needed to make a decision and follow through.

Some of my anger was directed at those in my congregation who had turned their backs on me and, in some cases, lashed out at me. I was angry at the ones who telephoned at all hours to harass me or, to harass Dot, if I was not at home. I was furious at the ministry. I was greatly upset by fellow clergy who not only disagreed with what I believed, but attacked me through letters and resolutions. How dare that little bastard in my in-law's church read a statement condemning what we had done. How dare the pastor of my hometown church use our statement to sway people to his side so they would overlook his lousy ministry. Then there was the bishop and members of the cabinet who spoke at one of the churches served by the "twenty-eight". He said we were like the Billy goat standing on the railroad tracks facing an approaching train, chewing on red underwear and thinking he could stop the train. I heard he received a lot of laughter. This man was supposed to be my brother in ministry, the two of us standing tall against the social injustices of the community. The bishop simply did nothing. He left us "hanging out to dry". This was the bishop and cabinet who would determine my future appointments. They could all go to hell, I suddenly realized. I was now as determined to leave Mississippi, as I had been to remain, even if I had to change careers.

Starting a Mail Crusade

I began writing letters to every conference in the southeast and a few out west. I chose the western conferences because I had heard some of the twenty-eight were making inquiries about relocating out there. I even changed sending an inquiry to Florida, even though I had heard they were not taking transfers. I sent some of the letters from the Laurel Post Office because of Ms. Hinton.

It did not take long to receive responses to my letters. I got positive feelings from the Southern California and Arizona Conference. No promises, but they would consider me if there were any openings. The same was true of Indiana and a couple of other conferences. North Georgia, a place I would have dearly loved to serve, did not offer any encouragement. The same was true of Florida. I had written to six of the twelve District Superintendents in the Florida Conference. One of them wrote to say I would love living in Florida.

"The only problem is a lack of space. We hardly ever receive people from other areas."

Bruce Gannaway, District Superintendent of Orlando, was more direct. "There is no way you will ever get into Florida."

Another door slammed shut.

Wilton and Dolores were also experiencing a frustrating search for a new conference. Wilton was still interested in the California and Arizona Conference where a few of the signers had moved. The West was appealing in many ways, and we would know those who had already transferred. But there were bigger considerations for me. Dot was pregnant and, if we moved to California, she would be far away from her family. Being so far away would be difficult for her. Besides, I had never traveled west of New Orleans. Moving to California was a possibility. The offers were there, but it would not be our first choice.

In the meantime, Wilton was also exploring Florida as a place to relocate. It was a fast growing state, and the attitudes there might be better. Rumor had it that new churches were being built all the time. But I had ruled out Florida because they had, in effect, closed their doors to transfers. That did not stop Wilton from trying. (In fact, Wilton was eventually accepted by the Florida Conference and moved to serve a church in Ormond Beach, Florida.)

"Why don't you try again? We might end up in the same conference."

I decided to give it another shot. What the heck, the worst they could do was say no, and they had already said as much. Again, I went through the process of writing letters to the District Superintendents in the Florida Conference. While I had been to Mobile, Alabama, which is close to Florida, I had never set foot in the Sunshine State.

One response came from a D.S. in the West Palm District telling me how great it was to serve in Florida. In fact, he wrote, it is so nice that everyone wants to come to Florida. However, we are not receiving any transfers this year. I assumed it was his way of telling me just how much I was missing by not coming to Florida where I could not go even if I wanted. Florida sounded great but out of reach. I reminded myself of my "bird in the hand" South Carolina offer. Discouraged, I wrote off Florida. That left Indiana, California, and somewhere with the National Council of Churches. My choices were getting slimmer.

Then one evening, when I got home from some pastoral visiting, I was greeted by an excited wife. I'd had a phone call from Cocoa, Florida. The caller was the pastor of a church there. David Cathcart was looking for an associate minister and wanted to talk with me about the position. His message was to call him as soon as I came home. I was reluctant to telephone him from the house because of the party line. Even before the controversy people listened in on conversations. Now I was the evening's party line entertainment. There was little doubt that all my calls were monitored. Throwing caution to the wind, I telephoned Reverend Cathcart.

I shall never forget his deep bass voice. He had heard about some ministers in Mississippi who wanted to move to another conference.

"I'm looking for an associate. We have a new building and the area is booming. Are you interested?"

Because of my party line paranoia, I was evasive but indicated I would like to discuss the position.

"Why don't you let us fly you to Cocoa and we can meet face to face. We'll send you tickets and pick you up in Orlando."

"Is it too far to drive?" I asked. I had never flown before and it did not appeal to me.

"Oh," he mused, "it's about 700 miles from your place to our place."

I decided I would take a chance and fly. Before hanging up the phone, I heard the clicks as my uninvited guests hung up their own. I knew calls were made all over the community that evening to report on my latest situation.

After the call, Dot and I talked about and planned my trip to Cocoa. She was excited. So was I. But, I had never flown before. I came from the school of thought, "if God wanted man to fly, he would have given him wings."

I only knew of Florida from travel brochures which promised oceans and skimpily-clad beach-goers. Dot had at least been to Pensacola in the Florida Panhandle. I felt a surge of excitement tempered by fear. I was going to see Florida at someone else's expense and possibly get a job. My feelings were mixed. I was afraid of flying, and yet, it was Florida.

In just a few days I received mail from Reverend Cathcart. There was a round-trip ticket from the Hattiesburg/Laurel Airport to Orlando, Florida. It was going to happen. I had an entrée into Florida. Having never flown in an airplane before, I was quite nervous. Now I had a plane ticket, a scheduled flight, and someone waiting to meet me at the airport in Orlando. I tried to block out newspaper accounts of airplane crashes. It didn't work, but I kept trying. It occurred to me that I had weathered death threats in person with a minimum of fear. Now, as I thought about getting on a plane with no death threats, I was scared to death.

Dot helped me pack for my two day stay in Cocoa. It was not difficult to determine what I would wear. I had a black suit for preaching, so I would wear that to make a good impression. I would take some casual clothes just in case people in Florida wore casual clothing. The plane ride would be a good time to work on a sermon so I took a couple of books along,

As the day of my flight drew nearer, my anxiety increased. I was to depart from the Laurel/Hattiesburg airport on Southern Airways. Dot drove me to the airport. I bravely got out of the car, perspiring, ready to turn and run. However, I wanted to be a man about this situation, so I acted calm, cool, and collected.

The Laurel/Hattiesburg airport terminal was not much larger than a double wide mobile home. After presenting my ticket to the agent, I sat down and began reading one of my books. I glanced around the room to see if any other person was waiting for the flight. I was the only one. As I looked about, I noticed a brown box on the wall with a coin slot. It was a machine that dispensed flight insurance from Mutual of Omaha. My anxiety soared. If flying was so safe, why do they have life insurance machines in the terminals? Still, just in case something happened, I deposited a few coins and bought $50,000 of life insurance. That should take care of Dot and our unborn child for a while.

The plane arrived on time and taxied to the terminal. The airport had a single runway and the daily traffic consisted of two flights, one to New Orleans and the other a return flight from New Orleans. If you were going anywhere else, you had to change planes in New Orleans, not something I was looking forward to.

Two people got off the flight. The agent announced that all passengers could board and the plane would be taking off shortly. I walked outside the terminal and saw a DC-3, twin-engine prop plane. It sat at a steep angle because the only landing gear was at the center and tail of the plane. I climbed up a few steps and took my assigned seat. Just as I sat down, another passenger rushed aboard, doubling the number of passengers. There were four seats across and about twenty rows of seats. I glanced at the interior of the plane and immediately went back to the book I held in my hands. "Held" is the most appropriate word to use because, even though I saw the words, I did not read a single one. I just wanted to focus on something, anything, that would take my mind off the fact I was in an airplane about to take off.

I learned a lot of things in the few minutes it took for the plane to taxi to the end of the runway. Planes taxi slowly. They also encounter bumps on the runway that raise your heart rate. Just before we took off, the pilot revved up one engine then the other. My heart rate rose again. Then he revved up both engines at the same time and the plane began to move. Slowly at first, accelerating until the tail wheel rose off the ground and the plane leveled out as it raced down the runway.

I never looked up from my book. I could feel the lift of the plane as it cleared the runway. I was airborne. I was flying. I did not know how high because I refused to look up. I was finally forced to lift my head when the stewardess tapped me on the shoulder and wanted to know if I wanted a coke or coffee. I looked around the cabin. Everyone was calm. Everything seemed to be working. My anxiety abated some. I ordered a coke.

We had been in the air for about twenty minutes when I mustered all my courage and quickly glanced out the window. It was not as bad as I thought. I peered at the ground and realized we were higher than the twenty-two story bank in Atlanta, the highest off the ground I had ever been up until now. We were flying, the stewardess told me, at around 10,000 feet. I looked out the window again and realized the plane was over Picayune. My anxiety almost disappeared as I looked for landmarks I could recognize. Within minutes we approached Lake Pontchartrain. Below was the Highway 11 bridge that my uncle worked on as bridge tender. We flew over my mother's house, my uncle's workplace, and the lake where we fished many, many times. Almost totally relaxed now, I began to enjoy the flight.

We landed in New Orleans just as darkness approached. I deplaned and went to the waiting area for the next leg of my flight which would take me to Orlando. As I sat in the waiting room, I thumbed through the pages of my book when a gentleman sat down next to me.

"Are you going to Orlando?" he asked.

"Yes, then Cocoa," I responded.

He pointed to the window in front of our seats. "That's the damn plane we'll be taking."

It was much larger than the plane I had just flown in from Laurel. It was a four-engine prop plane.

My new friend kept talking. "It has a pretty good record. Not many crashes. I was on one of those goddamned planes last week and it was a lousy ride. The s.o.b. bounced all over the sky."

My newfound confidence in flying began to wane. I wished he had sat somewhere else. He described the air business with graphic terms. He was a typical construction type. Every other word was a profane remark.

"What is your profession?" he asked. Without waiting for an answer he volunteered that he was a construction superintendent out of Baton Rouge.

At the first break in the conversation I said I was a Methodist minister. For a moment he looked shocked and embarrassed. Then the strangest thing happened. His whole demeanor changed.

"Is that right?" he asked. "I have a family member who is Methodist." The remainder of the conversation took on a sanitized air.

The PA system announced the boarding for the flight to Orlando and I, along with my new "converted" friend, found our seats and made ready for the takeoff. It was now raining that light, misty rain that so often invades New Orleans. It was my luck to sit next to the construction super from Baton Rouge. My seat was in the middle of the row and he was next to the window. I was just a little envious, but since it was dark I doubted I could see anything. The now "God-fearing" construction super pointed to the window and told me that it was a good spot to sit because it was an escape hatch in case of a crash. That remark was immediately followed by preflight instructions from the flight attendant. She caught my attention the moment she announced that most of our flight would be over water. She then removed a life preserver from a package and demonstrated how it should be used in case the plane had to land in water. That was more information than I needed. As we taxied along, I was fascinated to see the propeller forced the rain into a huge circle of spray. The flight attendant then announced that most of the flight would be over water.

"There are," she said, "rafts under some of the seats and a life preserver under each seat."

My friend felt under his seat and announced we were lucky. We had a life raft.

I didn't feel lucky, despite sitting by an exit window with a life raft. I felt nervous. We taxied down the runway, and I watched the props make huge rings of rain as they spun in the wet night air. We took off and were soon nearing our planned altitude. My friend pointed out the window at the exhaust coming from the motors. To my surprise, there was a finger of flame coming from each exhaust pipe. My mind played out the many movies about planes being shot down in war and leaving a long trail of flame as they plummeted into the ground or ocean. My heart pounded as I leaned back in my seat.

The flight continued along without incident for the next hour. Then I noticed we had slowed a bit. I tried to rationalize that we were getting to our destination too quickly and the pilot decided to back off the throttle. But my new friend gave me a nudge and said to look out the window. One prop was working but the other was dead still. It did not take a seasoned flyer to know that something was not right. Almost immediately the pilot came on the intercom and announced that a slight problem had developed in the engine and, to be on the safe side, he turned it off.

My mind traveled back to the South Carolina trip. Was God again intervening in my plans to leave Mississippi? At least in South Carolina we could park the car and wait out the storm. Where do you park an airplane? In the ocean? I was gasping and could feel my heart pounding in my chest. As if that weren't enough, my companion offered a comment.

"Good thing we're not on one of those propjets. The engine would have exploded."

Again, it was more information than I needed or wanted.

I leaned my head back and tried to focus my mind on something less threatening. I noticed the book I had brought with me. It was written by a minister from Miami named Roy Angel. The title was "Shoes of Iron". I read the information on the book jacket. The messages contained in the book dealt with difficult times and how one can cope. It was an answer to my prayers. Surely God had placed that book in my hands for this trip. I have often heard it said, and have said it in many sermons, "God never puts a problem before us without also providing a way through the problem." My anxiety did not go away, but at least I felt some peace.

We landed in Tampa to change planes for the trip to Orlando. The distance between Tampa and Orlando was less than eighty miles, and we were up and down in minutes. I did ask the flight attendant for an aspirin and a coke. She gave me the aspirin but said the flight was too short to provide a coke. Before I could protest we began our descent so I waited until I was on the ground.

I did look out the window once or twice, and noticed how beautiful Orlando was at night. The lights were bright and stretched for many miles in each direction. This was no Sandersville. We landed and taxied to the gate, walked down the steps, and I planted my feet on solid ground. Were it not so wet from the rain, I am sure I would have knelt and thanked God for delivering me to this new city. We had landed at the Herndon Airport, in the heart of the city.

Meeting Dave and Betty Cathcart

The Cathcarts were waiting to greet me. David was a big man with gray hair and a booming voice. Betty was younger looking than David and very lovely. David shook my hand firmly as he welcomed me to Florida.

Betty gently took my hand and, in a sweet and loving voice said, "We are so pleased to have you visit with us." Her smile was warm and, for a weary, anxious traveler, a most welcome smile. They led me to their car and we began a journey to Cocoa, about fifty miles east.

I was surprised by the lack of buildings between Orlando and Cocoa. I expected to see farms and houses, but all I saw was pine and palm trees. It was very different from Mississippi. Dave and Betty began to tell me about his church and the job opportunity he was offering.

"Now Reverend Kellar, I just want to tell you how proud we are of you and your friends for taking a stand in Mississippi. I know you must be having a rough time," Mrs. Cathcart said.

It was what I needed to hear. As it turned out, she had long been a champion of blacks.

"Now Florida will be more liberal than Mississippi, but we still have many who are prejudiced," David said.

We talked about Cocoa and the surrounding communities. I learned that it was not unusual for a church to take in a hundred members in a year, and the demand for housing was so great that some had to wait several months while their home was built. It was like being in another world. If God had been telling me not to leave

Mississippi, the encounter I had that evening with these two wonderful people seemed to contradict His message.

I stayed with the Cathcarts. That evening we made plans to meet some of his church members the next day and to tour the area. Early the next morning, we toured the community, met several different church members, had lunch and then visited the church. It was not what I expected a large church to be. Having grown up in the Deep South, I expected a church to be constructed with red brick with several steps leading to the sanctuary. The sanctuary would be filled with either white pews trimmed in mahogany, or dark oak pews on red carpet. First Methodist Church of Cocoa had none of that. It was a large, one-story building. The front was made of glass. Further, it did not have pews, but folding chairs. The floor was not done in red carpet but was a hard substance called terrazzo. It did not look like a church at all. The Sunday School rooms opened to the outside and reminded me of some of the small motels on the Gulf.

"What do you think, pal?" Dave asked.

"It's different from anything I have seen," was the only reply that came to mind.

Later that evening we met with several members of the congregation. Dave was one of the most energetic men I had ever met. He never stopped. We moved from one person to the next with Dave remembering some of the names and stumbling through the others. It was obvious that he was well liked by the congregation. It was a delightful evening, and I met many people and talked a lot about where I had come from. People asked about the church I served and were aghast to find that I served not one, but three churches. When I told them the total number of members was less than one hundred, they were amazed. But they were really surprised to learn that I preached three times every Sunday and drove almost a hundred miles each Sunday going from one church to another.

The evening ended with Dave and Betty taking me to the local Dairy Queen for ice cream. Later, when we returned to the parsonage, we talked about my coming to be Dave's associate. They would provide a house and over $4,000 a year.

"How far are we from Mississippi?" I asked.

We figured a bit and agreed we were about 700 miles from Dot's home. I wanted to know the distance for two reasons. One was to consider how long it would take to drive from one to the other. Another was the nagging realization that I had to fly back the next day and was wondering about the possibility of taking the bus. I gave the lame excuse that I wanted to experience the actual distance between Florida and Mississippi. Of course, Dave and Betty wouldn't hear of it.

The next day, the Cathcarts drove me to Herndon Airport. We said our goodbyes, and I told him I would let him know my decision as soon as I discussed the visit with Dot. I had told them she was pregnant and that would play a role in where we ended up.

This flight required a change of planes in Tampa too. This plane was larger than the other ones. I was told this flight would not take as long because it was a propjet. The first thought that came to mind was what my friend the construction super: "If this had been a prop jet," he had said when the engine failed on the flight from New Orleans, "it would have exploded." For the next two hours all I could think of was exploding engines. My level of anxiety was disquieting at best.

It was an uneventful flight even though I feared the engines would blow up. But we landed in New Orleans in the afternoon without incident. I deplaned and headed for the Southern Airways gate to board the DC-3 for the Hattiesburg/Laurel Airport. I remember two things about the flight. One was the attendant. She was tall, skinny and unattractive. The other was the bumpy ride from New Orleans to Biloxi, another stopover on the flight. The attendant served an Air Force man a cup of coffee. As he held the cup, the plane hit an air pocket. The plane dropped and the hot coffee exited the top of the cup. It hung in the air for a split second. In that short moment of time, the man tried to get out of his seat before the coffee came down. He didn't make it. The coffee landed square in his lap. It was both humorous and tragic. He let out a pained yelp as the attendant grabbed a damp cloth. She stood there for a moment looking at the coffee on the man's uniform, centered in his crotch area. She paused, seeming to consider whether she should hand him the cloth or use it on him. He was impatient, probably due to the pain, and took the cloth from her hand before she made a decision. By the time we landed at Keesler Air Force Base, he was a little more composed.

The flight to Hattiesburg/Laurel took only a few minutes. Dot was waiting at the airport, anxious to find out about Florida. I described Cocoa as well as I could. For every description Dot had two new questions. She had as many questions about Dave and Betty Cathcart. She was interested, and we began to give it serious thought and prayer. As we neared Sandersville, some of the unpleasant feelings returned. I realized I had not thought very much about Sandersville or Mississippi while in Florida. The weighted feeling in my soul returned with a vengeance, along with a sense of misery. If God had sent me a message about staying in Mississippi through storms, measles, and a wild plane ride, then what was my gut saying by heaping the ugly weight of my dilemma on me again so quickly? I had felt good in Florida. The couple I stayed with had been gracious and entertaining.

My status in Sandersville could best be described as "on trial." By that I mean, some people kept their distance but clearly retained an interest in me. I am confident that every sermon I preached was picked apart, in private and public. I continued visiting the Lion's Club and, much of the time, no one said anything to me. And I didn't say anything about my decision to leave Sandersville and Mississippi, and relocate my family to Florida, but as soon as I was accepted by the Florida Conference, our decision was made.

In preparation for the move, Dot and I visited with Wilton and Dolores every chance we got. We also visited with her parents more frequently. Her Dad was still vehemently opposed to any form of racial progress. He would chat with me as long as we stayed away from certain topics. Her mother worried about our well being.

Dot's pregnancy was something to behold. Having always been slim, her protruding stomach was very obvious. I loved the way it looked and could feel the baby kick. I do not recall Dot experiencing much nausea, but you will have to ask her about that. I and nausea do not get along. I was a thoughtful husband when she suffered. I would open the bathroom door and toss her a damp rag. It was the least I could do.

Church worship continued as usual. It is interesting to note that we didn't lose a single member over the entire time I was there. I believe they continued to come just to see what happened next.

I continued preaching as if everything was in good shape. At the same time, I prepared to leave Sandersville in June and move to Florida. Dot was getting bigger by the day. It was exciting to see her pregnant, and I grew more excited about becoming a father. We must have discussed a hundred or more names. He would carry my middle name as a boy. I could not bring myself to name a child Ned. Thomas would suffice, and we later agreed on Kent as a middle name. If it was a girl, it would be Katy or something like that.

I continued corresponding with Dr. Cathcart. Miss Hinton fielded letters from Cocoa on a regular basis. I had letters from many different places, but usually only one or two from a particular area. Every time I visited the post office, Miss Hinton would drop hints about the Florida mail. I knew, too, that others would know that I was getting most of my mail from a single source. They could put two and two together. I wondered how long it would be before they did. I made my decision

The attitude of the church had changed almost back to normal. One of the members, a low-key sort, once asked if I planned to leave.

"You're our only hope to make it as a single church" he had said.

I was as honest with him as I could. I said if I left it would not be because of Sandersville, but because of the politics of the Mississippi Conference.

He was obviously disappointed. I felt bad because they expected me to be their savior. I was in a balancing act, trying to be honest with my reasons for leaving, and trying not to give the impression I was getting even with the congregation for the way they had treated me. In all honesty, most of my anger toward the congregation had passed, or I had just grown indifferent. In either case, I was not as angry as I had been. I took time to reflect on my experience as pastor of Sandersville. I concluded that they had been good to me in spite of our differences. They had been nicer and more accepting than many of my brother clergy.

Chapter Twenty-two

Final Chapter

In May of that year I was approached by a representative of the school system. I was informed that the practice of the school system was to invite a local minister to preach the baccalaureate sermon for the senior class. The service was rotated between the three ministers: the Baptist, the Presbyterian, and the Methodist. As luck would have it, it was the Methodist preacher's turn. I was told that it was my choice. Did I want to preach? After giving it some thought, I said yes. I know that may surprise some, but it elated my church members. They loved being in the spotlight, and this was the only "joint" service of the year. And this year it would be a Methodist service.

The graduation service was scheduled for late May. No one knew I would be leaving Sandersville in a matter of days. This would be my farewell sermon to the community. In the meantime, we packed up some of our things. Living in a furnished parsonage meant we didn't have any furniture to pack or move. My belongings consisted of several books, a typewriter, and our clothes. I had bought a car while at Sandersville. It was a Chevy II and it had faithfully ridden the hills of south central Mississippi for me. In a few days, we would put all our worldly goods in that car and head for Florida.

The baccalaureate was on a Sunday evening and it was packed. The students, their parents, the church members, and the curious had gathered to hear the sermon. I do not know who was more nervous, me or the school board. Some were wondering if this would be a time to get even, to preach a sermon on integration, or say something that would upset the crowd.

My sermon was a take-off of my trip to Florida. I used an outline of Roy Angel's book, "Shoes of Iron", the book I had read while on my adventuresome flight to and from Florida. Dr. Angel wrote about those times when everything gets turned upside down. He was saying, in essence, that times get tough so tough men have to wear shoes of iron. It was appropriate for the group. I told of my trip to Florida and how frightened I had been. One passage spoke about having the assurance that "underneath are the everlasting arms." I joked that I really counted on those arms when I was 30,000 feet above the ocean. I also talked about how God gets us through difficult times, even when they are so hot that we have to wear shoes of iron. It was a well received sermon, and many came to say how much better it was than those they heard every Sunday. Even if I say so myself, I was on a roll that night.

It was the only time some of the citizens of Sandersville had ever heard me preach, and it would be their last. The Presbyterian Minister had the closing prayer. He used my outline for his prayer, which I took as a compliment. He told me that he had already planned to use those points, that it was a coincidence and nothing more. I believed it was just too hard for him to say "good sermon". He was one of the people who would be glad to see me go.

One Last Chance to Stay

The Mississippi Annual Conference met the last week of May. I had debated going. I had made up my mind to leave. Bishop Franklin had been informed and had released me to the Florida Conference. Brunner Hunt, my District Superintendent, had also been informed. I could just pack up and leave. However, I felt compelled to attend the annual conference. Maybe it was a way of saying that I was not ashamed of what I had been a part of. Maybe I wanted to make sure I was doing the right thing by leaving. Whatever the reason, I attended. It was held at Galloway Methodist Church in Jackson. I planned the trip and one overnight stay. The conference lasted for a full week, but I could not afford to stay that long. Two days would be ample.

I made it in time for the opening session. This was the first conference meeting since the "Born of Conviction" statement, and there was a lot of tension. The news media was present, waiting for some kind of statement about the turmoil that had developed in the past year. If they were looking for a profound statement from the bishop, they were sorely disappointed. He made little mention of the issue. It was business as usual. Some of the twenty-eight ministers were present but others had already left the conference. On one occasion when the issue was mentioned, it was quickly pushed aside. Some tried to resurrect it but to no avail.

I did see my District Superintendent who was surprised to see me.

"Are you staying? Sandersville would love to have you return but you need to let me know immediately."

My mind flashed back a full year when Dr. Hunt first told me I was going to Sandersville. He knew I did not want to go but I had no recourse. It felt different now because, this time, it was my call.

For my peace of mind, I had to give it some consideration. Mississippi was a known factor; Florida was unknown. I could make it through another year, I thought. I asked him for a few minutes to think it over.

"Let me know this afternoon."

I went outside to find a place where I could think, but it was not to be.

"I thought you boys would be long gone."

It was Ernest, a man who served a church in the conference. He was not impressive physically. He was not very accomplished and was somewhat a joke among most of the ministers I knew. He had led the singing at a revival I had while at Arnold Line Methodist a few years prior. I had not thought of us as friends, but rather an acquaintance. "I just wanted you to know that you all have really upset the

Conference. You come in here with your statement and make it hard for all of us." He sneered as he talked.

My insides were boiling. But I tried to be reasonable. "Look, it was a decision I made. You could have made it, too."

He became even more incensed. "You people really think you are something don't you? You will never go anywhere in this conference if I can help it."

That really set me off. "Who in the hell do you think you are? You're a joke and always will be." I was aware how close my face was to his, and how tightly I had clenched my fists. I was ready to punch this guy out on the steps of Galloway Methodist Church. I could not remember ever being so angry.

He gave a little half smile as if to say, "I got you." Only he did not say it. He tried to step back from my presence.

The hell with reason. "I'll kick the shit out of you right now."

He looked frightened and turned to walk away. His parting remark was, "People like you do not deserve to be in the ministry."

It took several minutes for me to settle down. I remembered what I was supposed to be thinking about, my conversation with Dr. Hunt. If I had doubts, the confrontation with Ernest the Jerk erased it from my mind. This is what it would be like if I stayed. I was again determined to pack and get out of Mississippi.

The following week I preached my last sermon at Sandersville. Some of the members came by to say goodbye, and others said they hated to see me go. One of them, by the grace of God, was Larry Hosey.

Dot and I moved out of the parsonage. Our "child," the dachshund Tracey, required little packing. She slept and ate her way to Florida. Dot and I drove to Hattiesburg to spend a day or two with Dot's parents before leaving for Florida. It wasn't easy for them to tell each other goodbye. We drove out of the driveway filled with apprehension and excitement. We were going to Florida to start a new life and ministry.

It is a Long Way to Central Florida

We had planned to break our trip into two legs. We would stop at Tallahassee for the night then drive to Cocoa the following day. I looked for palms and beaches along the way but the Panhandle offered little. Highway 90 passed through at least a thousand small towns, each with one stoplight. The road was predominantly broken concrete. We were completely exhausted when we arrived at the Holiday Inn in Tallahassee. Dot was six months pregnant, and the heat was more than we had imagined. She broke out in a heat rash and was miserable. Knowing the next day promised 300 more miles of driving did not help. I slept like a log that evening, though Dot wrestled with the heat, and the fact that her stomach was not as flat as it had been.

We left Tallahassee early the next morning. For the first 100 miles, it was much like driving through southern Mississippi. The scenery changed when we neared Clermont. The land was hilly and covered with citrus trees. We were both fascinated and ready to stop and pick a few oranges. Fortunately, we didn't because it was illegal. How would it have looked for the new associate minister of First Methodist of Cocoa to be arrested for stealing oranges? When we reached Orlando, I assured Dot that we were close to Cocoa. She was one relieved lady.

It was late in the day when we drove into Cocoa. Rev. Cathcart had given good directions. We were to go to Clearlake Road and turn left. The visual marker would be a bar with the intriguing name of "The Blue Matador." To fully appreciate the significance of using that landmark, you must understand that I came from an area that did not have bars. The few that did exist were denied existence by local Christians, and they would never use them as a marker for giving directions. We continued to Dixon Boulevard, turned right and then right again across from a shopping center. No more Mr. Harvey's. We would shop at an A & P. We found the home on Greenwood Way. It was a small house, a concrete block with a flat roof. There was a retarded palm tree in our front lawn. We were home.

There are a couple of experiences that I want to share because they meant so much to me. Both involved meeting ministers from the area. The first man I met was the longtime pastor of First Baptist Church in Cocoa. His name was David Sawyer and had pastored the church for more than twenty-eight years. He was an icon in the area. We met at his church and talked for several minutes. He wanted to know everything about Mississippi and the experience I'd had. He was excited about the report I gave him. As I stood to leave, he called in his secretary and announced that they had a hero in town. Me. I was extremely uncomfortable and it must have shown.

"Brother Kellar, we do think of you as a hero."

I was not a hero. I had left in the midst of the battle. Those who stayed were the real heroes. I thought of the civil rights activist and Methodist preacher, Eddie King, who had been beaten and jailed for his beliefs and actions.

The next person I wanted to meet was Dr. Hugh Brockington, a black minister who served the Metropolitan Baptist Church in Cocoa. He was a leader among the black community and had the respect of the white community. He, too, was an icon in the area. Rev. Cathcart spoke highly of him, and I wanted to speak with him very much. In all of my time in Mississippi, I had never met nor talked with a black minister. I felt guilty about that.

Dr. Hugh Brockington was a tall man with a deep bass voice that was just plain inspiring. I had heard him pray at a ministerial meeting, and was awed by what he said and the manner in which he said it. The man fascinated me with his stature, his voice, and his influence in the community. I liked him from the moment we met, and my appreciation grew every time I was with him. I mention Hugh because he was a hero. He had fought to integrate this community and succeeded with little violence. He was respected by all who knew him.

But the reason I shared my experience with Dr. Brockington was something he said to me after I told him of the guilt I felt about leaving Mississippi in the midst of turmoil.

"I feel like I ran away from the struggle."

With that, he leaned over, put his hand on my knee and said, "Brother Kellar, you made your witness when few others were willing to do so. It is now for someone else to take up the challenge and move it to the next level. You have done your job and done it magnificently."

I shall never forget that moment, and I shall never forget Hugh Brockington. I spent many hours with him as I worked in the community. What a wonderful influence he was to the community, and what an inspiration he was to me.

There was a third person that also became a friend and an inspiration. His name was W. O. Wells, pastor of Saint Paul's Baptist Church. W. O., as I learned to call him, was a young vocal leader in the black community. He would easily have been a freedom rider in Mississippi. He was representative of the young blacks and was known as one who pushed for integration, much to the consternation of the white community. We, too, became friends. I always admired his commitment toward making the community aware of the black man's plight.

Tomorrow's Hope "... and a child shall lead them."

At the outset of this book, I mentioned how much hatred and prejudice had been drilled into the minds of almost every child in Mississippi. I have to admit that I heard some of those teachings. I remember well the water fountains being labeled as colored and white. Restrooms at the bus station were labeled as white and colored. I never understood why that was. No one ever told me that I should not drink from the colored fountain or use the colored restroom. You can understand how stupid this sounded to a young man who did not have indoor plumbing until I was five or six years old. I have concluded that separation of the races has been in existence for so long that parents forget to teach their children the reasons for it. It was simply the way it was done. I have shared my experiences with young black kids and the repercussions I experienced. It seemed natural to play with other kids, black or white. In retrospect, I realize I was an aberration. No other member of my family thought as I did.

Sandersville

A lot of years have passed since I served the Sandersville Methodist Church. In 2007, I attended the reunion of the signers of the "Born of Conviction" statement. It was the first time I had seen most of them in forty years. Some of the group have passed away including Dot's brother Buford. He had transferred to the Southern California Conference and was an administrator at Clermont School of Theology, in Clermont, California. Others had also transferred to other conferences. In all, about two thirds of the twenty-eight left Mississippi.

So much has changed in Mississippi. Blacks and whites go to school together. Ole Miss, the school that had experienced hours of upheaval and violence on the eve of allowing a black man to enroll in 1962, now has a fully integrated campus. The same is true with all the colleges and universities in the state. Mississippi Southern changed its mascot from the Confederate General Forrest who established the Klan to the Golden Eagles. Ole Miss no longer uses the "largest confederate flag in the world" at its football games. These are only some of the numerous changes that have been incorporated into daily life in the South today.

Someone asked me recently if the "Born of Conviction" statement had much to do with all the changes. I honestly do not know. I do know that I was changed by the statement, as were a number of people in Sandersville. Perhaps because it was not presented by outside agitators, but by their sons, natives of Mississippi, who threw down the gauntlet. History must determine the impact the statement had on the State of Mississippi.

I wish I could tell you that we have made great progress in racial relations. I don't think we have. I still find an undercurrent of racism as I work with older groups of citizens. The "n" word is not as prevalent as it used to be, but you can hear it if you listen. It took a long time for people to develop the hatred and prejudice I lived with in my home state. It will take a long time for it to disappear. Many will take it to their grave. I still find people who are bothered by my attitude or outright offended. Some hide it well, but I've been around long enough to recognize the bias, see the prejudice. In my forward, I wrote about a man who told a racial joke. That occurred after I had moved to Cocoa, and it was told by a leading layman of a Cocoa church. So, you see, I am not sure just how far we have come.

For the past forty years, I have lived in Florida, near the Space Center. We have several black friends with whom we socialize. I celebrated the thrill of accepting a black family into the congregation of a church I served as pastor for four years in Rockledge, but I found that prejudice is not unique to Mississippi. It's everywhere. I know that intellectually, but it is still difficult for me when faced with it. It reminds me of a bad time in my life. Nor is it a "redneck" disease, which many still believe. An acquaintance of mine who was born "up North" into a wealthy family who never knew financial need, speaks about the "niggers" with the same venom of the poorest redneck in Mississippi.

I need to share one other experience. It occurred on a ski trip. I remember it very well because so many of my "friends" were present. We had gathered for an after-ski party. Someone mentioned a news report about a black man who had committed a crime. One of the men suggested that the suspect's penis be cut off.

"Man, that is harsh thinking," I said.

Almost immediately the party turned into a heated debate. I was on one side of the argument, up against the other thirteen men present. One close friend was sort of sympathetic for my position, but he maintained a low profile. The wealthy Northerner who speaks regularly about the "niggers," became almost irrational. It was, as Yogi Berra once said, "déjà vu all over again."

This man paced about the room railing about "niggers." Then he stopped and asked pointedly if I had ever attended school with a "nigger".

"No," I replied.

"Well," he doggedly announced, "I went to school with them."

I finally got in a word. "I lived a block from many black families when I was a kid. And you know what, my family couldn't have afforded to live that close to you back then."

My comment sailed right over his head, or he decided to ignore it. He deemed himself more qualified to speak about blacks because he had attended an integrated school. It was a real bummer of an evening. There have been other times when I have become involved in arguments about blacks, but that experience stands out. I want to be like Martin Luther King Jr. and not let those remarks rattle me or turn me into an angry person. I am still working on that part of me that wants to strike out against people like that. I shall never understand what makes a person think like that.

One of My Proudest Moments

There have been many good experiences, too. My son, Kent, was born three months after we arrived in Florida. He is a Floridian, not a Mississippian. As a person who loves a happy ending, I am pleased to say to you that this book also has one. And, before I die, I suspect I will have many more good experiences that I may or may not convey to you in writing. But a recent experience will remain with me for as long as I live. It involves my children and my grandchildren.

I visited my son and two granddaughters in Atlanta. I continue to find something in Atlanta to lure me back. Now the lure is my son, Kent, conceived during that stormy year in Sandersville, his wife, and two of the most beautiful granddaughters in the world, Phoebe and Madison. Phoebe is eleven and Madison is seven. Phoebe is the cautious one, and a born actress. Madison is all energy and seemingly knows little fear.

While there, I accompanied my son Kent to a PTA meeting at their school. The school is a Magnet school, attracting students from different cultures and races. It was Black History Month and the children were to present a program. We separated from the girls so they could get changed and made our way to the auditorium. It was filled with proud parents and school staff. The crowd looked much like a mini United Nations. There were Hispanics, Blacks and Caucasians, American Indians, Asians, all sitting side-by-side, chatting about their children and the school. I kept pinching myself to see if I was awake or dreaming.

Earlier that evening I had asked Madison who her best friend was. According to her, she had lots of best friends. But her very best friend was Monesia.

"Is Monesia black, Oriental, Hispanic or white?"

"Poppa, I don't know," she said. "She has black hair and her skin is dark."

Madison and Phoebe genuinely seem to be color blind when it comes to skin.

The best was yet to come. The program was a series of choral presentations and cultural displays celebrating Black History Month. Madison was in the first group that marched onto the stage. The group sang a song that sounded vaguely familiar. The words gave me chills.

> Ain't nobody gonna turn me around, turn me around
> Ain't nobody gonna turn me around.
> I'm gonna keep on walking, Lord.
> Keep on talking, Lord
> Marching up to freedom land,

(This song was taught to a mass meeting of the black community at Mount Zion Baptist Church in Albany, Georgia in 1962.)

It was a protest song and my little blonde headed, blue-eyed granddaughter was belting it out. She had already told me about the song, so I wasn't surprised. What cheered me so, was seeing my granddaughter sing it.

The program did not end there. Soon, Phoebe and her group came to the stage. I watched with proud grandfather eyes as she looked out at the audience with the brightest smile of them all. And then she and the choral group began singing "Martin's Dream". The song is about Dr. Martin Luther King, Jr's speech. titled "I Have a Dream". The words of my granddaughter's song were as clear to me as the air I was breathing:

> "I have a dream that one day on the red hills of
> Georgia the sons of former slaves and the sons of
> former slave owners will be able to sit down together
> at a table of brotherhood.

I have a dream that one day even the state of Mississippi, a desert State, sweltering with the heat of injustice and oppression, will be transformed into an oasis of freedom and justice."

The concluding words of that great speech sounded in my mind like the clanging of a great bell.

Let Freedom ring…
But not only that, let freedom ring from Stone Mountain Georgia!

I was a short fifteen minute drive from Stone Mountain where, as a student at Emory, I read about the almost weekly meetings of the Ku Klux Klan that assembled on top of that mountain.

Let freedom ring from every hill and every molehill of Mississippi, From every mountainside, let freedom ring.

I sat there as a native of Mississippi, the father of a child conceived in Mississippi, with a long heritage of Mississippi blood in my veins, listening to my granddaughters singing songs of praise for black people. There was a wide range of emotions that flooded my very soul. There was a twinge of pain as I remembered the past. But it was quickly swept away by the flood of joy and pride that inundated me that evening. I wanted to shout and cry at the same time. The tears that filled my eyes were tears of happiness.

If someone had told me forty years ago that I would witness children, black and white, red and yellow, Protestant, Catholic and Jewish, holding hands and singing together, I would have had trouble believing it could happen, never mind would happen. But I saw it and I heard it and I felt it.

I could not wait to telephone Dot and share what I had experienced. As we drove home, I asked the girls if they would sing the songs again and they did.

"Do you know what those songs are?" I asked. And before they could answer I said, "They're civil rights songs."

"Poppa, we know that."

The only thing that was left to be said was, "Duh."

I was never so proud as I was on that evening. I cannot help but think about a verse from Rogers and Hammerstein's musical "South Pacific".

> You've got to be taught to hate
> Before you are six or seven or eight.
> To hate the people your parents hate.
> You've got to be carefully taught.

How pleased I am to learn that my children have taught their children to love all people. My son and daughter-in-law are rearing the girls without passing along the old refrain of hate, or that they were better than others. They learned their lessons well.

I still bask in the warmth of that evening. I felt a sense of victory. Remembering the experiences, the pain, the rejection, the threats, having to leave my home state, always brings a bit of pain. I have sometimes wondered what would have happened if I had never signed that statement. I have been asked, "Was it worth all of the hurt?" Yes, it was. I would never have fit in with the system, the attitudes that were so prevalent. I could not have kept my mouth shut. My granddaughters' school program reinforced my resolve. I had seen on that evening Dr. King's dream become reality. The best way to explain how I feel now is summed up with one word: victory. The audience gathered that evening were parents of different races, cultural groupings, and religions, sitting side by side, applauding all the children. The Ross Barnett's, the White Citizens Councils, the KKK, and all the state councils and committees created for the sole purpose of preventing integration, were soundly defeated that evening. Perhaps it was an aberration, and the next day would bring the hatred and prejudice back to life. But for that moment, all the efforts, all the hurts and rejections, were worth it. Our future is in good hands with these children. Indeed, "a child shall lead them."

I cannot tell you of the pride I have knowing these are my grandchildren. Dot and I have been richly blessed. Our two children are gifted with the capacity to care deeply about humankind. Our grandchildren are not burdened with the hate and prejudices that caused so much pain for so many people. What more can anyone ask for?

Well, one other thing. I have been writing this book for several years. I would pick it up then put it away. I have already confessed to you that the sequence of events may not be completely accurate. While some letters may have come earlier than listed, they all came. Most I have quoted word for word. Now, I am finishing this epistle on November 25, 2008. In the past few weeks I watched as Barack Obama, a black man, was elected President of the United States! Forty short years ago, a black person voting risked his life. It's not paradise but man, we have come a long way.

Or have we? I spent so much time dealing with hardcore racist that I fear they will rise again, given the slightest opportunity. Until that opportunity arises they will remain quiet At most they will make veiled racial remarks. They have to. It is in their upbringing. I paid a price as did so many. Some paid the ultimate price. Has it been for ought? I pray not.

Bibliography

Sadler, Lew, "Say Dixie Whites Are Not Bad Folks" Published in Eyes On The Prize, Williams, Juan, Editor, Viking Penguin Inc., New York, New York, 1987, pp. 54-55

Williams, Juan, Eyes on the Prize p. 208

Williams, Juan, Eyes on the Prize .216-217

Ashmore, Sam: The Mississippi Methodist Advocate, 1963

Laurel Leader Call, Laurel Mississippi Newspaper

Jackson (Mississippi) Times, January 11, 1963 Issue
East, P. D., The Petal Paper

Abernathy, Ralph, "Ain't Nobody Gonna Turn Me Around", Civil Rights Song

Rogers and Hammerstein, "You Have to be Taught". From the musical, South Pacific

(Many quotes came from different Newspapers including but not limited to: The Clarion Ledger, (Mississippi), The Times Picayune (New Orleans), The Hattiesburg American (Hattiesburg, Mississippi) and the Associated Press and UPI.

www.ingramcontent.com/pod-product-compliance
Lightning Source LLC
LaVergne TN
LVHW091533060526
838200LV00036B/586